THE
BUSINESS POLICY GAME

Third Edition

PLAYER'S MANUAL

Richard V. Cotter

University of Nevada, Reno

David J. Fritzsche

University of Portland

Prentice Hall, Englewood Cliffs, New Jersey 07632

Library of Congress Cataloging-in-Publication Data

Cotter, Richard V.
    The business policy game : player's manual / Richard V. Cotter,
David J. Fritzsche. — 3rd ed.

        p.   cm.
    Includes index.
    ISBN 0-13-099359-X
    1. Management games. 2. Decision-making. I. Fritzsche, David J.
II. Title.
HD30.26.C67   1991
658.4'0353—dc20   90-43760
                                                       CIP

Editorial/production supervision: *Carol Burgett*
Cover design: *Mike Fender*
Prepress buyer: *Trudy Pisciotti*
Manufacturing buyer: *Robert Anderson*

 © 1991, 1986, 1973 by Prentice-Hall, Inc.
A Division of Simon & Schuster
Englewood Cliffs, New Jersey 07632

Printed in the United States of America

10 9 8 7 6 5 4 3 2 1

ISBN 0-13-099359-X

Prentice-Hall International (UK) Limited, *London*
Prentice-Hall of Australia Pty. Limited, *Sydney*
Prentice-Hall Canada Inc., *Toronto*
Prentice-Hall Hispanoamericana, S.A., *Mexico*
Prentice-Hall of India Private Limited, *New Delhi*
Prentice-Hall of Japan, Inc., *Tokyo*
Simon & Schuster Asia Pte. Ltd., *Singapore*
Editora Prentice-Hall do Brasil, Ltda., *Rio de Janeiro*

CONTENTS

LIST OF FIGURES

PREFACE

The first edition of the <u>Business Policy Game</u> was published in 1973, at a time when computers were just starting to be used as instructional aids in the classroom. Instructors who wished to use the computer had to make a big time investment in learning to program and use a mainframe computer, and computer programs developed for one brand of computer were difficult to transport and install on computers of another brand. Students who participated in this simulation in those days had to do all of their analysis with a mechanical calculator. Even electronic calculators did not come into widespread use until the late seventies.

In the eighteen years since the first publication of this work technology has changed rapidly, and the authors have attempted to keep up with the changes. Personal computers have largely supplanted mainframe use for computer-aided instruction. Many students now have their own computers, and computer laboratories are widely available. Student analysis now should take place with statistical and spreadsheet programs on the personal computer rather than mechanical calculators. Instructors no longer need to become experts in programming in order to use personal computers. Installation of programs is much simpler and the programs, themselves, are much easier to use.

During this same period, the Association for Business Simulation and Experiential Learning (ABSEL), formed in 1974, has done much to further the development and use of simulations for business education. Simulations now provide an exciting, meaningful experience for students by placing them in the role of top management in simulated firms, thus giving them an experience which approximates that of the "business world."

The computer programs for this edition have been completely re-written to take advantage of the changing technology. Several changes have been made to the model to make it more realistic to the players. The Player's Manual, too, has been re-written in an attempt to make the manual and the programs more user-friendly.

The <u>Business Policy Game</u> is a general management simulation that provides students with a challenging decision-making exercise. It has been used successfully with groups of upper-class undergraduates and graduate students in business administration and in executive development programs. The simulation also has been used successfully for many years in the International Collegiate Business Policy Games competition held annually at the University of Nevada, Reno.

Each simulation participant requires a <u>Player's Manual</u>; the <u>Instructor's Manual</u> is to be used only by the instructor, along with the computer programs available on floppy disks from Prentice Hall. The game is available in two versions, for use on IBM and compatible computer systems, or on Apple Macintosh systems.

The <u>Business Policy Game</u> has been patterned, in part, after similar games which preceded it. Particular acknowledgement is given to Dr. John E. Van Tassel, whose "Boston College Decision-Making Exercise" inspired the senior author to become interested in business simulation and influenced the development of the model of this game and the <u>Player's Manual</u>. This revision is the result of experiences with the first two editions, as well as numerous other simulations and discussions with ABSEL members and colleagues. We would like to thank all of those authors and friends for their contributions. Most of all, we we each want to thank our spouse, Carolyn Cotter and Nan Fritzsche, respectively, for their patience and counsel. Without their assistance, this project could never have been completed.

AN OVERVIEW OF THE <u>BUSINESS POLICY GAME</u>

<u>Educational objective</u>. An instructional supplement for courses dealing with strategic management and policy. Formulation of objectives and strategy are emphasized, with opportunity to implement policies that will lead to the realization of objectives. A premium is placed on successful integration of functional area concepts. The model is challenging to upper-division undergraduate and graduate business students.

<u>The simulation</u>. A computer-based simulation of a manufacturing firm. Student teams compete with each other as members of management of simulated companies producing and selling a consumer durable good. The model is interactive so that marketing decisions, for example, may influence the sales of competitors as well as the sales of the firm making the decision.

<u>Course use</u>. Strategic management and policy at the upper-level undergraduate or graduate level, suitable for use independently or as supplementary material; seminars for management development. Variations of the model have been used successfully in the classroom and in intercollegiate competition for more than 20 years.

<u>Number of participants</u>. Twelve or more. An industry world may contain from three to six firms (student teams), with each firm's management consisting of four to eight participants. For more than six teams, separate industries may be run concurrently.

<u>Time required</u>. Sixteen to twenty sessions of about fifty minutes each (later sessions typically may require less time). Outside preparation will reduce the time required in group sessions. Preparation by participants before the first session may require six to eight hours.

<u>Space required</u>. Ideally, each company might have a separate "board room" for decision-making sessions. Grouping of teams in different parts of a large room works satisfactorily.

<u>Materials and equipment needed</u>. A copy of the <u>Player's Manual</u> for each participant and the <u>Instructor's Manual</u> for the administrator. The administrator should arrange to have the computer programs and history files installed on a personal computer system. Access to a computer system by players is helpful, but not required. A spreadsheet program is useful for student analysis and a decision support system.

<u>Administrator's role</u>. To provide an environment which maximizes the learning experience; and to arrange for materials, physical facilities, and computer processing of student decisions. Instructions and suggestions for all phases of the simulation is provided in the <u>Instructor's Manual</u>.

CHAPTER 1

INTRODUCTION

The Business Policy Game has been designed as a strategic
management simulation to provide a challenging, complex decision-
making exercise. As a strategic management simulation, it requires participants to set objectives, develop strategy to
realize the objectives and create operating policies to ensure
that operating decisions support the strategy. Participants are
also responsible for making quarterly operating decisions for
each of the functional areas of finance, marketing and production
and to integrate those decisions for the purpose of meeting the
firm's overall goals and aspirations. Participation in the simulation requires that a student of business administration review
information and techniques that have been learned in other
courses and/or in practical on-the-job experience, and put into
practice many of the principles of management decision making and
strategic planning. To be successful, participants need to adopt
the viewpoint of top management in the simulated business firm
which they operate. They must carefully specify the goals and
objectives which guide their firm's operation. The participants
are required to make quarterly decisions concerning the operations of their manufacturing firm as they compete with the
management teams of other firms in the industry.

The Business Policy Game is not intended to duplicate any
actual industry. Rather the simulation model was designed to
include general relationships that might exist in any competitive
industry. One might say it is generic. Participants need to
utilize their knowledge and experience in order to make certain
deductions about the economy in which they are operating and
about general relationships which exist within the simulation.
These deductions must be combined with knowledge about specific
relationships and with the participants' beliefs about the
actions that competitors are likely to take. A set of decisions
ideally would follow from utilizing a combination of different
types of data analysis and forecasting techniques and from

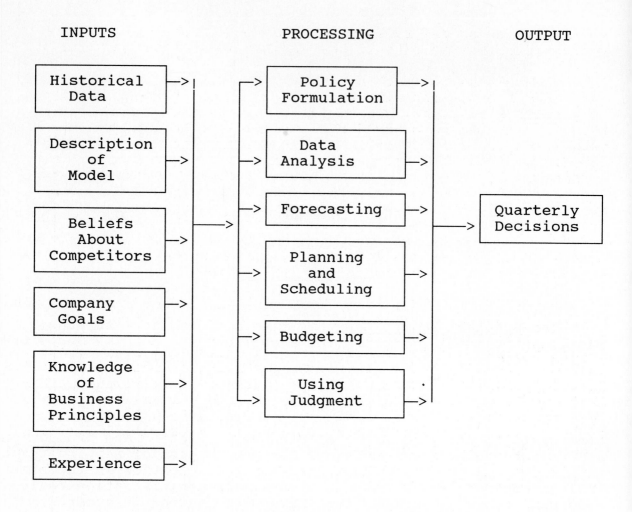

INPUTS   PROCESSING   OUTPUT

FIGURE 1-1
Flow Chart of Activities in Preparation for
Making Decisions in the Business Policy Game

development of strategies and policies to meet the goals and
objectives of the firm. (See Figure 1-1.)

The Simulated Environment

The computer program used to process the decisions made by
competing teams includes definitions of certain relationships
that have been abstracted from the economic environment of the
business world. This abstraction, or model, does not purport to
include all of the relationships that exist. To do so would make
the simulation too complex to handle. The relationships included
are those that contribute significantly to the degree of realism
required to provide a plausible simulation. These relationships
are outlined and described in subsequent sections of this manual.

A description of the rules which must be followed in order to successfully participate in the simulation is also included.

Some of the relationships that exist in the simulation and the rules for dealing with the relationships will be described only in general terms. These relationships are comparable to those in the business world that are subject to uncertainty and thus not completely specified. For example, if a manufacturer lowers the price of a product, sales of the product normally increase. The magnitude of the sales increase cannot be known with certainty. Thus, only the general relationship between price and sales volume will be described in this manual. The actual effect of a specific price change must be estimated by observing the relationship between price and sales volume which exists in historical data and by experimentation with the price variable during the course of the simulation.

Other relationships will be described in more precise terms in later chapters. These relationships are subject to less uncertainty in the business world. Cost functions, accounting relationships, and methods of deriving various entries in the income statement, funds statement, and balance sheet are included in this group. The cash balance at the end of the quarter, for example, is equal to the previous quarter's balance plus total cash receipts less total cash payments. Explicit descriptions concerning the constraints required by the simulation model are also provided which the participants may consider to be "rules of the simulation." One such rule states that only one plant may be built in any marketing area.

During the course of the simulation, the participants will encounter a variety of business and economic situations and administrative problems. In order to successfully cope with these problems, the participants will find it necessary to engage in economic forecasting, sales forecasting, and profit planning. Cash flow analysis and capital budgets must be prepared. Production planning and scheduling must be accomplished. Cost analysis, pricing, policy formulation, and the development and implementation of marketing programs will be necessary. In addition, participants must prepare and analyze financial reports, cash flow statements, cost and sales analyses reports, and informational reports regarding competitors and the economic situation. Most participants will find it necessary to review basic textbooks and materials from this and other courses, and to draw from their past experiences in order to complete these activities effectively.

Preparing for Action

The Business Policy Game will require a heavy investment in time on the part of the participant--TANSTAAFL. (There ain't no such thing as a free lunch.) This investment should be a prudent one, however, as participation in the simulation should significantly increase overall understanding of the operation of business enterprises.

In order to participate effectively in the simulation, one must understand the relationships within the simulation model as well as its rules and constraints. Sample historical data from the previous two years of the firm's operation are shown in Appendix A. Study the data thoroughly for relationships which will help the firm in managing its resources. Economic and sales forecasts must be made and plans must be formulated for the firm's continued operation. It should be obvious that these tasks require the delegation of specific jobs to different team members. Thus, members of each firm should organize to perform the management function effectively.

Getting Ready for the First Decision

Before preparing the first set of decisions and after carefully reading this manual, you and your colleagues are urged to complete the following set of activities and planning reports:

1. <u>Organize your management team</u>. You should assign members of your team to corporate offices and other critical posts, decide upon specific decision-making procedures to be followed, and divide the work load among the various members of your firm. Unless the simulation administrator prescribes an organizational structure, you may design the organization of your management team. Your organizational structure and your ability to work together as a management team will be important ingredients in the success of your firm.

You should weigh the advantages and disadvantages of various organizational structures when designing your organization. Company officers for a functional organization might include president; vice-presidents of finance, marketing, and production; vice-president for economic and sales forecasting; and corporate secretary for recording policies and decisions. A geographical structure might replace the functional heads with division managers for each of the market areas.

Some teams find centralized decision making to work well. Various company officers will normally make recommendations to the president regarding the operations of their particular departments. However, the final decision-making authority rests with the president. Other teams prefer to vest their decision-making authority in the management team as a group. Recommendations are provided by the various officers of the firm, but the actual decisions are made by the officers as a group. Still other teams find a decentralized form of organization to be effective. Final decision-making authority is vested with the head of the unit responsible for the decision. Under a decentralized functional organization, the marketing decisions would be made by the vice-president of marketing, production scheduling decisions by the vice-president of production, etc. Coordination of overall decision making would be undertaken by the president, and conflicts would be resolved by the president of the firm.

You should prepare an organization chart that shows the lines of authority in your firm's organization and the position of each member of your firm in the organization. Then, fill in the Corporate Charter from Appendix C with your company name, and the name and position title of each member of your team. The Corporate Charter should be turned in to the simulation administrator.

2. <u>Prepare a forecast of expected levels of economic activity</u>. Your firm's sales will be affected by the general level of economic activity in your industry world. As real Gross National Product (GNP) rises, you can expect sales to rise, too, and as real GNP falls sales are likely to fall at the same time. GNP forecasts are included in your quarterly reports. A forecast of real GNP will be helpful in estimating future sales. Specific suggestions for preparing such a forecast are contained in Chapter 6.

3. <u>Prepare a sales forecast</u>. Production scheduling, plans for investment in a new plant and in equipment, expected cash receipts, and selling expenses are all affected by the volume of sales your firm realizes. Suggestions for preparing a sales forecast using the Sales Forecast work sheet can be found under the "Sales Forecasting" section in Chapter 6.

4. <u>Prepare a production schedule</u>. Production must be scheduled for the first decision period as well as planned for subsequent quarters of business operation. Production planning will depend upon your firm's expectations of sales volume. The completed plan will provide the basis for determining production facility requirements. Suggestions for preparing production plans using the Production Plan work sheet together with descriptions of production costs and production possibilities are found under the "Production Planning and Scheduling" section in Chapter 7.

5. <u>Prepare an investment plan</u>. Alternative methods of expanding productive capacity and their associated costs may be analyzed using the Capital Investment work sheet. It is discussed under the "Evaluation of Alternatives" section in Chapter 9. The nature of the expansion your firm undertakes will depend upon your production plan.

6. _Prepare a capital budget_. Capital is required to finance any planned expansion. The Capital Budget work sheet discussed under the "Capital Budgeting" section of Chapter 10 may be used to analyze alternate sources of funding for your firm.

7. _Prepare a cash budget_. Sufficient funds must be provided to finance the expenses and cash outlays required by your operations and investment plans. Sources of funds and cash requirements are outlined in Chapter 10. Suggestions for preparing the Cash Budget work sheet also are included under the "Cash Budgeting and Funds Statement" section.

8. _Prepare pro forma financial statements_. Your projected balance sheet may be used to analyze how the composition and levels of assets and liabilities affect your financial condition. Your expected level of profitability is an important means of judging the success of your firm's planned operation. You should evaluate your decisions prior to submitting them by preparing a projected income statement and balance sheet. Income Statement and Balance Sheet work sheets, along with suggestions for their preparation, are found under the "Profit Planning and the Income Statement" and "Balance Sheet" sections in Chapter 10.

9. _Formulate objectives and outline initial strategies and policies_. As you complete the planning activities outlined above, tentative policies should be developed for the operation of your firm and for the decisions which must be made on a quarterly basis. We suggest that you state these policies explicitly in written form for future reference. As the simulation proceeds, you probably will decide to revise your policies based upon the experience gained from the operation of your firm and the changing conditions of the dynamic business environment.

We recommend that your firm be very specific in the formulation of objectives and operating policies. A corporate objective to "maximize profits" is laudable but provides little guidance for strategy and policy formulation and is of little value as a standard for achievement. At the end of the first year of the simulation, or any other year for that matter, you will have little idea whether profits were in fact maximized or whether you fell short. It would be better to seek an objective of, say, "15 percent after-tax return on equity." Then you could judge your achievement more adequately after a year's experience and take corrective action where necessary.

You may view many of your policies as decision rules to be followed in specific situations. An example of a specific policy might be: "Ignore price reductions by competitors when they amount to less than ten cents per unit; but when the reductions are greater, match their price immediately." Avoid such generalizations as "charge a fair price that is consistent with production costs and with competitors' pricing policies." That's pure cotton. The clear formulation and statement of your policies will help to assure the consistency and stability of your firm's operations and will save you a considerable amount of preparation time during the decision periods as you participate in the simulation. See Chapter 4 for additional help in the development of objectives and the formulation of strategies and policies.

The simulation administrator may require some or all of the above reports to be turned in as part of the material used to evaluate team performance. Work sheets, contained in Appendix C, can be used to facilitate the preparation of the reports. It is suggested that a most effective way to present the work sheets is to develop a decision-support system. The various Business Policy Game work sheets have been prepared as spreadsheet templates, and are available on disk. A decision-support system can be developed relatively easily by using these spreadsheet templates.

Your initial reports will provide a good basis for a more extensive strategic plan and policy manual that the administrator may require after you have some experience with the simulation.

Submitting Decisions

The next step is to formulate and submit an actual decision set for the first period of your firm's operation. The simulation administrator will specify the date and time when your decisions are due. It is important that your firm's decisions be submitted prior to that time. Failure to do so may hold up the simulation run or more likely will result in the decision submitted for your firm during the previous period being used as the decision for the current period. Such action would normally not be in the best interests of your firm. Chapter 2 outlines the decisions that must be made and describes the decision form. Copies of the decision form are included in Appendix C.

We hope that the experience of participating in The Business Policy Game will be both enjoyable and rewarding. More importantly, though, it should be a meaningful and challenging educational experience. The amount of serious effort that you put into the analysis, planning, and decision-making activities of the simulation will determine how much the simulation will contribute to your education. Remember TANSTAAFL!

CHAPTER 2

QUARTERLY DECISIONS

The management of each simulated firm must make a number of decisions for each quarter of simulated operations. This chapter summarizes the decisions that are required, and provides instructions for their entry on the decision form as well as indicating certain limits and restraints that have been placed upon specific decisions. Some restraints are a result of the limitations of the simulation model and some are imposed to add realism to the Business Policy Game. More detailed information about each type of decision will be provided in later chapters of this manual to assist participants in formulating their strategy and decisions. Blank decision forms are found in Appendix C. These may be detached, and one copy turned in to the simulation administrator for each decision. You are urged to include a written copy of your decision form if you submit your decisions on floppy disk. If the disk becomes damaged or, for some reason, the computer is unable to read the disk, the simulation administrator will have a hard copy of your decision and it can be re-entered.

The simulation administrator will specify the date, time, and place where each simulation decision set is due. Timely submission of simulation decisions (on computer disk and/or on the decision-entry form as specified by your administrator) is extremely important. If your decision set is not submitted properly, the processing of the simulation will be delayed, causing lost time and possible hardships for your competitors and the simulation administrator. Failure to submit a decision set by the appointed time will result in your previous period's decision set being used for the current quarter, with adjustments for decisions that may not be legal for the current quarter (i.e. constructing another plant in the same area would be outside of the constraints of the model).

8

The mode of data entry will be specified by the simulation administrator.

1. You may be asked to enter your own decisions via personal computer, saving them on a floppy disk. The disk should be labeled "PLAYER'S DISK" with your company and world numbers, and must be initialized by the simulation administrator to contain the decision-entry program (BPG.EXE) and several data files necessary to run the program. The decision set is entered via personal computer.

2. You may be asked to enter your decisions via a hard-disk system or local area network (LAN) using the decision-entry program. Decision data then would be saved on the hard disk or the LAN system.

3. The administrator may arrange to have all data entered centrally from information that your firm submits on a decision form from Appendix C.

After the simulation has been run on the computer you will receive a set of reports (see Appendix B) showing the results of your operations and those of your competitors. The report may be given to you in the form of a computer printout or you may be asked to print it yourself from a floppy disk or from the computer system that you used to enter the decisions.

If the first or second mode is utilized, you will be told where to find microcomputers which can be used to enter your decision or you may use your own computer if it is compatible with the one used to run the simulation. Follow the instructions for using the decision-entry program, found at the end of this chapter. You also may be asked to turn in your decision form to show the values that have been entered.

If the third mode is specified, submit your decision forms by the specified time for data entry. Invalid entries may be edited by the simulation administrator and/or the computer program. Even though adjustments to invalid entries may not reflect your intentions, the decisions of the administrator are not subject to appeal. You are responsible for the implementation of your decisions by correct entries on your decision form.

Data are entered directly from the decision form. Always be sure to fill it in completely prior to data entry. Then check it carefully. Incorrectly completed forms may result in incorrect data entry and thus simulation results which are somewhat different from what your firm anticipated. We suggest that you refer to Figure 2-1 as you read this chapter.

The BUSINESS POLICY GAME Decision Form

Company __1__   World __1__   Year __2__   Quarter __4__

	Price	Adv. (000s)	Salespeople Hire Trans Commission					(000s) Bank Loan $
Area 1	$ 10.00	$ 46	# 1	# __	# __			
Area 2	$ 10.00	$ 40	# 1	# __	# __			
Area 3	$ 10.00	$ 40	# 1	# __	# __			
Area 4	$ 10.00	$ 46	# 1	# __	# __			

Salespeople Commission **20** ¢   Salary $ **3000**

Bank Loan $ ____
Bond Issue $ ____
Stock Issue# ____
Dividends $ ____
Time CDs $ **100**

Model

Model	Area 1	Area 2	Area 3	Area 4
Model# __1__	# __6__	# __	# __	# __
Qual # __2__				

Production
Lines Hours # __6__ # __40__

Production scheduling

	Shut-down tivate	Deac-tivate	Reac-tivate		Construction New Lines	New Add	New Plant
	# __	# __	# __		# __	# __	# __
	# __	# __	# __		# __	# __	# __
	# __	# __	# __		# __	# __	# __
	# __	# __	# __		# __	# __	# __

R & D (000s)
Area 2 $ __
Area 3 $ __
Area 4 $ __

Prod $ __72__
Proc $ __68__

2d Shft

Figure 2-1
Decisions for Year 2, Quarter 4

The figure illustrates the completed decision form for Company 1, which was used to generate the historical data for Year 2, Quarter 4. Values for other companies were the same, except for advertising and production scheduling. In these cases the entries shown for Area 1 were in your home area, instead. The home area for Company 2 is Area 2, and for Company 3 is Area 3. If there are more than three companies, the home areas for Companies 4, 5, and 6 are Areas 1, 2, and 3, respectively. The computer reports for Year 2, Quarter 4 of simulated operations are shown in Appendix B.

As you complete the decision form, be sure to enter values within the limits shown below (and a plus or minus sign where appropriate) in each entry block. If no sign is entered, the numbers are assumed to be positive. When entering decisions with the decision-entry program, if you attempt to enter too many digits for a field, your computer will beep to indicate an error. If you enter a value outside of the limits noted below, an error message will appear in the middle of the screen requesting a legal entry. If no entry is made, the default value from the previous period's decision set will be used.

Decision Form

Company, World, Year, Quarter

Enter your Company, World, Year and Quarter numbers on the decision form. If you are using the decision-entry program to enter your decisions via microcomputer, enter these values when prompted.

Company ____	World ____	Year ____	Quarter ____

Marketing Decisions

Price

The wholesale price of your product must be set each quarter in each of the four marketing areas. During the last quarter of Year 2, each firm charged $10.00 per unit for its product in each marketing area. For price, as for all other decision variables, last period's value will be used if there is no entry for the current quarter. Company policy (and the simulation model) limits price changes to a maximum of 30 percent per quarter. Because the product price was $10.00 in each area during Year 2,

Quarter 4, the highest price that your company may charge in Year 3, Quarter 1 is $13.00 and the lowest is $7.00. A price change as large as this is discouraged because of the unknown effect that such changes may have on the market. Management may specify different prices for different areas. If your price is in whole dollars, enter zeros for the cents so that there is no question of whether you forgot to enter the cents figures.

Maximum change: 30 percent in any quarter
Limits: 1.00 to 99.99 (in dollars and cents)

	Price
Area 1	$____.____
Area 2	$____.____
Area 3	$____.____
Area 4	$____.____

Advertising

Advertising expenditures must be allocated to each of the four marketing areas. Enter the amount (in thousands of dollars) to be spent in each area. The amount must be specified even though no change is desired, and the default values from the previous quarter will be used if you make no entry.

Limits: 0 to 999 (in thousands of dollars)

	Adv. (000s)
Area 1	$_____
Area 2	$_____
Area 3	$_____
Area 4	$_____

Salespeople

The total number of active salespeople and salespeople in training in each marketing area is reported in the Operating Information Report each quarter.

	Area 1	Area 2	Area 3	Area 4
Active Salespeople	12	10	10	13
Salespeople in Training, Qtr 1	1	1	1	1
Salespeople in Training, Qtr 2	1	1	1	1

Salespeople may resign for a variety of reasons including insufficient compensation. Normal turnover may account for some resignations over which you will have no direct control.

1. To hire and begin training new salespeople, enter the number of people to be trained in each area under "Hire Salespeople." It takes two quarters of training in the area in which the salesperson is hired before a salesperson can be sent to the field to sell. Salespeople in training will be carried on the training roster for two quarters, and will automatically be assigned to their area when training is complete. No further decision-entry is necessary after the first quarter in which the salespeople were hired. If you make an entry in the following quarter, you will hire additional salespeople to begin their training period in that quarter.

Limits: 0 to 99

	Salespeople		
	Hire	Trans	Commission
Area 1	#_____	#_____	_____¢
Area 2	#_____	#_____	Salary
Area 3	#_____	#_____	$_____
Area 4	#_____	#_____	

2. If your firm desires to transfer a salesperson from one area to another, this can be accomplished by making the appropriate entries under "Transfer Salespeople" on the decision form. To transfer salespeople from one area to another, you should enter a negative number for the area from which the salespeople are leaving, indicating the number of salespeople you are moving out of the area. This must be balanced by one or more positive numbers in the area(s) to which the salespeople are moving.

Your positive moves in may not exceed the total value of negative moves out. That would signify increasing the size of your sales force, and an increase only may be accomplished by hiring new salespeople in training (See paragraph 1, above). If your

13

negative values total more than your positive values, the additional salespeople will be fired (see below).

In order to limit the entries in this field to transferring salespeople (and not firing them), all individuals who move out must have a place to move in, and all individuals who move in must have come from another marketing area. Remember, the sum of the negative (people moving out) and the positive (people moving in) numbers must equal zero.

You may transfer salespeople from several areas at the same time. However, you may not transfer salespeople in and out of the same area in one quarter. They must either go into an area or out of an area. Not both. Transfers take place immediately. A transferred salesperson, however, may not be very effective until he or she has moved and settled into a new marketing area. The salesperson will, however, continue to draw a salary. In addition, the salesperson will be provided with a moving allowance of $5,000 (shown under "other selling expenses").

Maximum: to be transferred out: number of active salespeople minus 1.

Maximum: the sum of positive numbers may not exceed the sum of negative numbers.

Limits: -9 to 99

    3. You may fire salespeople in an area by entering the number of people you want to fire under "Transfer Salespeople." You indicate that the salespeople are to be fired by entering a negative number in an area, with no balancing positive number indicating a transfer to another area. Thus, if you decide to fire 2 salespeople in Area 3, enter -2 under the "Trans" column for Area 3.

Maximum to be discharged: Number of active salespeople minus 1

Limits: -9 to 0

Changes in Sales Force Compensation

    The compensation rates for salespeople may be changed by entering the new compensation levels on the decision form. If no entries are made, default values (rates from the previous quarter) will be used.

    1. The salary for each active salesperson at the end of Year 2 amounted to $3,000 per quarter. Sales salary may be increased or decreased. Enter the total amount of the desired

14

salary level, in dollars per quarter, under "Salary" on the decision form.

Limits: 1 to 9999 (in dollars)

   2.   Sales commissions are paid to salespeople in addition to their basic salary. Commissions amounted to 20 cents per unit sold at the end of Year 2. Sales commissions may be increased or decreased during any quarter. Enter the new amount for the desired commission rate in number of cents per unit under "Commission" on the decision form.

Limits: 1 to 99 (in cents per unit sold)

Model Number

   Enter the model number to be produced. For Year 3, Quarter 1 the only model available is number 1 and you are producing it at Quality level 2 (see below). The latest model number developed by the research and development department, together with the applicable labor and materials costs, will be reported in the Operating Information Report each quarter.

```
Latest Model Developed: 1       Model Produced This Quarter:  1  Quality: 2
Standard Cost per Unit for Next Quarter (includes inflation, cost savings):
       Model  1 Quality 2 Labor Cost:  2.46  Materials Cost:  1.23
```

   Model numbers are sequential (models 1, 2, 3, etc.). Your company's model 2 (when it becomes available for production) will have different marketing characteristics than another company's model 2. If more than one model number is available, there is no marketing advantage in skipping a model to produce the highest numbered one, unless your next model is two or three models behind those offered by competitors, making it technically obsolete.

   If a new model is available and your company wishes to put it into production, enter the new model number. Otherwise enter the same model number that was produced in the previous quarter. If model number 4 is reported to be available, and your firm decides to introduce it, enter "4" on the decision form. The new model will be put into production immediately and will be available for sale in the following quarter.

Maximum: Highest model number reported available from the R & D Department.

Minimum: Same model number as was produced during the previous
            quarter. Once a new model has been placed in produc-
            tion an earlier model may not be reinstated.

Limits: 1 to 12

```
┌─────────────────────┐
│ ┌─────────────────┐ │
│ │      Model      │ │
│ ├─────────────────┤ │
│ │                 │ │
│ │ Model#____      │ │
│ │                 │ │
│ │ Qual #____      │ │
│ └─────────────────┘ │
└─────────────────────┘
```

Model Quality

    When a new model is introduced, its quality level must be
specified. You may choose from three levels of quality:

    (1) deluxe
    (2) average
    (3) economy

    The quality level of a model is determined when the model is
introduced and may not be changed during the production run. The
choice of quality level is yours. Quality level is determined by
manufacturing tolerances and the quality and quantity of raw
materials used. It is not related to whatever you may have spent
on research and development in order to bring the new model to
market. When introducing a new product, enter the desired
quality level in the "Qual" space on the decision form. If you
continue to produce the same model as in the previous quarter,
you must also continue the same quality level.

Limits: 1, 2, or 3
           May be changed only when introducing a new model

Finance Decisions

Bank Loan

    If your firm wishes to take out a short-term bank loan by
drawing against your $2.5 million line of credit, enter the
amount desired (in thousands of dollars) under "Bank Loan" on the
decision form. Short-term loans are made for a period of three
months, and repayment is automatic during the quarter following
that in which the loan is made. However, interest must be paid
on the loan during the quarter in which it is outstanding. The
annual interest rate will be the short-term rate that is avail-

16

able during that quarter to a company with your credit standing. Your account will automatically be charged one-fourth of the annual rate.

Bank loans are secured by inventory and receivables, and may not exceed 50 percent of the value of receivables plus inventory at the end of the previous quarter. Your line of credit requires an annual cleanup, so a loan request will be denied if there has been a loan outstanding during each of the past three consecutive quarters.

Maximum loan: 50 percent of receivables + inventory

Maximum loan: 0 if a loan was outstanding in each of the previous three quarters

Limits: 0 to 2500 (in thousands of dollars)

```
        (000s)
Bank Loan    $_____

Bond Issue   $_____

Stock Issue# _____

Dividends    $_____

Time CDs     $_____
```

Sale or Redemption of Bonds

1. Bond issue. Secured long-term borrowing may be undertaken by issuing new bonds in amounts that are multiples of $1,000,000. New bond issues are callable ten-year bonds carrying the long-term rate of interest that is available to a company with your credit rating during the quarter of issue. Bonds must be secured by plant and equipment and the value of existing bonds plus new bonds to be issued may not exceed 75 percent of net fixed assets. Furthermore, your investment banker will consider an issue too risky to underwrite if the existing bonds, plus new bonds to be issued, exceed 50 percent of total equity (consisting of the previous quarter's total equity plus the proceeds of new shares to be sold simultaneously with the bonds). Enter the amount of new bonds to be sold (in thousands of dollars) on the decision form under "Bond Issue." If you decide to issue $1,000,000 worth of bonds, enter 1000 on the decision form. Do not include commas in your entry.

Maximum issue: 50 percent of equity or 75 percent of net fixed
                 assets, whichever is less

Limits: 0 to 9000 (in thousands of dollars), in million dollar
          lots

    2.   <u>Bond redemption</u>.   Bonds that are outstanding may be
called and redeemed in amounts that are multiples of $100,000
except that there is a restriction in the bond indenture that
prohibits the redemption of more than $500,000 of the face amount
of bonds in any one quarter.   If your firm has more than one bond
issue outstanding, the bonds carrying the highest interest rate
will be redeemed first.   If bonds are to be redeemed, enter the
face amount of the bonds for which redemption is desired (in
thousands of dollars), <u>preceded by a minus sign,</u> under "Bond
Issue" on the decision form.   If you decide to redeem $500,000
worth of bonds, enter -500 on the decision form.   The 5 percent
call premium will be charged automatically.

Maximum redemption: Total amount of bonds outstanding (if less
                      than $500,000)

Limits: -500 to 0 (in thousands of dollars) in hundred thousand
          dollar lots

<u>Sale of Common Stock</u>

    1.   <u>Stock issue</u>.   New shares of common stock may be issued
through an investment banker in multiples of 100,000 shares,
provided the new issue will be large enough to raise at least <u>$1
million</u>.   The investment banker will make a firm offer at any
time of a price that will be determined by the following formula:

$$\text{Issue price} = \frac{(\text{shares outstanding}) \times (\text{latest market price})}{(\text{shares outstanding}) + (\text{shares to be issued})}$$

    If your firm's credit rating is 2, this is the issue price.
If your firm's credit rating is 3, subtract 10 percent of the
formula value from the issue price.   If your credit rating is 1,
add 10 percent.

    Enter the number of new shares to be issued (in thousands of
shares) on the decision form under "Stock Issue."   If your firm
decides to issue 4,000,000 shares of stock, enter 4000 on the
decision form.   Do <u>not</u> include commas in your entry.

Minimum issue: Enough shares to raise $1 million

Limits: 0 to 9000 (in thousands of shares) in 100,000 share
          blocks

18

2. Stock repurchase. Shares of your firm's common stock may be repurchased by placing a purchase order with the firm's stock broker. The shares will be purchased at a price that is 10 percent above the market price reported at the end of the previous quarter. Stock is repurchased by entering the number of shares to be repurchased preceded by a minus sign in the "Stock Issue" section of the decision form. Repurchase must be made in multiples of 100,000 shares. If your firm decides to repurchase 500,000 shares of stock during the current quarter, enter -500 on the decision form. Your corporate charter requires that there be at least 3 million shares outstanding so repurchases are limited to an amount that would leave at least 3 million shares after the repurchase. Shares may not be repurchased if there are insufficient retained earnings to fund the repurchase.

Maximum repurchase: to leave at least 3 million shares outstanding

Limits: -900 to 0   (in thousands of shares)

Dividends

Cash dividends may be paid to stockholders; but a restrictive bond covenant provides that the dividends paid in any quarter, taken together with dividends paid in the previous three quarters, may not exceed the total amount of earnings in the previous four quarters of operations. In addition, the board of directors of your company has decided that if all bonds should be repurchased this restriction on dividend policy would be maintained. Thus if total earnings in the previous four quarters amounted to $200,000 and dividends already paid in the previous three quarters amounted to $190,000, the maximum dividend that could be paid in the current quarter would amount to $10,000. Enter the amount of cash dividends to be paid (in thousands of dollars) under "Dividends" on the decision form. If your firm decided to declare the permissible amount of $10,000 in dividends in the above example, you would enter 10 on the decision form. Dividends may not be declared if the retained earnings account on the balance sheet has a negative balance.

Maximum: Net income last 4 quarters minus dividends last 3 quarters

Maximum: 0, if retained earnings are negative

Limits: 0 to 9999 (in thousands of dollars)

Certificates of Deposit

Three-month time Certificates of Deposit (CDs) may be purchased in multiples of one hundred thousand dollars. Purchases may be made at the beginning of any quarter. CDs mature at the beginning of the next quarter, three months later. Interest will be earned on deposits at the rate reported in the industry report for 3-month time CDs during the quarter in which they will be invested. Interest will be credited to your account on the last day of the quarter in which the deposit is made, with quarterly interest calculated at one-fourth of the annual rate.

Note that while interest is credited on the last day of the quarter that the deposit is made, the funds from the deposit itself are not available until the next day--the first day of the subsequent quarter. Thus if your firm should need emergency cash during the quarter in which the funds are invested in CDs, the funds will not be available to meet the need.

To purchase time CDs, enter the amount of the purchase in thousands of dollars on the decision form under "Time CDs." If your firm decides to purchase $400,000 worth of CDs, enter 400 on the decision form. Do not include commas in your entry. Repayment of the CDs, as well as crediting your account with earned interest, will be done automatically by the bank.

Limits: 0 to 9900 (in thousands of dollars), in hundred thousand dollar lots

Production Decisions

Research and Development Expenditures

Research and development expenditures should be allocated between new product development and research for improved production processes that may result in lower costs. Enter the amount (in thousands of dollars) to be spent for each category.

Limits: 0 to 999 (in thousands of dollars)

R & D (000s)
Prod $_____
Proc $_____

Production Scheduling

    At the beginning of Year 3, six production lines are available in your home area. On each quarterly decision form, all available production lines in each plant and for each shift must either be scheduled for production, be shut down, or be deactivated. See Chapter 7 for certain restrictions on production scheduling and shutdowns. If a line is available for production but is not scheduled to produce, the line must be shut down or deactivated.

    1. Schedule production lines and hours. Production lines to be scheduled for first-shift operation should be entered on the decision form for the area in which they are located. Enter the number of production lines that are to be producing (not more than the maximum available) and the number of hours that are to be scheduled per week (from 40 to 48). Make sure your entry is for the area or areas in which you have a plant. The decision-entry program will not accept an entry for an area where no production lines are available. If new lines are desired, an entry must be made under "New Lines" two quarters before production may be scheduled. See paragraph 1 under "Investment in Production Facilities and Equipment" below.

Limits: Lines -- 0 to maximum number of lines available
            Hours -- 0, 40 to 48

Note: Lines scheduled + lines shut down + lines deactivated must be equal to the number of lines available.

Production Scheduling		
	Production Lines	Hours
Area 1	#_____	#_____
Area 2	#_____	#_____
Area 3	#_____	#_____
Area 4	#_____	#_____
2d Shft	#_____	#_____

    2. Second shift. Production on a second-shift operation is possible only in a firm's home area plant (see Chapter 7). Enter the number of production lines that will be producing on the second shift and the number of hours that are to be scheduled per

week (see paragraph 1, above). Note: Second shift lines are not available and may not be scheduled until workers for the shift have been trained according to paragraph 2 under "Investment in Production Facilities and Equipment" below. An entry must be made under "New Lines" in the Construction section of the form one quarter before second-shift lines may be scheduled for production.

Limits, Lines: 0 to maximum number of lines available

Note: Lines scheduled + lines shut down + lines deactivated (permanently ended) must be equal to the number of lines available.

Limits, Hours: 0, 40 to 48

    3. Shut down lines (for one quarter only). Production lines that are available but not scheduled for production, and have not been deactivated, should be shut down. Enter the number of lines which you plan to shut down on the decision form under "Production Scheduling--Shutdown." Be sure that all lines (both first-shift lines and second-shift lines) are accounted for. If you shut down a first-shift line, a corresponding second-shift line must be shut down or deactivated unless there remains at least as many first-shift lines as second-shift lines. A second-shift line may not continue operating unless there is a corresponding line on the first shift. Check to be sure that your entry is for the area in which you want to shut down lines.

Limits: 0 to maximum number of lines available

Note: Lines scheduled + lines shut down + lines deactivated must be equal to the number of lines available.

Production Scheduling			
	Shut-down	Deac-tivate	Reac-tivate
Area 1	#_____	#_____	#_____
Area 2	#_____	#_____	#_____
Area 3	#_____	#_____	#_____
Area 4	#_____	#_____	#_____
2d Shft	#_____	#_____	

4. Deactivate first-shift lines. Any line that is available for production may be deactivated and removed from production until such time as you choose to reactivate the line. Enter the number of lines that you desire to deactivate in the appropriate area on the decision form under "Production Scheduling--Deactivate." Deactivated lines may not be scheduled for production until they have been reactivated (see paragraph 6, below).

Limits: 0 to the number of lines available for production

Note: Lines scheduled + lines shut down + lines deactivated must be equal to the number of lines available.

5. Deactivate (terminate) second shift. Production lines available for second-shift production may be deactivated (terminated) by entering the number of lines you desire to deactivate under the "Production Scheduling--Deactivate" column for the "2nd Shft" area on the decision form. Second shift lines must be deactivated if the corresponding lines on the first shift are deactivated.

The deactivation of second-shift lines effectively fires the current second-shift workers. To reactivate a second-shift line you must train new workers utilizing the same process as was used to originally create the second-shift line (see 2, above).

Limits: 0 to number of second-shift lines available

Note: Lines scheduled + lines shut down + lines deactivated must be equal to the number of lines available.

6. Reactivate first-shift lines. First-shift production lines that have been previously deactivated (but not second-shift lines) may be reactivated and made available for production. Such lines are reported in the Operating Information Report.

	Area 1	Area 2	Area 3	Area 4
Lines Previously Deactivated	2	0	0	0

Reactivation requires one quarter of preparation before a line may be scheduled for production. Enter the number of lines to be reactivated under the appropriate area on the decision form. Lines may not actually be scheduled for production until the following quarter.

Limits: 0 to number of lines previously deactivated

Investment in Production Facilities and Equipment

Investment in new facilities or equipment may take the form of construction of new lines in existing plants, training workers for second-shift operation, constructing a new addition to an existing plant, or constructing a new plant. For details of these alternatives, see Chapter 8.

1. <u>New First-Shift Lines</u>. Plant space that is available for new line construction is reported in the Operating Information Report.

	Area 1	Area 2	Area 3	Area 4
Space Available for New Lines	2	0	0	0

Construction and preparation of new lines requires two quarters before they become available for production. In Year 3, Quarter 1 as many as two new lines may be added in the existing home area plant. If a new addition or new plant is under construction, the construction of new production lines may be undertaken as early as two quarters before completion of the new plant capacity (see below). In this way, production lines may be made available for production as soon as the new addition or new plant is completed.

Enter the number of new lines to be added in the area where a plant with additional capacity is located. After the construction has begun, no further entry is necessary (that is, enter "0" in subsequent quarters) until the lines are ready and available for production. Positive entries in subsequent quarters will result in starting <u>additional</u> new lines at that time (if space is available). When ready for production, and not before, new lines must be scheduled for production, shut down, or deactivated.

Limits: 0 to space available

Construction		
New Lines	New Add	New Plant
#___	#___	#____
#___	#___	#____
#___	#___	#____
#___	#___	#____
#___		

24

2. <u>New Second-Shift Lines</u>. Where production lines are already producing on the first shift in a home area plant, second-shift operations can be added. You may add second-shift operations to one or more first-shift lines which currently are in operation. To add second-shift lines, enter the number of second-shift lines you wish to add on the decision form in the "New Lines" column under "2d Shft." The line(s) will be available for production during the <u>following</u> quarter.

Limits: 0 to number of 1st shift lines operating in home area

3. <u>New Additions</u>. Additions may be constructed by adding on to existing plants. Capacity may be added in units of <u>two</u> production lines per addition unless the maximum plant size of twelve lines has already been reached. Three quarters are required to construct an addition. An addition may be added to a plant under construction if it is not started prior to the last 3 quarters of plant construction. To begin construction, enter "2"--the number of lines of capacity--under "New Add" on the decision form in the area in which you wish to construct the new lines.

After construction has begun, no further entries are necessary (that is, enter "0" in subsequent quarters unless space is available within the 12-line maximum and you wish to begin construction of another addition). If you wish, you may begin construction of the production lines (paragraph 1, above) so that the lines will be available for production when the new plant is completed. New line construction may be started as soon as the first quarter after construction of the new addition was begun.

Limits: 0 or 2 lines (to a maximum of 12 lines in a plant)

4. <u>New Plant</u>. To begin construction of a new plant, enter the number of lines of capacity that are desired (6, 8, or 10) in the area in which the new plant is to be located. Only one plant per company is permitted in each of the four marketing areas. It takes five quarters to complete the construction of a new plant. After construction has begun, no further entry is required except to begin construction of new lines (see paragraph 1 above) prior to the start of production. New production lines may be started during the fourth quarter of plant construction.

Limits: 0 in home area; 0, 6, 8, 10 lines in other areas

New plants may only be built in areas where there is no existing plant.

Entering Decisions & Printing Reports

You may be asked to use a computer to enter your decisions directly, saving them on a floppy disk or on a hard disk (which may be part of a PC network), and to print your firm's reports. To print reports, see option #3 under "Running the BPG Computer Program" (below).

Your decision set will be stored in a file on the disk and saved for use when the simulation program is run by the administrator. If your decision set is stored on floppy disk, you will need to give your disk to the simulation administrator prior to the time the simulation is to be run.

Before entering your decision on the computer, the following tasks should be performed:

1. <u>Complete decision form</u>. The decision form always should be completed before entering decisions on the computer. The decision form helps to organize your firm's decision set in the order in which the values will be entered. The form centralizes the decision variables in one place, thus easing the chore of checking for decision completeness. The form also serves as the original record of your team's decision. It is recommended that you turn in a copy of your decision form (if you use floppy disks) in case the computer has trouble reading your disk.

2. <u>Obtain access to decision file</u>. Your firm's decision set will be stored on magnetic disk. The simulation administrator will tell you the type of computer system, the type of disk you will use (floppy or hard) and how to access the disk. If you are using an IBM or compatible computer system, read the next section. If you are using a Macintosh computer system, skip to the section labeled "Macintosh Users."

Running the BPG Computer Program
IBM and Compatible Users

<u>Floppy Disk Users</u>

If you are to enter your decision set to be saved on a floppy disk, your team will need a decision disk initialized for your simulated world and company. Your decision file, several data files necessary to run the program, and report files will be stored on the floppy disk. As each team will have a separate decision disk, it is important to know your company and world numbers in order to obtain the correct disk. The simulation administrator will tell you where to obtain your disk.

26

A word about disk etiquette. Handle the disk carefully. Do not touch the surface. Do not bend it or spill coffee or other liquids on it. Do not play frisbee with it. Treat the disk as you would a good friend, gently and carefully.

When entering data using a floppy disk, first put the disk in the disk drive. NEVER PUT A DISK IN A DRIVE WHICH IS SPIN-NING. Open the disk drive door if it is not already open. Grasp the disk, holding it with your fingers on the label end and, for 5 1/4 inch disks, remove the disk from its dust jacket. Be very careful not to touch the surface of the disk which is inside the plastic cover you are holding. Take special care not to bend it. Gently slide the disk into the disk drive with the label side up. After the disk is in the disk drive as far as it will go, close the disk-drive door.

If the computer is off, turn it on after placing a DOS "boot disk" in drive A: unless you are told to use some other drive by the simulation administrator.

If the computer is already running, check the computer prompt showing the active drive (most likely either A:> or B:>) to make sure your disk is in the active drive. If your disk is not in the active drive, either move your disk to the active drive or change the active drive by typing the letter of the drive containing your disk and a colon. Then press <ENTER>. For example, if your disk is in drive B, type:

B: <ENTER>

All Users

First, be sure that the DOS prompt showing on your monitor is for the disk drive and directory containing the Business Policy Game decision-entry program (BPG.EXE) and data files. If you are running from a floppy disk, the DOS prompt may be

A:>

If you are running from a hard disk or local area network, the prompt may also show a directory path, like

C:\BPG2>

If you are not sure of the correct directory, see your simulation administrator.

To run the BPG computer program, type BPG. The program will load from disk and the main menu screen will appear.

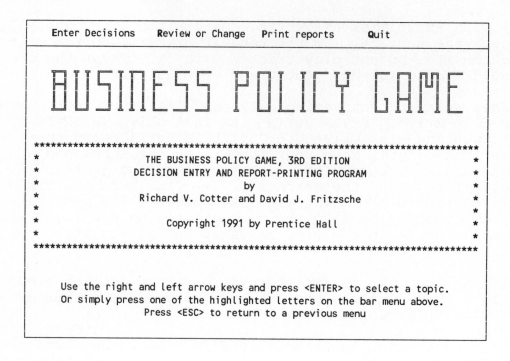

The main menu offers four options, listed across the top of the screen:

    Enter Decisions
    Review or Change
    Print Reports
    Quit

Use the right or left arrow keys to highlight your choice and press <ENTER>, or simply press the first letter of your choice. Each choice is described in detail below.

To enter your first set of decisions, press "E," for ENTER DECISIONS. After choosing your first menu item, an identification (ID) screen will prompt you to enter your Company number, World number, and the Year and the Quarter numbers for your decision set (or if you choose PRINT REPORTS, the Year and Quarter of the reports). The entries in the ID screen example shown below are for Company 1, World 1, Year 3, Quarter 1.

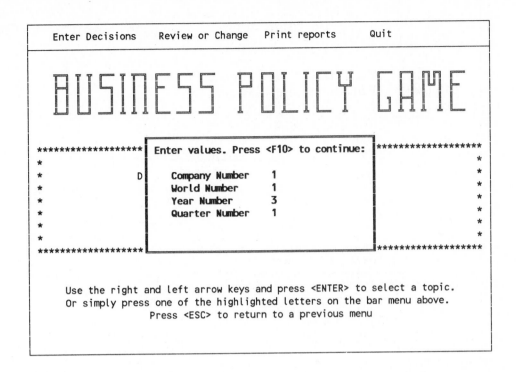

```
     Enter Decisions    Review or Change   Print reports      Quit


     ┌──────────────────────────────────────────────────────────────┐

          BUSINESS POLICY GAME


     *******************┌─────────────────────────────────┐*******************
     *                  │ Enter values. Press <F10> to continue: │                  *
     *               D  │                                 │                  *
     *                  │   Company Number     1          │                  *
     *                  │   World Number       1          │                  *
     *                  │   Year Number        3          │                  *
     *                  │   Quarter Number     1          │                  *
     *                  │                                 │                  *
     *                  │                                 │                  *
     *******************└─────────────────────────────────┘*******************


             Use the right and left arrow keys and press <ENTER> to select a topic.
             Or simply press one of the highlighted letters on the bar menu above.
                      Press <ESC> to return to a previous menu
```

Press the <u><F10> function key</u> to exit the ID screen. If the
values that you entered for identification matched those on your
decision disk or directory, the program will proceed to execute
your choice from the main menu. If they did not match, an error
message will show on the screen and you will have to try again.
The computer will presume that you do not know what you are doing
or that you are an undercover agent for another company. But it
also is possible that you <u>are</u> an honest citizen and inadvertently
picked up the decision disk for another company (if using floppy
disks) or obtained incorrect information from your administrator.
In either case, check with your administrator.

     1.   <u>Enter Decisions</u>. The data entry screen which appears,
shown below, is in a format similar to that of the decision forms
in this manual. The default entries on the screen are values
from your decision set for the previous quarter. For your first
set of decisions, Year 3, Quarter 1, the values should be the
same as those shown on the sample decision form, Figure 2-1.
They are the same ones that were used to generate the reports for
Year 2, Quarter 4.

     Decision values are entered by moving the cursor to one of
the variables on the screen and entering the new value for that
variable. Move the cursor to the next field by pressing <ENTER>
or move it back one field by pressing the <up-arrow> key.   Other

cursor-movement keys may be used to move around the input screen.
They are as follows:

<ENTER>	Forward one field
<Down-arrow>	Forward one field
<Up-arrow>	Back one field
<Tab>	Forward one column
<Shft-tab>	Backward one column
<Page down>	Move to last field
<Page up>	Move to first field
<ESC>	Return to the main menu without saving values

```
╔══════════════╦═══════════════╦═══════════════════╦═══════════════════════════╗
║  F1 - Help   ║  ESC - Back   ║  ENTER - Next Field ║  F10 - Exit or Save Decision ║
╠══════════════╩═══════════════╩═══════════════════╩═══════════════════════════╣
║  Company 1 World 1 Year 3 Quarter 1 -- Default values are from last quarter   ║
║                                                                               ║
║         ┌Price     Adv.        Salespeople        ┐  ┌                       ┐║
║         │                  Hire  Trans  Commission │  │Bank Loan        0     │║
║  Area 1 │10.00     46        1     0        20     │  │Bond Issue       00    │║
║  Area 2 │10.00     40        1     0               │  │Stock Issue      00    │║
║  Area 3 │10.00     40        1     0      Salary   │  │Dividends         0    │║
║  Area 4 │10.00     46        1     0      3000     │  │Time CDs        100    │║
║         └                                          ┘  └                       ┘║
║                                                                               ║
║     Model           Production Scheduling              Construction           ║
║   ┌          ┐   ┌                                  ┐ ┌                     ┐ ║
║   │Model  1  │   │Production Shut- Deac-  Reac-     │ │New  New  New        │ ║
║   │Qual   2  │   │Lines Hours down tivate tivate    │ │Lines Add Plant      │ ║
║   └          ┘   │                                  │ │                     │ ║
║           Area 1 │  6    40    0     0     0        │ │ 0    0    0         │ ║
║     R & D  Area 2 │  0     0    0     0     0        │ │ 0    0    0         │ ║
║           Area 3 │  0     0    0     0     0        │ │ 0    0    0         │ ║
║   ┌          ┐ Area 4 │ 0   0    0     0     0       │ │ 0    0    0         │ ║
║   │Prod  72  │ 2d Shft│ 0   0    0     0             │ │ 0                   │ ║
║   │Proc  68  │       └                              ┘ └                     ┘ ║
║   └          ┘                                                                 ║
╚═══════════════════════════════════════════════════════════════════════════════╝
```

If you should enter an illegal value, or one outside of the range
permitted by the rules of the game, an error message will appear
in the middle of the screen, suggesting the range of values that
you may enter. If you have a question about the range of values
for a particular decision variable, move the cursor to the
numeric field for that variable and press the <F1> function key
for context-sensitive help. A help screen will be superimposed
on the input screen with information about that variable. For
example, the help screen for the Price variable is shown below.
Press <ESC> to restore the decision-input screen.

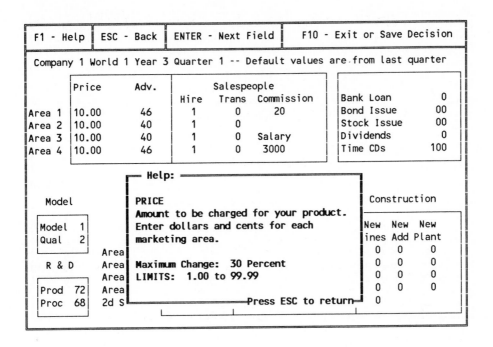

```
┌─────────┬───────────┬────────────────────┬───────────────────────────┐
│ F1 - Help │ ESC - Back │ ENTER - Next Field │  F10 - Exit or Save Decision │
└─────────┴───────────┴────────────────────┴───────────────────────────┘

 Company 1 World 1 Year 3 Quarter 1 -- Default values are from last quarter

        │ Price    Adv.        Salespeople          │
        │                  Hire  Trans  Commission  │ Bank Loan      0
 Area 1 │ 10.00     46      1      0       20        │ Bond Issue    00
 Area 2 │ 10.00     40      1      0                 │ Stock Issue   00
 Area 3 │ 10.00     40      1      0     Salary      │ Dividends      0
 Area 4 │ 10.00     46      1      0      3000       │ Time CDs     100

                 ┌─ Help: ──────────────────────────┐
    Model        │ PRICE                             │  Construction
                 │ Amount to be charged for your product. │
  ┌───────────┐  │ Enter dollars and cents for each  │  New  New  New
  │ Model  1  │  │ marketing area.                   │  ines Add Plant
  │ Qual   2  │  │                              Area │   0    0    0
  └───────────┘  │ Maximum Change:  30 Percent  Area │   0    0    0
     R & D       │ LIMITS:  1.00 to 99.99       Area │   0    0    0
  ┌───────────┐  │                              Area │   0    0    0
  │ Prod  72  │  └────────────────Press ESC to return┘   0
  │ Proc  68  │  2d S
  └───────────┘
```

When you have finished entering your set of decisions,
carefully check the values on the screen against the values on
your decision form to make sure that you have entered all of the
values and that they are correct. Each value that has been
changed from the default value will be highlighted. While you
may have been called a "good kid," you do not want to become the
team goat for entering an incorrect decision which causes your
firm to lose thousands of dollars.

After you are satisfied that your firm's decision set has
been entered correctly, press the <u><F10> function key</u>. There will
be a short pause while all values from the screen are checked for
conformation to the rules of the game. If any values fall
outside of legal ranges you will be returned to the decision-
entry screen with the cursor located in the field in question. A
message at the middle of the screen will identify the problem.
Additional help can be obtained by pressing the <F1> function
key. If all values pass the test, the menu shown below will be
superimposed over the data entry screen. Press "Y" to save the
decision. If you decide to return to the menu screen without
saving the decision, press the "N" key. If you would like to
stay with the data entry screen (as you would if you pressed
<F10> by mistake), press the "D" key. Pressing "Y" or "N" will
return you to the main menu screen. If you return without saving
values, don't forget to run the program again, later.

Company 1 World 1 Year 3 Quarte

```
                                  Press Y to Save Decisions
          Price      Adv.         Press N to Return to Menu without Saving
                           Hire   Press D to Return to Decision Input Screen
Area 1   10.00       46    1
Area 2   10.00       40    1      0                 Stock Issue    00
Area 3   10.00       40    1      0    Salary       Dividends       0
Area 4   10.00       46    1      0    3000         Time CDs      100
```

Model		Production Scheduling					Construction		
Model 1		Production		Shut-	Deac-	Reac-	New	New	New
Qual 2		Lines	Hours	down	tivate	tivate	Lines	Add	Plant
	Area 1	6	40	0	0	0	0	0	0
R & D	Area 2	0	0	0	0	0	0	0	0
	Area 3	0	0	0	0	0	0	0	0
Prod 72	Area 4	0	0	0	0	0	0	0	0
Proc 68	2d Shft	0	0	0	0		0		

   Good luck. May your decisions be wise and your entries be
error free. But just in case you discover, too late, that you
have entered incorrect values; or in case you change your mind
about some of the decisions that you have entered, read the next
section.

   2. Review or Change. You may review or change your current-quarter decision set as many times as you like prior to the
time designated by your administrator to run the simulation.
After the simulation has been run it is too late--you will have
to live with the decision that was entered. This option is
available only if you already have entered a set of decisions for
the current quarter. If no decisions have been entered previously, you will receive an error message. In this case, try the
first option from the menu, ENTER DECISIONS.

   After selecting the REVIEW OR CHANGE option, the data entry
screen showing your current decision set which has been previously entered for this quarter will appear. You may change any of
the variable values shown on the screen by moving the cursor to
the variable and entering the new value. The cursor is moved
down by pressing <ENTER> and is moved up by pressing <ESC>.
Other cursor-movement keys are the same as those shown above
under ENTER DECISIONS.

   After you are satisfied that your firm's decision set has
been entered correctly, press the F10 function key. There will
be a short pause while all values from the screen are checked for
conformation to the rules of the game. If any values fall

outside of legal ranges you will be returned to the decision-
entry screen with the cursor located in the field in question. A
message at the middle of the screen will identify the problem.
Additional help can be obtained by pressing the F1 function key.
If all values pass the test, the menu shown below will be superimposed over the data entry screen. Press "Y" to save the
decision. If you decide to return to the menu screen without
saving the decision, press the "N" key. If you would like to
stay with the data entry screen (as you would if you pressed
<F10> by mistake), press the "D" key. Pressing "Y" or "N" will
return you to the menu screen.

F1 - Help	ESC - Back	ENTER - Next Field	F10 - Exit or Save Decision

Company 1 World 1 Year 3 Quarter

Press **Y** to Save Decisions
Press **N** to Return to Menu without Saving
Press **D** to Return to Decision Input Screen

	Price	Adv.	Hire				
Area 1	10.00	46	1				
Area 2	10.00	40	1	0		Stock Issue	00
Area 3	10.00	40	1	0	Salary	Dividends	0
Area 4	10.00	46	1	0	3000	Time CDs	100

Model

Model	1
Qual	2

R & D

Prod	72
Proc	68

Production Scheduling

Construction

	Production Lines	Hours	Shut-down	Deac-tivate	Reac-tivate	New Lines	New Add	New Plant
Area 1	6	40	0	0	0	0	0	0
Area 2	0	0	0	0	0	0	0	0
Area 3	0	0	0	0	0	0	0	0
Area 4	0	0	0	0	0	0	0	0
2d Shft	0	0	0	0		0		

A note of caution is in order. It is possible to overwrite
a new decision file on your disk with old data. When you choose
ENTER DECISIONS from the main menu, the default values on the
decision screen are from the previous quarter. If you have
previously entered new decision values for the current quarter,
they may be retrieved as default values only when you select
REVIEW DECISIONS. If you wish to review them later, but mistakenly should select ENTER DECISIONS you may have a problem.
The default values on the screen will not be the ones that you
previously entered, but rather the values that were used for the
past quarter. Press <ESC>, return to the main menu, and start
over. Otherwise, you may inadvertently clobber your previously-
entered decision file. If, without changing any default values,
you press <F10> and SAVE the default values, last quarter's
decision values will be overwritten to your current-quarter's
decision file. Any previously-entered values will be overwritten
and lost forever. BE CAREFUL!

3. Print Reports. After the simulation has been run, your report files may be returned on your decision disk or directory. To print the output, select this option. Sample reports for Year 2, Quarter 4 may be found in Appendix B, or you may be asked to print copies from your disk. If your printed copies are different from those in the appendix, you should rely on the newly printed copies.

After choosing PRINT REPORTS, the menu for printing company reports will appear on your screen.

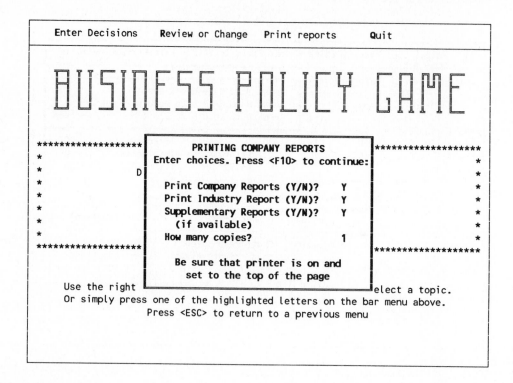

Choose which reports you wish to print by entering "Y" for Yes or "N" for No. Indicate the desired number of copies. Then press <F10> to continue. Your printer must be on-line and the paper should be positioned to start printing at the top of the page. When all reports have been printed, you will be returned to the main menu.

4. **Quit**. Select this option when you want to end your current session with the computer. The menu shown below will appear superimposed over the menu screen. Press the "Y" key to end the session. Press the "N" key to return to the menu.

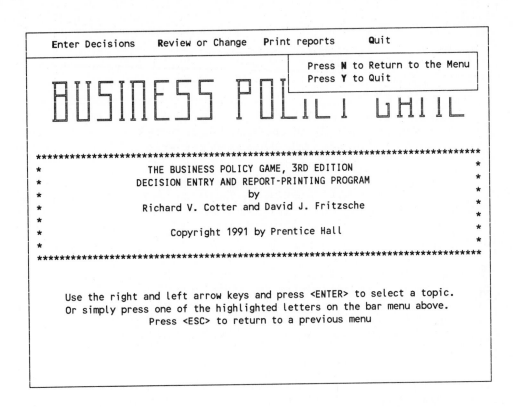

```
Enter Decisions     Review or Change    Print reports      Quit
                                        ┌──────────────────────────────┐
                                        │ Press N to Return to the Menu │
                                        │ Press Y to Quit               │
BUSINESS POLICY GAME ──────────────────────────────────────────────┘


**************************************************************************
*                                                                        *
*                THE BUSINESS POLICY GAME, 3RD EDITION                    *
*                DECISION ENTRY AND REPORT-PRINTING PROGRAM               *
*                                 by                                      *
*                 Richard V. Cotter and David J. Fritzsche                *
*                                                                         *
*                   Copyright 1991 by Prentice Hall                       *
*                                                                         *
**************************************************************************


           Use the right and left arrow keys and press <ENTER> to select a topic.
           Or simply press one of the highlighted letters on the bar menu above.
                     Press <ESC> to return to a previous menu
```

Floppy Disk Users

After you have received the message that your current session has ended and the disk drive has stopped whirring (the disk light is off), open the disk drive door and carefully remove the disk. Then shut the computer off. DO NOT REMOVE THE DISK UNTIL THE DISK DRIVE HAS STOPPED SPINNING. YOU CAN DESTROY THE CONTENTS OF A DISK IF YOU REMOVE IT WHILE THE DRIVE IS RUNNING.

Place the disk back into its protective sleeve if it is a 5 1/4 inch disk, and return it to the security of your firm's records area. Arrange for delivery of the disk to the administrator prior to the simulation run!

Note: Your firm is responsible for providing the administrator with a disk containing the current Quarter's decision set prior to the simulation run time. Failure to do so will result in the previous Quarter's decision set being used for your current decision.

35

Running the BPG Computer Program
Macintosh Users

Floppy Disk Users

To enter your decision on floppy disk, your team will need a decision disk initialized for your simulated company and world. Your decision file, several data files necessary to run the program, and report files will be stored on the floppy disk. As each team will have a separate decision disk, it is important to know your company and world numbers in order to obtain the correct disk. The simulation administrator will tell you where to obtain your disk.

A word about disk etiquette. Handle the disk carefully. Do not spill coffee or other liquids on it. Do not play frisbee with it. Treat the disk as you would a good friend, gently and carefully.

When entering data using a floppy disk, first put the disk in the disk drive. Grasp the disk, holding it with your fingers on the label end. Be very careful <u>not</u> to touch the surface of the disk which is inside the plastic cover you are holding. Gently slide the disk into the disk drive with the label side up. The drive will take control of the disk after it is pushed about half way into the drive.

If the computer is off, turn it on and wait until the desktop appears prior to inserting your disk in a floppy drive.

All Users

The disk icon for the drive containing your Player's Disk (when using floppy disks for data entry) or your folder (when decisions are to be saved to a hard disk) should be named BPGcw, where:

> c = your company number
> w = your world number.

Thus, if your firm is Company 3 in World 2, your disk (or folder) should be named BPG32.

Double click on the disk icon to open the disk or folder. Find the application file named

> BPG.BAS APL

Double click on this file and the main menu screen will appear.

The main menu offers three options, listed across the top of the screen:

The main menu offers three options, listed across the top of the screen:

    Decisions
    Reports
    Quit

Click on one of the menu options to pull down the menu. Then move the cursor to your choice and release the mouse key. Or you may hold down the command key and press the letter associated with your choice.

To enter your first set of decisions, click on DECISIONS and move the cursor to ENTER NEW DECISIONS, or hold down the command key and press "E." After choosing your first menu item, an identification (ID) screen will prompt you to enter your Company number, World number, and the Year and the Quarter numbers for your decision set (or if you choose PRINT REPORTS, the Year and Quarter of the reports). The entries in the ID screen example shown below are for Company 1, World 1, Year 3, Quarter 1.

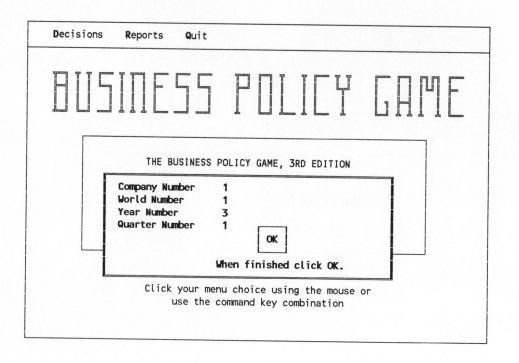

Click on OK to exit the ID screen. If the values that you entered for identification matched those on your decision disk or directory, the program will proceed to execute your choice from the main menu. If they did not match, an error message will show on the screen and you will have to try again. The computer will presume that you do not know what you are doing or that you are an undercover agent for another company. But it also is possible that you _are_ an honest citizen and inadvertently picked up the decision disk for another company (if using floppy disks) or obtained incorrect information from your administrator. In either case, check with your administrator.

1. _Enter Decisions_. The data entry screen which appears, shown below, is in a format similar to that of the decision forms in this manual. The default entries on the screen are values from your decision set for the previous quarter. For your first set of decisions, Year 3, Quarter 1, the default values on the screen should be the same as those shown on the sample decision form, Figure 2-1. They are the same ones that were used to generate the reports for Year 2, Quarter 4.

Decision values are entered by moving the cursor to one of the variables on the screen and entering the new value for that variable. Click on the desired field using the mouse. Other cursor-movement keys may be used to move around the input screen. They are as follows:

<ENTER>	Forward one field
<Tab>	Forward one column
Mouse click	Any field

```
┌──────────────────────────────────────────────────────────────────┐
│   Help     Exit                                                    │
├──────────────────────────────────────────────────────────────────┤
│ Company 1 World 1 Year 3 Quarter 1 -- Default values are from last quarter │
│                                                                    │
│        Price    Adv.        Salespeople                            │
│                         Hire  Trans  Commission   Bank Loan      0 │
│ Area 1 10.00     46      1      0       20        Bond Issue    00 │
│ Area 2 10.00     40      1      0                 Stock Issue   00 │
│ Area 3 10.00     40      1      0     Salary      Dividends      0 │
│ Area 4 10.00     46      1      0      3000       Time CDs     100 │
│                                                                    │
│                                                                    │
│     Model          Production Scheduling        Construction       │
│                                                                    │
│  Model   1      Production Shut- Deac-  Reac-    New  New  New      │
│  Qual    2      Lines Hours down  tivate tivate Lines Add Plant     │
│              Area 1   6    40    0    0      0     0  .0    0        │
│     R & D    Area 2   0     0    0    0      0     0   0    0        │
│              Area 3   0     0    0    0      0     0   0    0        │
│  Prod  72    Area 4   0     0    0    0      0     0   0    0        │
│  Proc  68    2d Shft  0     0    0    0            0                 │
└──────────────────────────────────────────────────────────────────┘
```

If you should enter an illegal value, or one outside of the range permitted by the rules of the game, an error message will appear in the middle of the screen, suggesting the range of values that you may enter. If you have a question about the range of values for a particular decision variable, move the cursor to the numeric field for that variable and pull down the HELP menu for context-sensitive help. Then, select VARIABLE INFORMATION. Or hold down the command key and press "H." A help screen will be superimposed on the input screen with information about that variable. For example, the help screen for the Price variable is shown below. Click on OK to restore the decision-input screen.

Company 1 World 1 Year 3 Quarter 1 -- Default values are from last quarter

| | Price | Adv. | Salespeople | | | | | |
			Hire	Trans	Commission			
Area 1	10.00	46	1	0	20	Bank Loan	0
Area 2	10.00	40	1	0		Bond Issue	00
Area 3	10.00	40	1	0	Salary	Stock Issue	00
Area 4	10.00	46	1	0	3000	Dividends	0
						Time CDs	100

Model

| Model | 1 |
| Qual | 2 |

R & D

| Prod | 72 |
| Proc | 68 |

Area
Area
Area
Area
2d S

PRICE
Amount to be charged for your product.
Enter dollars and cents for each
marketing area.

Maximum Change: 30 Percent
LIMITS: 1.00 to 99.99

Click [OK]

Construction

| New | New | New |
ines	Add	Plant
0	0	0
0	0	0
0	0	0
0	0	0
0		

When you have finished entering your set of decisions, carefully check the values on the screen against the values on your decision form to make sure that you have entered all of the values and that they are correct. While you may have been called a "good kid," you do not want to become the team goat for entering an incorrect decision which causes your firm to lose thousands of dollars.

After you are satisfied that your firm's decision set has been entered correctly, pull down the EXIT menu and select either SAVE DECISION or WITHOUT SAVING DECISION. You may also hold down the command key and press either "S" or "X." There will be a short pause while all values from the screen are checked for conformation to the rules of the game. If any values fall outside of legal ranges you will be returned to the decision-entry screen with the cursor located in the field in question. A message at the middle of the screen will identify the problem. Additional help can be obtained by using the help menu. If all values pass the test, you will be returned to the main menu screen. If you return without saving values, don't forget to run the program again, later.

There is additional help for data entry, which can be accessed by pulling down the HELP menu and selecting INSTRUCTIONS FOR DATA ENTRY, or the command key plus "I."

Good luck. May your decisions be wise and your entries be error free. But just in case you discover, too late, that you have entered incorrect values; or in case you change your mind about some of the decisions that you have entered, read the next section.

2. Review or Change. You may review or change your cur-rent-quarter decision set as many times as you like prior to the time designated by your administrator to run the simulation. After the simulation has been run it is too late--you will have to live with the decision that was entered. This option is available only if you already have entered a set of decisions for the current quarter. If no decisions have been entered previous-ly, you will receive an error message. In this case, try the first option from the DECISIONS menu, ENTER NEW DECISIONS.

After selecting the REVIEW OR CHANGE option, the data entry screen showing your current decision set which has been previous-ly entered for this quarter will appear. You may change any of the variable values shown on the screen by moving the cursor to the variable and entering the new value. The cursor is moved down by pressing <ENTER> and is moved up by clicking on a field, using the mouse. Other cursor-movement keys are the same as those shown above under ENTER NEW DECISIONS.

After you are satisfied that your firm's decision set has been entered correctly, pull down the EXIT menu and select SAVE DECISION or WITHOUT SAVING DECISION. There will be a short pause while all values from the screen are checked for conformation to the rules of the game. If any values fall outside of legal ranges you will be returned to the decision-entry screen with the cursor located in the field in question. A message at the middle of the screen will identify the problem. Additional help can be obtained by pulling down the HELP menu. If all values pass the test, you will be returned to the main menu screen.

A note of caution is in order. It is possible to overwrite a new decision file on your disk with old data. When you choose ENTER NEW DECISIONS from the main menu, the default values on the decision screen are from the previous quarter. If you have previously entered new decision values for the current quarter, they may be retrieved as default values only when you select REVIEW OR CHANGE DECISIONS. If you wish to review them later, but mistakenly should select ENTER NEW DECISIONS you may have a problem. The default values on the screen will not be the ones that you previously entered, but rather the values that were used for the past quarter. Pull down the EXIT menu and select WITHOUT SAVING, return to the main menu, and start over. Otherwise, you may inadvertently clobber your previously-entered decision file. If, without changing any default values, you select the EXIT menu and SAVE the default values, last quarter's decision values will be overwritten to your current-quarter decision file. Any previously-entered values will be overwritten and lost forever. BE CAREFUL!

3. Print Reports. After the simulation has been run, your report files may be returned on your decision disk or directory. To print the output, select this option. Sample reports for Year 2, Quarter 4 may be found in Appendix B, or you may be asked to print copies from your disk. If your printed copies are different from those in the appendix, you should rely on the newly printed copies.

After choosing PRINT REPORTS, the menu for printing company reports will appear on your screen.

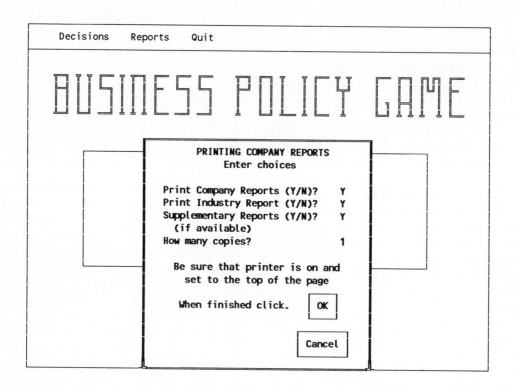

Choose which reports you wish to print by entering "Y" for Yes or "N" for No. Indicate the desired number of copies. Then click on OK to continue. Your printer must be on-line and the paper should be positioned to start printing at the top of the page. When all reports have been printed, you will be returned to the main menu screen.

4. Quit. Select this option when you want to end your current session with the computer. Pull down the QUIT menu and select EXIT PROGRAM, or hold down the command key and press "Q."

Floppy Disk Users

After you have received the message that your current session has ended and your disk is visible on the desktop, move the disk icon to the trash can to eject it from the computer. If you want to shut the computer off, pull down the SPECIAL menu and select SHUT DOWN. In a minute a message will appear indicating that it is safe to turn off the computer, or the computer may turn itself off, depending upon the Macintosh model you are using.

Return the disk to the security of your firm's records area. Arrange for delivery of the disk to the administrator prior to the simulation run!

Note: Your firm is responsible for providing the administrator with a disk containing the current Quarter's decision set prior to the simulation run time. Failure to do so will result in the previous Quarter's decision set being used for your current decision.

Summary

Steps for entering decisions and printing output.

    1.   Complete Decision Form

    2.   Run BPG computer program

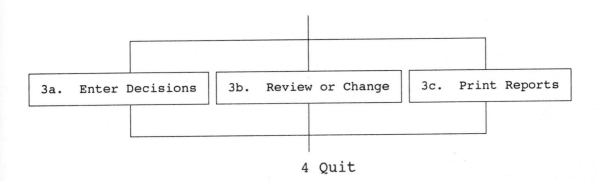

4 Quit

Quick Reference

A quick reference guide to the variable definitions and valid entry limits for each of the variables may be found in Figure 2-2. The variables are listed in order of their appearance on the decision form. A quick reference guide to operating costs may be found in Figure 2-3.

PRICE
Amount to be charged for your product. Enter
dollars and cents for each marketing area.
Maximum change: 30 percent
Limits: 1.00 to 99.99

ADVERTISING
Amount to be spent for advertising in each
marketing area (thousands of dollars)
Limits: 0 to 999

HIRE NEW SALESPEOPLE
Number of new salespeople to be hired. Those
hired now will be in training for two quarters,
then become active salespeople in the third
quarter.
Limits: 0 to 99

TRANSFER OR DISCHARGE SALESPEOPLE
Number to be transferred or discharged
Negative: fire or transfer out.
Positive: transfer in.
A negative balance will be fired.
Maximum number to be fired or transferred is the
number available minus 1.
Limits: -9 to 99

COMMISSION
Amount of commission (in cents) to be paid to
each salesperson for each unit sold, in addition
to salary.
Limits: 1 to 99

SALARY
Quarterly salary (in dollars) to be paid to
 salespeople in addition to commissions.
Limits: 1 to 9999

BANK LOAN
Short-term loan for one quarter.
Maximum: 50% of receivables plus inventory
Minimum: 0 if a loan was outstanding in each of
         the last three quarters.
Limits: 0 to 2500 (in thousands of dollars)

BOND ISSUE (Sold in million-dollar lots)
Positive: Sell new 10-year bonds.
Maximum: 50% of equity or 75% of net fixed
         assets, whichever is less.
Limits: 0 to 9000 (in thousands of dollars)

Negative: Redeem outstanding bonds.
Limits: -500 to 0 (in thousands of dollars)

STOCK ISSUE (Sold in 100-thousand share lots)
Positive: Number of common shares to be issued
Minimum issue: $1 million
Negative: Number of shares to repurchase
Maximum repurchase: to leave at least 3 million
         shares outstanding, with positive
         retained earnings
Limits: -500 to 9000 (in thousands of shares)

DIVIDENDS (Declared and Paid)
Amount to pay (in thousands of dollars)
Maximum: Net income last 4 quarters minus
         dividends paid last 3 quarters.
Limits: 0 to 9999

TIME CERTIFICATES OF DEPOSIT (CDs)
Short-term 3-month investments, purchased in
100,000 dollar lots.
Limits: 0 to 9900 (in thousands of dollars)

MODEL NUMBER
Model number to produce this quarter. New model
goes on sale next quarter.
Minimum: Same model number as last quarter.
Maximum: Highest number reported available.
Limits: 1 to 12

QUALITY (of product)
May be changed only on introduction of new
model.
Enter 1 for deluxe
Enter 2 for standard
Enter 3 for economy
Limits: 1 to 3

(Continued on next page)

PRODUCT RESEARCH & DEVELOPMENT
Amount to spend on developing new product
models.
Limits: 1 to 999 (in thousands of dollars)

PROCESS RESEARCH & DEVELOPMENT
Amount to spend on developing improved
production processes (to reduce production
costs).
Limits: 1 to 999 (in thousands of dollars)

SCHEDULING PRODUCTION LINES, HOURS (First Shift)
Lines: Number scheduled in each plant.
Lines not scheduled must be shut down or deacti
vated.
Limits: 0 to number of lines available

Hours: Number of hours scheduled per week.
Limits: 0, 40 to 48

SECOND-SHIFT LINES, HOURS
Lines: Number scheduled for Second Shift.
Limits: 0 to number of first-shift lines
        available. New lines must be prepared
before production may be scheduled.
Hours: Number of hours scheduled per week.
Limits: 0, 40 to 48

SHUT DOWN PRODUCTION LINES
Number to shut down (for one quarter only).
Available lines not scheduled for production
must be shut down or deactivated.
Limits: 0 to number of lines available

DEACTIVATE PRODUCTION LINES (First Shift)
Number of lines to be deactivated (not available
for production until reactivated). Lines not
scheduled for production must be shut down or
deactivated.
Limits: 0 to number of lines available

DEACTIVATE SECOND-SHIFT LINES
Number of 2nd-shift lines to terminate
(permanently not available for production). If
2nd-shift production is desired later you may
construct new 2nd-shift lines.
Limits: 0 to number of lines available

REACTIVATE PRODUCTION LINES
Number of first-shift lines (previously deactivated) to be prepared for production next
quarter.
Limits: 0 to number previously deactivated

NEW PRODUCTION LINES (First Shift)
Number of new lines to be prepared for
production. Preparation continues for 2
quarters. Lines will be available for
production in the 3rd quarter.
Limits: 0 to space available

NEW SECOND-SHIFT LINES
Number of new or reactivated lines to be
prepared for 2nd-shift production. Lines will
be available for production next quarter.
Limits: 0 to number of first-shift lines

NEW ADDITION
Number of lines capacity to add to plant. Construction takes 3 quarters. New lines are not
automatic. They may be prepared next quarter
(or later). Maximum plant capacity is 12 lines.
Limits: 0 or 2 (to a maximum of 12 lines)

NEW PLANT
Number of lines capacity desired for a new plant
to be constructed. New plants may only be built
in areas where there is no existing plant.
Limits: 0, 6, 8, or 10

FIGURE 2-3
SUMMARY OF THE BUSINESS POLICY GAME COSTS -- Year 2, Quarter 4
(Costs change over time because of inflation and changes made by management.)

Marketing Expenses

Salespeople -- Salaries and commissions: $3,000/quarter + 20 cents/unit
                Training: $5,000/quarter/trainee
                Moving expense: $5,000/salesperson transferred
                Severance expense: $5,000/salesperson fired

Inventory storage: In-plant warehouse -- 10 cents per unit up to 300,000 units
                Public warehouse: 30 cents per unit

Transportation within area produced: 10 cents/unit
              To Area 4: 40 cents/unit
           To Other areas: 70 cents/unit

General selling expenses: $150,000/quarter + $4,000/salesperson + 20 cents/unit

---

Production Costs

Labor costs/line for Model 1, Quality 2

		Standard costs/unit	
(Other models, as reported)			
Straight time:	$240/hour for Model 1	Labor	$2.40
Second shift:	110% of straight time	Materials	1.20
Overtime:	150% of straight time	Maintenance	.25
		Total (Qual 2)	$3.85
Maintenance:	$25/hour/line	(Qual 1)	+ 10%
		(Qual 3)	- 10%

Shutdown standby cost: $52,000/quarter/line
Deactivation cost: $100,000/line (1st shift)
Reactivation cost: $50,000/line (1st shift)

Construction:
     New line -- $500,000/line + Worker training: $100,000/line--1st shift or 2nd shift
     Equipment replacement costs: $106,000 in Year 2, Quarter 4
         1/28 of existing equipment replaced each quarter at current costs
     New plant addition: $900,000 per 2-line addition
     New plant construction: 6 lines: $2,600,000
                        8 lines: $3,300,000
                    10 lines: $4,000,000

Finance Expenses

Bank loan: Interest for quarter at current short-term interest rate
Bonds: existing -- 10% interest, new -- current long term interest rate.
       Interest paid quarterly. Callable at 5 percent call premium
Common stock: issue price determined by formula in text
Income tax: 39% of net income; paid 1st quarter of following year

---

Other Expenses

Executives' salaries: $150,000/quarter
Plant depreciation (Y2,Q4): $32,000/quarter (existing plant) in Year 2, Quarter 4
      Straight-line basis over 31.5 years, no salvage value (0.7936% per quarter)
Equipment depreciation: $110,000 in Year 2, Quarter 4 (existing equipment)
      Straight-line basis over 7 years, no salvage value (3.5714% per quarter)

CHAPTER 3

THE BUSINESS ENVIRONMENT

As the Business Policy Game begins, you and your fellow team members are assuming the management of a simulated corporation that has been in existence for a number of years. Your firm's principal business activities are the production and distribution of an unnamed product that has the general marketing characteristics of a consumer durable good. The product's characteristics represent a composite of the characteristics of a number of products in the "business world" and thus cannot be accurately described by any unique existing product. The same product type is also manufactured and sold by other firms in direct competition with your firm. However, these products are differentiated in the minds of consumers.

The firms in your industry have surprisingly similar histories during past years. Examination of the financial statements and other historical data that are presented in Appendix A will highlight the fact that there has been little, if any, difference among the products sold by the various companies in your industry. Each company has maintained substantially the same level of sales; production levels for each company have been about the same; the pattern of financing has been similar; and profits have differed by a relatively small amount. One almost could guess that the various companies have been operating under the same management, unless collusion were present--an unlikely assumption in view of the antitrust laws that exist in our simulated world.

As the simulation develops, you may be sure that the different operating strategies that will be developed by your firm and its competitors will cause a divergence among the production, sales, financing, and profit performance of the various competing companies. Furthermore, as you and your competitors place new models on the market, you will find that there is a difference between the way your product is received by the market and the way in which your competitors' products are received. Consumers will demonstrate brand preference. You may prefer to think of the differences as akin to the differences between a new IBM PS/2 and a new Compaq or perhaps even an Apple Macintosh microcomputer.

Economic Environment

The firms in your industry are conducting business in a simulated environment with an economy that is similar to the economy of your country during recent years. Because of this similarity, a knowledge of the characteristics of your nation's economy will enable your firm to make certain inferences about the simulated economic environment. Your country's gross national product (GNP) for example, has generally increased over time. However, unless your country is highly unusual, this growth has not been constant over time as indicated by the historical record. The gross national product, as well as other economic time series indexes, has fluctuated considerably.

The current-dollar GNP index for the Business Policy Game is reported in the Quarterly Industry Report, unadjusted for inflation. In addition, a four-quarter forecast of real GNP, adjusted for changes in the Consumer Price Index, is purchased every three months by your marketing department and reported each quarter.

	REAL GROSS NATIONAL PRODUCT FORECAST							
	Actual Values for Last 4 Quarters				Forecast Values, Next 4 Quarters			
	Qtr 5	Qtr 6	Qtr 7	Qtr 8	Qtr 9	Qtr 10	Qtr 11	Qtr 12
HIGH					105.03	107.94	110.74	113.73
MEAN	98.51	101.02	101.44	101.98	103.99	106.52	108.93	111.50
LOW					102.95	105.10	107.12	109.27

As you might expect, the quality of the forecast is best for the quarter immediately ahead, with a wider range of possible values as time becomes more distant. These are, in fact, excellent forecasts and may be relied upon. The interval between the high and low values of forecasted GNP may be considered as a 95 percent confidence interval--that is, the actual value of nominal GNP can be expected to fall within this interval about 95 percent of the time.

Other economic time series also are included in the Business Policy Game. The impact of price level changes is shown by the Consumer Price Index (CPI), also reported quarterly. The stock market index may be considered as roughly comparable to the Dow Jones Industrial Average, the Tokyo Stock Exchange Nikkei 225 average, the Frankfort Stock Exchange FAZ index or the Sydney

Stock Exchange All Ordinaries index of the business world. Interest rates in the simulation will rise and fall in much the same manner as rates in your country during the last several years. You will find that knowledge of these economic times series data is helpful as you forecast future levels of simulated economic activity. Suggestions for using techniques to forecast future economic activity are found in Chapter 6.

GNP Index (Current $	110.55		---Credit Rating---		
Consumer Price Index	108.41	Interest Rates:	No. 1	No. 2	No. 3
Stock Market Index	109.12	Long-Term	7.60	8.80	9.80
Stock Market Earnings Yield	6.09	Short-Term	6.00	6.40	7.80
3-Month Time CD Rate	4.50				

Marketing Areas

The simulated country in which The Business Policy Game is set is divided into four marketing areas as shown on the map in Figure 3-1. If the shape of the simulated country does not match the shape of your country, you may want to divide a map of your country into four areas to represent the four marketing areas of the simulation. For purposes of the simulation, numerical designations have been given to each area. The Northeast portion of the country is known as Area 1, the Southeast portion as Area 2, the Northwest portion as Area 3 and the Southwest portion as Area 4. The level of economic activity in each of these areas is growing along with that of the country as a whole. The rate of growth, however, is not the same for each area. Areas 1, 2 and 3 are growing 20 percent slower than the economy as a whole, while Area 4 is growing much faster--at a rate about 50 percent greater than the entire economy.

The numerical designations for the marketing areas correspond to the home areas of the companies that are competing in the simulation. Company 1 has a production plant located in its home area, Area 1. Company 2 is located in Area 2 and Company 3 in Area 3. If more than three teams are competing, company 4 has Area 1 for its home area along with Company 1. Company 5 is located in Area 2, and Company 6 is located in Area 3. As yet, no company has located any production facilities in Area 4. The administrator of the simulation will assign team numbers to each company and will let you know how many companies are competing.

Production, Research and Development, Distribution

While each company has been producing goods only in its home area, marketing activities have been ongoing and its sales force has been operating in each of the four marketing areas. During

49

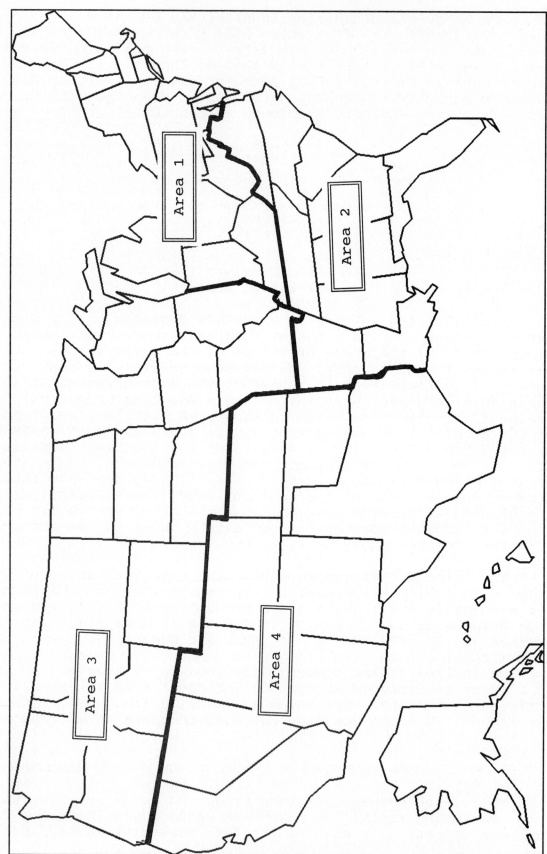

FIGURE 3-1
Map of Marketing Areas

the fourth quarter of Year 2, each company posted a wholesale price of $10 per unit in each marketing area. Advertising, salespeoples' salaries and commissions and other distribution costs have averaged approximately $3.25 per unit sold. Transportation costs vary according to the distance of the shipment. Shipping costs on goods that are shipped to points within the home area amount to ten cents per unit. Freight is somewhat higher on goods shipped to points in non-home areas with total shipping charges amounting to forty cents per unit for goods shipped to Area 4 and seventy cents per unit for goods shipped to other non-home areas.

Research and development outlays have been restricted somewhat during the past year. The director of research and development, however, has been very optimistic. He recently reported to the board of directors that he believes the new model on which his staff currently is working should significantly enhance sales and, perhaps, bring substantial savings in production costs. The former management had threatened his department with a substantial budget cut. He has requested that you continue his present budget and gradually increase the amount allocated for research and development expenditures. He will then be able to retain and expand his competent professional staff and continue research efforts, which he believes will bear fruit within a relatively short period of time--perhaps within a few months, but most likely by the end of Year 3. See Chapter 5 for additional details about research and development, marketing, and distribution.

In order to match production output more closely with sales volume, the former management of your company had deactivated two of its production lines in your home area about three years ago (prior to the period shown in the historical data that are appended). Recent sales trends have been sharply upward, however, and both of these lines were reactivated to increase production during Year 2. The plant in your home area now has six production lines available, each with a capacity of 52,000 units per quarter under normal operating circumstances. Production costs at present are about $4.30 per unit. Details of costs and production capacity adjustments are described in Chapters 7 and 8.

Other operating expenses, for which plans must be made, include inventory storage costs and interest on bonds and loans. The government taxes corporate income at 39 percent of net profits. Taxes, accrued quarterly, must be paid during the first quarter of each year. The tax laws contain no provisions for carry-back of losses to reduce tax liabilities in prior periods. Losses, however, may be carried forward indefinitely to reduce tax liabilities in the future.

Each company has issued 6 million shares of capital stock, which is traded in the over-the-counter market. The bid price for each company's stock, along with earnings and dividends per share, is quoted regularly in the Quarterly Industry Report. None of the firms in the simulation, however, has declared a dividend yet. Chapter 9 includes additional details about the financial environment.

Reports

Computer-generated reports will be provided to your management team following each quarter of simulated operations. The reports for the fourth quarter of Year 2 are reproduced in Appendix B, along with a summary of data from Years 1 and 2 in Appendix A. Two types of reports will be provided each quarter:

I. Reports about individual companies, distributed confidentially only to the company concerned.

   A. Financial Statements Report, including

      1. Income Statement
      2. Cash Flow Statement
      3. Balance Sheet

   B. Operating Information Report, including

      1. Production Cost Analysis
      2. Output, Inventory, and Sales Analysis
      3. Other Operating Data, such as a report on the results of research and development activities (availability of new models and changes in production costs), size of the sales force, construction activity (new plants, new lines, etc.)
   C. Current Period Decisions and GNP Forecast

II. Reports about competitors that are distributed to each company in the simulation.

   D. Quarterly Industry Report, providing information about each competitor of the type that could be gleaned from industry sources, quarterly financial statements, and public reports.

   E. Annual Industry Report, distributed in the fourth quarter of each year, contains annual data on operations of competitors. This information is the type that could be obtained from annual reports.

   F. Historical and Financial Data for Years 1 and 2, distributed only in Year 2, Quarter 4, includes a summary of pertinent information for the last eight quarters leading up to the beginning of the competition. These reports are similar to those found in Appendix A.

Data that are reported in the various reports are described in subsequent chapters. Sample copies of each report are included in Appendices A and B.

CHAPTER 4

DEVELOPING THE STRATEGIC PLAN
AND SELECTING STANDARDS OF SUCCESS

Your simulated firm may be viewed as a single business corporation or as a strategic business unit (SBU) of a diversified corporation. In either case, you are calling the shots without interference from above. Your responsibility is to stake out the direction the firm will take in terms of its mission, develop realistic goals and objectives, create a strategy which will enable your firm to obtain its stated goals and successfully implement the strategy. Your reward could be mega salaries and a golden parachute.

Mission

The firm's mission serves as the crystal ball for the organization. It describes what business the firm is in and the type of business it is aspiring to become. The mission deals with the scope of activities performed and the purpose of the activities. The mission statement may focus upon products and/or services being provided, major ingredients in a line of products, central technology of an organization, customer groups served, customer needs, etc. (Thompson and Strickland 1987). Be sure to leave your rose-colored glasses home when you develop the mission statement. This one requires some realistic thought.

Defining Goals and Objectives

The manner in which the performance of your simulated firm is evaluated will depend, in part, upon your ability to meet the goals and objectives that your firm has set. We recommend that your firm explicitly develop a written set of goals upon which your management can agree very early in the simulation. The simulation administrator may require your firm to submit a written document defining your goals and objectives, along with

54

the policies and strategies which you have formulated to achieve
these goals and objectives.

Many students, and business managers as well, tend to define
their goals and objectives in very general terms. For example,
an objective might be "to make a satisfactory profit on a minimum
investment in physical and financial assets." While this may
sound fine on the surface, a closer examination reveals that this
statement really doesn't provide very much guidance for the
operation and evaluation of your company.

Explicit Definition

Strategic goals and objectives should set the hurdles for
your firm to jump when pursuing its mission. They provide the
specific level of accomplishment desired. If you don't know the
exact height of the hurdle, how high should you jump? Imagine
the glory and fame obtained from jumping five feet to clear a one
foot hurdle, or consider the possibility of jumping three feet to
clear a ten foot brick wall.

We think of goals as desired long-term performance levels
and objectives as short-term performance targets. Both goals and
objectives state _what_ is to be achieved and _when_ it is to be
accomplished (Quinn 1980). Your strategic goals and strategic
objectives should contain the following four components (Hofer
and Schendel 1978):

1.   the goal or attribute sought

2.   an index for measuring progress
      toward the goal or attribute

3.   a target or hurdle to be achieved

4.   a time frame within which the tar-
      get or hurdle is to be achieved.

We urge your firm to provide explicit definitions of your
goals and objectives. An explicit definition can be made in
either absolute or relative terms. Examples of absolute definitions include:

1.   Maintain a rate of return on stockholders'
      end-of-Year 2 investment in your company's
      stock (goal) of at least 20 (hurdle) percent
      (index) through year seven (time).

2.   Maintain a growth rate for assets (goal) of
      at least 5 (hurdle) percent (index) each year
      (time).

55

3. Generate sufficient sales to maintain a share of the market (hurdle) equal to at least 30 (hurdle) percent (index) by year five (time).

Examples of comparative statements of objectives (relative to competitors) include:

1. Maintain a larger (hurdle) share (implicit index) of the market (goal) than any of our competitors by year five (time).

2. Maintain a net return on the book value of owners' investment (goal) at least equal (hurdle) to the median return (index) of the industry through year seven (time).

Your firm's objectives and goals may be defined in terms of some of the quantitative measures that have been described, or in some other terms that your management may prefer. They should, however, be related to the variables that actually are included in the simulation model. Realizing a company objective of "maintaining high morale," while a noble objective, could only be partially inferred from reported results in the computer output by examining, perhaps, the turnover rate in salespeople. Your firm does not actually have overt control over most working conditions which affect employee morale.

After goals and objectives have been set for your business, goals and objectives need to be set for the functional areas of your firm. The goals set for the finance, marketing and production functions must reinforce and be consistent with the goals set for the business. Similarly, the functional-area objectives should lead toward the realization of the functional-area goals.

Your goals and objectives should appear reasonable, and their realization should be possible in light of the historical data available to you. It is possible that your firm may wish to revise its hurdles after you have gained several quarters of experience with the simulation. However, give your goals some time to work before you give up on them. Changing goals every quarter will lead you in circles and you run the risk of becoming the last of the big wheels with no destination.

Formulating Strategies

It is important, once your objectives and goals have been defined, to formulate strategies for attaining these objectives. Operating without a clear strategy is like driving in an unfamiliar state without a road map. Both are only recommended for the extremely faithful. Your strategy is your plan for utilizing the firms resources to attain your stated goals. Your firm's strategy should be set forth explicitly so that it will provide guidance for the day-to-day operation of your firm by your management team and its subordinates. One test of the clarity of your strategy is to ask yourself if another management team could operate your firm as your team would if the other team was provided with only your firm's written statement of its goals, objectives, strategies and policies. Would they make the same set of decisions in your absence? If the answer is affirmative, your document is acceptable. If not, it's back to the drawing boards.

You may want to think of strategy as (Hofer and Schendel 1978):

> the fundamental pattern of present and
> planned resource deployments and environmen-
> tal interactions that indicate how the or-
> ganization will achieve its objectives.

The four components of strategy which follow from this definition are:

1. Scope: products offered and market segments served.

2. Resource deployments: planned use of funds, equipment, materials, personnel, etc.

3. Competitive advantage: unique position created relative to competition by the scope and resource deployment decisions.

4. Synergy: added advantage obtained by the specific combination of resources and/or scope decisions.

As you develop your strategy, include all four components to strengthen your final plan. Interrelationships which might go unnoticed when simply planning for resource utilization become important elements. The resulting strategy should enable your firm to successfully interact with its environment.

There are a number of generic strategies which your firm may follow. The strategies consist of the combinations of the following three dimensions: scope of your market, types of competitive weapons used and segmentation of the market (Chrisman, Hofer and Boulton 1988). The scope can be either narrow, serving one market, or broad, serving more than one market. The competitive weapons consist of price, user benefits and some combination of price and user benefits. User benefits are created through product development, product availability and promotion. The market may be either segmented, using different competitive weapons in different markets, or unsegmented, using the same competitive weapons for all markets.

To develop your firm's strategy, select a generic strategy and then tailor the dimensions to your specific environment. For example, scope will specify the market areas in which you plan to compete. Your competitive weapons consist of price, product-- model and quality, advertising and sales force. You may choose to segment your market or treat all market areas as one area.

In addition to general business strategy, your firm needs to develop functional-area strategies in finance, marketing, and production. The guiding forces behind functional area strategies are functional-area goals. Functional-area strategies consist of the plans made by the functional areas to meet the functional goals discussed above. Functional-area strategies taken together determine the success of your firm's overall business strategy.

Setting Policy

Company policies are the internal, working rules of the organization. They are guidelines developed by management to set limits for or otherwise control day-to-day tactical decision making and other actions of subordinates. Policies may be used to simplify the decision making process by eliminating specific alternatives from consideration. For example, if your company has a policy of not introducing a new product until at least two new models are available, no time would be spent debating whether to introduce a new product if only one new model were available.

We again want to caution you against using vague generalities when developing policy. "Maintaining a reasonable price for our product in relation to production costs and competitors' pricing activities" does not provide much guidance for your marketing department as it sets product prices. A more useful policy might be "to maintain a markup of 50 percent over production cost, with the constraint that in no event should the whole-sale price exceed that of the highest priced competitor by more than 5 percent." Other examples of an explicit pricing policy might be "to maintain a markup of 40 percent over production costs plus transportation costs to each market area without regard to competitors' pricing policies", or "to match competitors' prices in each market area without regard to markup over production cost." Hopefully these examples will provide you with a starting point for the development of your firm's policies.

Keep in mind that the purpose of developing policies is to enable your firm to meet the objectives which the management team has set for the firm. Policies are tools for management to use in the day to day operation of the firm. Policies should be formulated for each of the decision areas for which your firm will be responsible (as described in Chapter 2). As the simulation progresses and your firm obtains additional information concerning conditions in the industry and the activities of competitors, you may wish to revise your existing policies.

Even though your initial policies may be revised during the simulation, they will be valuable in providing guidance and direction to your management team and subordinates as decisions are being made. Policies serve as management's stabilizer. Your firm will discover that establishing clearly defined policies will save much time in the decision-making process. If top management decides to adopt a specific policy when faced with a management issue, the next time the issue arises the decision will simply follow the established policy. Management can spend its time on analysis and the development of new policies rather than on rehashing the same issues over and over again.

Strategic Plan

The simulation administrator may request that your firm submit a strategic plan prior to the start of the simulation or the plan may be developed during the course of the simulation. Alternatively, the plan may be considered as part of a term project for your firm's management.

In order to complete a strategic plan, your firm must conduct a situation analysis. This consists of a thorough examination of the industry, the competition and your firm. The plan then flows from the findings of the situation analysis. We like to include this analysis as a supporting part of the strategic plan. However, your administrator may decide to include only the actual plan itself. The components of our full strategic plan (including the situation analysis) follow:

I. Situation Analysis

    A. Industry

        1. stage of life cycle

        2. structure - description of important factors which shape the industry

        3. driving forces - forces which change the industry structure

        4. economics - cost, price and profit relationships

        5. key success factors - key requirements for success in the industry

6. problems - current or potential problems facing the industry

B. Competition

    1. intra-industry

        a. rivalry among existing competitors

        b. threat of new competitors - existing products & services

        c. threat of competitors offering substitute products & services

        d. bargaining power of suppliers

        e. bargaining power of customers

    2. individual competitor

        a. company 1 - position in industry
        b. company 2 - position in industry
        c. etc.

    3. forecasted changes in competitive conditions

C. Company

    1. past performance - significant ratios

    2. current conditions

        a. external opportunities
        b. external threats
        c. internal strengths
        d. internal weaknesses

    3. significant issues and problems which must be faced

II. Strategic Plan

A. Mission statement

B. Business level

    1. goals & objectives
    2. strategy

C. Functional level

1. finance

   a. goals & objectives
   b. strategy

2. marketing

   a. goals & objectives
   b. strategy

3. production

   a. goals & objectives
   b. strategy

D. Implementation plan - action timetable

E. Policies

   1. finance
   2. marketing
   3. production

At a minimum, the plan should consist of your mission statement, your business-level goals, objectives and strategy, your
functional-area goals, objectives and strategies, an implementation plan and your firm's policies. Each element of the plan
should be well thought out and should be integrated with all of
the other elements of the plan. The plan serves as your operations map.

Your firm's operations will be judged according to how well
your management team performs in competition with the management
teams of the other firms in your industry. This evaluation will
be based in part, upon your firm's ability to set and achieve
reasonable goals. During the evaluation process, comparisons
will be made with other companies in the industry regarding
profitability, efficiency, and financial standing. Certain
ratios and quantitative measures will be reported regularly in
the computer-generated reports that your firm will receive at the
end of each quarter. These will be described below.

There also is a subjective element to performance evaluation
requiring a judgment of the quality of planning and goal-setting
activities, the quality of the plans and goals themselves, the
faithfulness of the company's management in meeting goals and
objectives, and the ability to submit successfully to board or
shareholder reviews. Some of these qualitative factors are
discussed in the third section of this chapter.

<u>Avoid End Play</u>

At times, teams involved in a simulation exercise such as the <u>Business Policy Game</u> are tempted to adopt an unofficial strategy which is referred to as "end play." This strategy calls for the allocation of the firm's resources in such a manner as to build the best relative position among the competitors during the final period of the simulation. This procedure ignores the quarters preceding and following the final quarter of the competition. In fact, the firm is often left in a position from which it would be impossible to continue. A word to the wise! As "end play" is unrealistic in the business world, it is frowned upon and will likely result in a penalty in the final evaluation of the firm's performance.

Even though you have been told that the simulation will continue for only a definite number of quarters, you should take the attitude that your firm's operations will continue well beyond that time. Even if you plan to sell your interest in the company when you retire, you are likely to receive the greatest return on your investment if your firm's plans have been laid out in such a manner as to take maximum advantage of the situation existing at the end of the period. If this is done, successors will continue to have a commanding position in the industry and the greatest likelihood of continued profitable operations. Again, we emphasize that an end-of-play strategy is unwise and is likely to hurt your relative position in the industry as well as downgrade your firm's performance when final evaluations are made.

Profitability

The profits of a business firm usually are considered to be for the benefit of the firm's owners or stockholders. If a firm is profitable, it is reasonable to expect that the wealth of individual stockholders should increase as a result of that profitability. The wealth of a stockholder can be increased in two ways: through appreciation in the market value of stock and/or through receipt of dividend payments. Realization of a satisfactory growth in stockholders' wealth requires the firm's management to conduct its activities in such a manner that the combination of dividend payments and appreciation of the firm's stock meets the financial requirements of the firm's stock-holders.

<u>Rate of Return on Stockholders' Investment (Investor ROI)</u>

Given that the firm stays healthier when stockholders are willing to invest in its stock, one overall goal of your firm ought to focus on providing some level of additional incremental wealth to your stockholders. This especially should be the case if we assume that you and other members of your management team purchased a majority interest in your firm's common stock at the end of Year 2 in order to gain control of its management. Obviously then, dividend payments and stock price appreciation would benefit your management team as stockholders in your firm. Dividends and appreciation can be considered as incremental returns on your initial investment at the end of Year 2. One way to compare the incremental return on your stock investment with those of stockholders in other competing firms is to compute and compare the rate of return on initial investment. You may wish to set a goal of a minimum rate of return on your stock investment or to attempt, at least, to realize a greater rate of return for your stockholders than stockholders of competing firms may realize.

This rate of return may be considered as an overall measure of profitability to your stockholders on their initial investment. In addition, it should be noted that the ability of a firm to pay regular dividends and maintain an increasing stock price is dependent upon its ability to show regular earnings. Potential stock purchasers in the <u>Business Policy Game</u>, as in the business world, will put a premium on earnings growth and thus will tend to bid up the market price for a fast-growing company's common stock.

The rate of return on stockholders' initial investment will be computed at the end of each quarter and will be reported as Investor ROI in the Quarterly Industry Reports. Investor ROI assumes a purchase of common stock at the end of Year 2, Quarter 4, and shows the time-adjusted return (stock price appreciation plus dividends) to the end of the quarter of the report. The computation is made by solving the following equation for r, the time-adjusted rate of return:

$$P_8 = \frac{P_n}{(1 + r)^{n - 8}} + \sum_{t = 9}^{n} \frac{D_t}{(1 + r)^{t - 8}}$$

Where D_t is equal to the dollar amount of dividends paid in quarter t, P_n is equal to the price of your company's common stock at the end of the most recent quarter, n. P_8 is the price at the end of Year 2 (the eighth quarter of historical data) when you began the simulation. The rate, r, is that discount rate that equates the discounted value of dividends and current stock price (discounted quarterly) to the initial stock price. The rate then is annualized by multiplying it by 4 and reported as Investor ROI.

Other Profitability Ratios

While the rate of return on stockholders' investment provides an overall measure of profitability, it is by no means the
only one. Profitability can be considered in relation to the
historical, or book value, of the owners' investment in a business or in relation to the dollar value of sales that the business has made in a given period of time. These profitability
ratios will be reported each quarter in the Industry Report.

The net profit margin on sales (net income to sales) shows
the percentage of profit from each sales dollar. The return on
equity (net income to book value of equity) reflects the percentage return on funds invested by stockholders and earnings
retained in the business. Quarterly income and sales are used
for ratios in quarterly reports and the ratios are restated using
annual income and sales for the Annual Industry Report.

Ratio analysis can be a useful way to compare a firm's
performance with some standard. Standards of performance that
may be used include absolute norms, criteria reflecting the
performance of other firms in the same industry, or standards
derived from the historical performance of the firm for which the
ratios are computed. Some analysts use rule-of-thumb standards
with which to compare ratios of different companies. For purposes of the Business Policy Game, however, it probably will be
more useful to you (and to those who will judge your firm's
achievement) to compare your company's performance with your own
historical record and with the performance of other companies in
your industry. Your ability to increase your firm's rate of
return on invested capital, for example, and to increase it more
rapidly than that of the other companies in your industry will
reflect favorably upon the quality of your management.

Financial Standing

Three different credit ratings are possible for firms
competing in the Business Policy Game: superior (Number 1),
preferred (Number 2), and questionable (Number 3). Credit
ratings are reported each quarter in the Industry Report. Each
firm starts the simulation with a preferred credit rating (Number
2). During the course of the competition, this rating may be
improved to a superior rating or reduced to a questionable rating
according to the way the firm handles its financial affairs. The
credit rating is a composite figure that reflects demonstrated
ability to meet a company's financial obligations and the likelihood of continuing to meet those obligations in the future.
Interest rates on bank loans and new bond issues, as well as the
selling price of new common stock issues, are determined, in
part, by a firm's credit standing.

In the Business Policy Game, credit analysts normally recompute and assign new credit ratings only once each year, at the end of the fourth quarter. A shortage of cash which necessitates emergency borrowing, however, usually will result in the immediate reduction of a firm's rating (during the quarter in which the emergency borrowing occurs).

Factors Affecting Credit Ratings

Many factors normally are considered by a credit analyst in judging the financial standing of a business firm. Among those that will be used to determine your firm's credit rating are the demonstrated ability to:

1. Meet repayment obligations on bank loans and other commitments, and avoid emergency borrowing.

2. Show significant growth of total resources (as reflected in the value of total assets).

3. Increase the market acceptance of your product (as shown by an increasing share of the market).

4. Show a reasonable return on book value of owners' investment in the firm (net income to equity).

5. Pay a reasonable proportion of profits to stockholders in the form of dividends (Business Policy Game stockholders expect to receive dividends amounting to 40 to 60 percent of earnings).

6. Maintain a capital structure that shows a reasonable relationship between borrowing and net worth (bonds to equity).

7. Generate sufficient profits so that there will be a comfortable margin over and above the bond interest requirements (interest coverage).

8. Maintain sufficient liquidity to assure that near-term obligations may be met in the normal course of business operations (current ratio).

Business Policy Game analysts will consider your performance on these measures over an extended period, rather than just looking at a single quarter's performance. As in the business world, the management of your simulated firm will have no direct control over the determination of its credit rating. You may, however, influence the analysts' decision by control of the various items shown above. The precise way that these various factors actually influence the determination of credit ratings in the simulation will have to be determined by experimentation and observation.

Qualitative Standards

Successful performance in the various quantitative measures that commonly are considered as reasonable standards for business success is important, but by no means the only way in which success can be measured. In addition, your management team probably will be judged on the way in which you are able to accomplish your goals and the manner in which you may have reached the level of performance shown by the quantitative measures. These latter judgments are more qualitative and subjective in nature.

At the beginning of this chapter it was suggested that you should prepare a written statement of your goals and objectives and develop appropriate strategies and policies to reach those objectives. The quality of these statements is important, and the way in which you utilize your knowledge and understanding of management theory and are able to integrate your knowledge of the functional areas of business will contribute to development of superior reports. You likely will be judged on the quality of the reports themselves, including how realistic your goals and objectives may be in the light of the economic environment in which you are operating. In addition you may be judged on your success in actually realizing the goals that you have set for yourself.

How well has your management group done in developing an effective organization and in working together as a team? This is a question that must be asked after you have completed the simulation and one that should be addressed by your group from the beginning. In a very real sense, your ability to work together effectively will tend to determine how well you are able to accomplish your goals and how you are likely to stand in relation to the quantitative measures of success.

An overall strategy for your firm is important and your ability to integrate strategies for marketing, production, and finance is a hallmark of success. But also you need to ask the questions (because those who judge your success are almost sure to ask them):

1. "Is your marketing strategy effective and well-implemented?"

2. "Are your production planning and strategy effective and well-implemented?"

3. "Is your financial strategy effective and well-managed?"

Finally, appearances are critically important to those who look at your work and are likely to be judging your performance. This applies in business organizations as well as to almost any form of interpersonal or inter-organizational relationship. The style and professionalism of your reports will have a marked impact on the way in which you will be judged. The poise and professionalism of your team members as they relate to others is important. Team members need to be able to relate professionally to each other, to members of other teams (your competitors), to the simulation administrator, and to others who may be judging your performance. Your written and oral communications with each other, and with those outside of your management team, will be used to form the bases of many kinds of judgments about you and how well you have done.

References

Chrismann, J. J., Hofer, C. W. & Boulton, W. R. (1988) "Toward a System For Classifying Business Strategies," The Academy of Management Review, 13(3), 413-428.

Hofer, C. W. & Schendel (1978) Strategy Formulation: Analytical Concepts. St. Paul: West Publishing Company.

Quinn, J. B. (1980) Strategies for Change: Logical Incrementalism. Homewood, IL: Richard D. Irwin.

Thompson, A. A. & Strickland, A. J. (1987) Strategic Management: Concepts and Cases (4th ed.). Plano, TX: Business Publications, Inc.

CHAPTER 5

MARKETING: STRATEGY

Your firm's marketing department is responsible for providing a desirable product for the consumer, and for making it
available at a location convenient for purchase. In addition,
the consumer must perceive that the value of the product is at
least as great as the price your firm is charging. Finally, the
marketing department must communicate this information so that
the consumer is aware that a desirable product exists at a fair
price. In short, the role of the marketing department is to
serve the consumer. If it fails this responsibility, your firm
is likely to fail in its mission!

The marketing function in the simulation has been simplified
somewhat from that found in the business world so that the
simulation will be tractable. A sufficient number of elements
have been included so that you can deepen your understanding of
the role marketing plays in the firm and in the business world.

Your firm's marketing management should begin the simulation
by setting marketing (functional level) goals and objectives, and
developing marketing strategy to accomplish these goals (see
Chapter 4 for a discussion of goal and objective setting and
strategy development). Marketing goals should support the
overall goals developed at the business level. The goals should
focus upon what marketing can contribute to achieving the business level goals. The following business-level goal was used as
an example in Chapter 4.

> Generate sufficient sales to maintain a share of the
> market (hurdle) equal to at least 30 (hurdle) percent
> (index) by year five (time).

Marketing goals and objectives that could support this business-
level goal might be:

Goal: Sell only product models (goal) which represent the
            current (hurdle) state of technology (index)(time
            implicit).

Objective: Introduce a new model (goal) at the beginning
                (hurdle) of each (time) calendar year (index).

Goal: Increase sales (goal) 10 (hurdle) percent (index)
            faster than our nearest competitor during our manage-
            ment tenure (time).

Objective: Increase sales (goal) by 15 (hurdle) percent
                (index) per year (time).

Other marketing goals and objectives may focus upon selling
expense cost reductions, transportation cost control, sales
forecasting, etc.

    Marketing strategy should be designed to enable your market-
ing department to attain its goals and objectives. The strategy
should plan for the allocation of marketing resources to gain a
competitive advantage and to achieve a synergistic effect. The
strategy for the model goal would focus upon the timing and size
of research and development expenditures. The effects of inflation should be taken into account. The strategy for increasing
sales would involve the size, timing and geographical allocation
of resources for promotion and pricing. An effective marketing
strategy should include all of the marketing variables which
require resources.

    The quarter to quarter tactical decisions which your market-
ing management must make are described below. These decisions
are guided by your marketing strategy and company policy. You
will have an opportunity to select a product which management
believes to be attractive to a large number of consumers. Your
firm must set a wholesale price for your product which is competitive in the marketplace. Advertising expenditures must be
established each quarter for each of the marketing areas. Finally, management must specify the number of salespeople working in
each area and how the salespeople will be compensated. This
includes hiring and training additional salespeople to compensate
for losses through normal attrition. Salespeople can also be
terminated.

    In addition to managing the marketing mix, the marketing
department is responsible for forecasting sales. Accurate sales
forecasts are critical to the success of the firm. Sales forecasts will be the basis for estimating cash receipts, variable
costs, plant expansion requirements, production requirements, and
inventory levels. An inventory which is too small results in
lost sales and lost customers. An inventory which is too large
results in excessive storage and interest costs.

This chapter contains a description of the marketing activities found in the Business Policy Game and the costs and expenses associated with these activities. The next chapter contains suggestions to assist in forecasting sales and economic activity. A careful reading of both chapters will help you understand the marketing function as it relates to the Business Policy Game. This knowledge, together with careful planning, will enable your firm to design and maintain an effective marketing mix which will provide a synergistic boost to your firm. Keep in mind, however, that customers' needs and desires change over time. An optimal mix will not necessarily remain optimal over your entire management tenure.

Advertising

The role of advertising is to communicate with consumers. This communication may focus upon the advantages and features of your product that are stressed by your functional marketing strategy, or it may announce the availability of a new model. The specific message to be carried in your advertising is beyond the scope of this simulation. However, rest assured that the advertising agency which creates your advertising will promote your product in the best possible light.

The level of advertising expenditures is completely under the control of your firm's management. Expenditures must be specified separately on the decision form for each of the four marketing areas. The relative effectiveness of a firm's advertising tends to follow an "S" shaped curve as shown in Figure 5-1. Small expenditures will tend to have little affect on the market. (No one can hear you when you whisper.) As expenditures are increased, advertising effectiveness tends to increase at an increasing rate. At some level, the point of inflection on the curve is reached and further increases in expenditures tend to yield relatively smaller benefits. As expenditures continue to be increased, a position is reached where additional expenditures yield no additional effectiveness. Expenditures beyond this level will eventually lead to an area where additional expenditures will actually decrease advertising effectiveness. What would be your reaction to watching 24 advertisements for the same product during half an hour of television viewing?

The secret to successful advertising is to keep advertising expenditures at a level where the returns realized from each dollar spent on advertising significantly exceed the expenditure. The problem then becomes: "At what levels of expenditure do we realize this condition?" If your firm becomes somewhat frustrated in its attempts to find this ideal range don't feel lonely. The major Fortune 500 firms don't know exactly where they are on the effectiveness curve either.

Advertising expenditures have a <u>carry-over effect</u> in that expenditures in one quarter will continue to affect sales for several quarters into the future. When planning your promotional campaign, be aware of this fact so that your firm can use it to best advantage. Your company may decide to engage in a constant or steadily increasing level of advertising each quarter. On the other hand, it may decide to engage in a seasonal strategy where expenditures are heavier in some seasons and lighter in others. Alternatively, your firm may decide to utilize a pulse strategy where it advertises heavily for several quarters, decreases expenditures for several quarters and returns to a heavy sequence for several quarters. You will want to avoid large fluctuations in advertising expenditures which we refer to as the "yo-yo strategy." Such expenditure patterns may succeed in earning your firm the title of yo-yo champion of the world.

Advertising expenditures for each of the firms in the <u>Business Policy Game</u> were $172,000 during the last quarter of Year 2, with about 15 percent more being spent in the home area and Area 4 than in the other two areas.

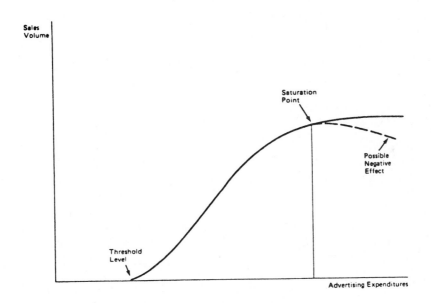

Figure 5-1
Advertising Effectiveness Curve

On an annual basis, past advertising expenditures have averaged between 65 and 70 cents for each unit of product sold. However, keep in mind that the purpose of advertising is to stimulate sales; thus past sales volume should not be used as a basis for setting future advertising expenditure levels. Advertising expenditures should be based upon the amount of sales the

firm wishes to generate. This will depend upon the amount of
inventory available, production capacity and time of year. Be
sure to purchase advertising for _every_ marketing area. This is
done by entering advertising expenditures on your decision form
for each area. Remember, you aren't likely to sell much of your
product if you don't advertise it. You also are not likely to
sell as much as you expect if you don't advertise very much.

Advertising expenditures must be allocated to each of the
four marketing areas. Enter the amount (in thousands of dollars)
to be spent in each area. The amount must be specified even
though no change is desired from the previous quarter.

Limits: 0 to 999 (in thousands of dollars)

	Adv. (000s)
Area 1	$_____
Area 2	$_____
Area 3	$_____
Area 4	$_____

Price

Your company is responsible for setting the wholesale price
for its product in each marketing area. There are no legal restrictions on charging different prices in different areas. Past
prices charged by firms in your world have tended to hover around
the $10 level. Econometric studies have indicated that prices
tend be to somewhat elastic in this range. Thus increases in
price would tend to decrease total revenue while decreases in
price would tend to increase total revenue, all other things
remaining equal.

It should be obvious that your firm is part of an oligopoly
and your pricing actions should reflect this knowledge. Pricing
in an oligopoly is somewhat treacherous. Each firm generally has
a narrow range over which it may vary its price without competitor reaction. When your firm lowers its price beyond this range,
your competitors are likely to follow suit. This may result in
an expanded market with all firms sharing in the expansion. This
movement could also set off a price war with rapidly falling
prices. If the industry price continues to drop, there will come
a point where one or more firms will engage in profitless pros-
perity. As price drops below a certain level, consumers may view
the product as being inferior and decide not to purchase it. A

reduction in price may also decrease the funds available to spend on enhancing sales through other marketing activities.

As a general rule, firms in a mature industry tend to avoid price competition and instead develop a strategy to compete on the basis of product, promotion and distribution. Price competition can be met overnight. A change in the other three variables of the marketing mix takes more time to copy. Thus a comparative advantage gained through altering one of the other variables of the marketing mix is longer lived than an advantage gained through a price change.

The wholesale price of your product must be set each quarter in each of the four market areas. Management may specify any price that it desires, except that company policy limits price changes to a maximum of 30 percent per quarter. Large price changes are discouraged, given the unknown effect that they may have on the market. Different prices may be specified for different areas. If your price is in whole dollars, enter zeros for the cents so that there is no question of whether you forgot to enter the cents' figures.

Maximum change: 30 percent in any quarter

Limits: 1.00 to 99.99 (in dollars)

	Price
Area 1	$_____._____
Area 2	$_____._____
Area 3	$_____._____
Area 4	$_____._____

Product

The products sold by the firms in your industry world are quite similar. However, there are quality and other perceived differences among the products which create customer preferences for each firm's product. Thus firms may pursue a differentiation strategy. From time to time, a firm's research and development department may create a new model which it hopes will be more desirable than the older version of the firm's product. If the new model is introduced into the marketplace, the firm's market share will often increase given no other change in the marketplace. Thus, companies that introduce new innovative models will generally be more successful than firms that continue to rely upon their older, somewhat obsolete products.

The model life cycle for the consumer durable good produced by your firm is relatively short. Thus we advise your firm to engage in an aggressive R & D program so that it will have replacement products available when the sales of an existing model start to slide. The products developed by your R & D department may be entirely new models or they may be variations in features and/or packaging of existing products. A few years back, Quaker State introduced a packaging innovation with its new screw-on top cans of oil which gave it a packaging advantage in the marketplace. This packaging innovation (for motor oil) eliminated much of the mess of adding oil to a car and allowed the user to safely store partly used cans. Now most other brands have copied this innovation, but Quaker State held the competitive advantage for several years. Product innovation does not, however, guarantee success. Anheuser Busch brought out a new nonalcoholic drink several years ago called Chelsea. It bombed badly! A word to the wise. When introducing a new model, it is advisable to be working on another new model which can be introduced quickly if the new introduction is not a winner.

A major advantage of pursuing a differentiation strategy through product innovation is that it is difficult to copy. A classic example is the Volkswagen Beetle which was the envy of the automotive world for many years. It was a unique design which cornered a significant share of the new car market. Unfortunately for Volkswagen, its innovative Rabbit did not fare as well after several successful years due to the competition copying the product with improvements. While innovation may provide a temporal advantage, the advantage is not permanent. However, product innovation is much more difficult to copy than price. Changes in promotion or in the sales force are generally easier to make than product changes. They are also more difficult to copy than price changes. As changes are made in the marketing mix, management should keep in mind the ease with which such changes may be matched by competitors.

New Model

When a new model is released by your firm's research and development department, its availability will be shown in the firm's Operating Information Report. For example, a new model number 5 might be shown as follows:

```
Latest Model Developed: 5     Model Produced This Quarter: 3  Quality: 2
Standard Cost per Unit for Next Quarter (includes inflation, cost savings):
      Model 5 Quality 2 Labor Cost: 3.45  Materials Cost: 1.66
      Model 4 Quality 2 Labor Cost: 2.97  Materials Cost: 1.43
```

74

Each new model will have a different labor and material cost associated with it which will be reported along with the release of the model. The costs that are reported are for the same quality level that currently is in production. The costs for other quality levels may be calculated easily, as shown below under "Model Quality." The inflation-adjusted standard costs reported for labor and materials will reflect any available cost savings that may have been achieved by your company's process research and development efforts. A new model may be introduced immediately or it may be held for introduction at a later date. Once a new model has been introduced, production of an earlier model cannot be continued or restarted. This constraint holds even if the older model was never produced. Special tools and dies which were required to produce the older model will have been sold when the new product is put into production thus making it impossible to produce the older model.

Each model released from the R & D department is assigned a number with higher numbers indicating more recent releases. It is possible for the firm in the above example to be producing Model 3 and have Models 4 and 5 available for introduction. If the firm decides to introduce Model 5, it will not be possible to introduce Model 4 in the future or to restart production of Model 3 as the tools and dies required to produce those models will have been sold as stated above. In addition, the Board of Directors adopted a firm policy several years ago that older models of the company's product will not be produced once a newer model is introduced. The Board wanted to avoid the possible bad image which could be created if consumers believed that the firm was producing and selling obsolete products.

Please note that while more than one firm may be producing a product with the same model number, the model number is a unique identifier for each company. The products will not be perceived to be identical by consumers. For example, both Lee and Levi Strauss make blue jeans. The jeans made by these two companies are not perceived as being identical by consumers.

The research and development department works closely with the marketing research department. Prior to the release of any new model, the marketing research department will assess the sales potential of the new model under development. Management of your firm has a long established policy that research studies must indicate at least an 80 percent likelihood that the new model's sales will exceed sales of the model currently in production perhaps by as much as 20 percent. Note: Management should be aware that research information is never totally accurate. Thus there is up to a 20 percent probability that sales of the new model will not match the sales volume of the current product. It is unlikely that sales will decrease more than 5 percent from the current model sales level.

To introduce a new model, enter the number of the new model on the decision form. Production of the new model begins immediately and thus the production costs for the quarter will be those of the new model. However, the new model will not be sold until the following quarter. Sales for the current quarter will be from the inventory on hand of the old model. If inventory of the old model is depleted, the remaining demand will be filled with units of the new model sold at the price you had set for the old model for that quarter. Thus, purchasers during the latter part of the quarter will get a bargain if you stock out of the old model earlier in the quarter. Any units of the old model not sold during the quarter will be sold to a liquidation agent at a price of 50 percent of the firm's cost, that is, at 50 percent of the value shown on the balance sheet. These units will be shipped overseas and will be recorded in your sales reports as foreign sales. Thus, all available inventory for the following quarter will be of the new model. The disposal of the old model units will have no effect upon consumer demand in the domestic market.

Enter the model number to be produced, even if it is the same as the last quarter. For Year 3, Quarter 1 the only model available is number 1.

If a new model is available and your company wishes to put it into production, enter the new model number. Otherwise enter the same model number that was produced in the previous quarter. If model number 4 is reported to be available, and your firm decides to introduce it, enter "4" on the decision form. The new model will be put into production immediately and will be available for sale in the following quarter.

Maximum: Highest model number reported available from the
          R & D Department

Minimum: Same model number as produced during the previous
          quarter. Once a new model has been placed in
          production an earlier model may not be reinstated

Limits: 1 to 12

Model
Model#___
Qual #___

Model Quality

When a new model is put into production, the quality level at which the product will be produced and sold <u>must</u> be specified. A new model may be sold as a deluxe (superior quality), standard (average quality), or economy model. Your board of directors long ago set a policy that the quality level of a product model would not be changed as long as the model is in production. They wanted to prevent customer confusion and the potential ill will which could be created by selling different quality levels of the same product. Quality levels can be changed each time a new model is introduced.

As you would expect, quality costs money. More costly material must be used and more care in assembly is required with each increase in quality. The relative costs for the three quality levels are:

    Deluxe (1)   110% of standard cost for quality 2
    Standard (2)   100% of standard cost for quality 2
    Economy (3)   90% of standard cost for quality 2

Note that the demand for your product is price-elastic, or sensitive to price changes. That is, a price increase can be expected, all other things being equal, to result in fewer units being sold. As you also might expect, the demand for higher quality products is less price sensitive than the demand for lower quality products. Therefore, if you change to a deluxe version (quality number 1) when you introduce model number 2 you can expect price increases to depress sales less than they would if you stayed with a standard version (quality number 2). Conversely, if you change to an economy version (quality number 3) you can expect demand to be more price sensitive than with the standard version (quality number 2).

When specifying the quality level of a new model on the decision form, enter the number of the quality level you have chosen:

                1 -- deluxe
                2 -- standard
                3 -- economy

If you continue to produce the same model as in the previous quarter, you must also continue the same quality level.

Limits: 1, 2 or 3
          May be changed only when introducing a new model

Salespeople

You have two types of decisions to make regarding the sales force. First, you must decide how many salespeople are required in each area. Second, you are required to develop a compensation package for the salespeople. This package consists of salary and commission rates.

Hiring Salespeople

The Operating Information Report for Year 2, Quarter 4, shows the number of salespeople working for the company at the beginning of the competition.

	Area 1	Area 2	Area 3	Area 4
Active Salespeople	12	10	10	13
Salespeople in Training, Qtr 1	1	1	1	1
Salespeople in Training, Qtr 2	1	1	1	1

Thus, adding the number of salespeople in the second quarter of training to those already active will give the number of expected active salespersons in Year 3, Quarter 1. Some of the salespeople previously working for your firm, however, may no longer be with the company by that time.

Each firm can expect to lose salespeople over time through normal attrition. They may leave due to better career opportunities in other industries, due to retirement or due to dissatisfaction with the compensation package being provided by the firm. Your firm has full control over the compensation package; however, you have no control over other factors which may cause a salesperson to leave the organization. We recommend that you plan for some resignations and maintain a sales force of sufficient size so that one or two resignations (or even more) during a quarter would not be devastating to the firm.

If your firm decides to hire additional salespeople, enter the number of salespeople to be hired under "Hire Salespeople" on the decision form in the areas the salespeople are to work. A salesperson must be trained for two quarters prior to being assigned to sell in the field. Thus, if you hire a salesperson in Quarter 2, the salesperson will be available to sell in the field in Quarter 4. Training costs will amount to $5,000 per quarter and the firm will be charged $5,000 in Quarter 2 and $5,000 in Quarter 3 for each salesperson in training. The new salesperson(s) would go on full salary and commission in Quarter 4.

Salespeople in training will be carried on the training roster for two quarters and will be automatically assigned to the area when their training is complete. No further entry is necessary after the first quarter in which the salespeople were hired. If you make an entry in the following quarter, you will hire additional salespeople to begin their training period in that quarter.

Limits: 0 to 99

```
┌─────────────────────────────────────────────┐
│┌──────┬──────────────────────────────────┐  │
││      │         Salespeople              │  │
││      │  Hire  Trans  Commission         │  │
││Area 1│ #____  #____        ____¢         │  │
││      │                                  │  │
││Area 2│ #____  #____                      │  │
││      │               Salary             │  │
││Area 3│ #____  #____                      │  │
││      │            $_____            │  │
││Area 4│ #____  #____                      │  │
│└──────┴──────────────────────────────────┘  │
└─────────────────────────────────────────────┘
```

Transferring Salespeople

Salespeople may be transferred from one area to another. If your firm hires a salesperson in Area 2 and decides that the salesperson is needed in Area 3 instead, it may transfer an <u>active</u> salesperson (not one still in training) to Area 3. The transfer can be accomplished by entering "-1" in Area 2 and "+1" in Area 3 under "Trans Salespeople" on the decision form. Your positive "moves in" to other areas may not exceed the value of negative "moves out." That would signify increasing the size of your sales force, and an increase may only be accomplished by hiring new salespeople. If your negative values are larger than your positives, the additional salespeople will be fired (see below).

You may transfer salespeople from several areas at the same time. However, you may not transfer salespeople in and out of the same area in one quarter. They must either go into an area or out of an area. Not both. In addition, you must maintain <u>at least one</u> salesperson in each area. Transfers take place immediately. A transferred salesperson, however, may not be very effective until he or she has moved and settled into a new market area. The salesperson will, however, continue to draw a salary. In addition, the salesperson will be provided with a moving allowance of $5,000 (shown under "other selling expenses").

Maximum negative (to be transferred out): number of active salespeople minus 1

Maximum positive (to be transferred in): the sum of positive numbers may not exceed the sum of negative numbers

Limits: -9 to 99

Firing Salespeople

You may fire salespeople in an area by entering the number of people you want to fire under "Transfer Salespeople." You indicate that the salespeople are to be fired by entering a negative number in the area with no balancing positive number indicating a transfer to another area. Thus, if you decide to fire 2 salespeople in Area 3, enter -2 under the "Trans" column for Area 3. A salesperson fired in a quarter is given $5,000 in severance pay and does not sell during the quarter. Remember, you must maintain at least one salesperson in each area and, thus, cannot fire your total sales force in any area.

Maximum to be discharged: Number of active salespeople minus 1

Limits -9 to 0

Sales Salaries

It is the custom in your industry to pay salespeople a base salary plus a commission. At the end of Year 2, each salesperson was receiving a base salary of $3,000 per quarter plus commissions. Salespeople have no expense accounts. Increases or decreases in salaries will affect the performance level and job satisfaction of your salespeople. Higher salaries will generally tend to increase the loyalty of the sales force and result in lower turnover. Lower salaries usually leads to employee dissatisfaction and increased resignations. When developing your compensation program, heed Armand Hammer's sage advice, "If you pay peanuts, you'll get monkeys." However, at some point, diminishing returns will set in as salaries are increased. How loyal and happy can you make a sales force? The higher the salary, the less the need to earn a commission by selling.

The salary for each salesperson must be entered on the decision form in the "Salespeople" section (see above). All salespeople are paid the same salary, which may be increased or decreased each quarter. Caution is urged, however. A yo-yo pattern here is likely to buy employee mistrust.

Limits: 1 to 9999 (in dollars)

Sales Commissions

In addition to a base salary, salespeople recently have been paid a commission amounting to 20 cents for each unit sold. Increases in the level of commissions will normally serve as a sales incentive leading to an increase in the number of units sold. Decreases often have the opposite effect. As with advertising expenditures and sales salaries, the effect of increasing commissions is subject to the law of diminishing returns. You may adjust the level of sales commissions or change the relative emphasis on salary and commissions each quarter. Enter the amount of the desired commission in number of cents per unit under "Commission" on the decision form (see above).

Limits: 1 to 99 (in cents per unit sold)

Managing the Sales Force

Managing the sales force involves resolving three questions: (1) how many salespeople should we employ? (2) how should we deploy the sales force? and (3) how should we compensate the sales force?

In order to determine the number of salespeople to employ, your firm must develop a sales forecast. Well managed firms develop a sales quota which they expect their salespeople to meet. The number of salespeople to employ is then determined by dividing the forecasted sales for the quarter by the sales quota. In the past, salespeople have often sold between 6,000 and 7,500 units per quarter. Your salespeople may or may not match these figures depending upon the economic conditions in your industry, the aggressiveness of your competitors, and your management skills.

If you develop a sales quota for your sales force, you can use the sales quota to allocate your salespeople among your market areas. Simply allocate your sales force by dividing the sales forecast for each area by the sales force quota and you have the required number of salespeople for the area. Unfortunately, your actual management activity is not quite that simple. You may have already recognized that salespeople are allocated in lumps of one person. Thus if you forecast 104,000 units to be sold in an area and your sales quota is 10,000 units per salesperson, you're left looking for 4/10ths of a salesperson. Here's what you get paid the big bucks to do, make wise decisions!

After your sales force is functioning in the field, it is wise to monitor the average number of units each person is selling in each area. You will likely find all is not going according to plan. A quick calculation or two will normally show that salespeople in some areas are producing a much higher return than those in other areas. This would suggest that you transfer some salespeople out of the low producing areas into the high producing areas to balance more evenly the return obtained per salesperson in each area.

While both salaries and commissions provide compensation for the salesperson, their uses are somewhat different. The salary provides security for the salesperson in that, regardless of the number of units sold, the salesperson is guaranteed a fixed salary. Salary is not a strong motivator to create additional sales. On the other hand, the commission is not paid unless a sale is made. It provides no security for the salesperson. It does provide a strong motivator for increasing sales. Each unit sold provides more money for the salesperson. Some mixture of the two compensation options is recommended. Your firm may want to place the emphasis of your compensation package upon one or the other of the two alternatives. However, be sure that your sales force can make a decent living or they will be looking for another job. It should come as no surprise that some people work better when the emphasis is upon salary, and other people work better with the emphasis upon commission.

Promotional Balance

You spend your promotional budget on advertising and salespeople. What is the proper balance? Marginal analysis would call for shifting dollars from the lower contributing area to the higher contributing area. In effect, that is what we discussed above when we suggested that you shift salespeople among areas to balance the number of units sold per salesperson. The proper allocation is more difficult when deciding whether to take money from advertising and put it into enlarging the sales force or vice versa.

There is a somewhat crude measure you can use to help determine whether you have the proper balance between your promotion tools. Calculate the number of dollars of sales obtained per dollar spent on advertising and the number of dollars of sales obtained per dollar spent on salespeople. However, don't shift dollars to balance these returns yet! The actions of your competitors can cause these returns to bounce all over the place while you hold your expenditures constant. (I SAID THIS METHOD WAS CRUDE.) Calculate these returns for at least a year and take the average before you make any changes. Then you may decide to shift expenditures in the indicated direction gradually while continuing to monitor the resulting returns. Sorry folks, this is as close as we can get in an operational setting. (Of course you could always try some econometric techniques.)

Marketing Expenses

Expenses related to selling and distribution activities will be reported as "Selling Expense" each quarter in the company Income Statement, illustrated in Figure 5-2. Current levels of these expenses may be found in the reproduction of the reports for Year 2, Quarter 4 in Appendix B.

INCOME STATEMENT	$000s
Gross Revenue from Sales	3450
Less Cost of Goods Sold	1530
Gross Profit	1920
Selling Expense:	
Advertising	172
Sales Salaries	135
Sales Commissions	69
General Selling Expense	399
Transportation Expense	161
Other Selling Expense	39
Total Selling Expense	975
Admin and General Expense:	
Research and Development	140
Storage Expense	16
Executive Compensation	148
Loan Interest	0
Bond Interest	50
Other Expense	0
Total Admin and Gen Exp	354
Total Operating Expense	1329
Operating Profit (Loss)	592
Other Income:	
CD Interest	1
Net Profit (Loss Before Tax)	592
Less Income Tax	230
Net Profit (Loss) After Tax	362
Less Dividends Paid	0
Addition to Retained Earnings	362

FIGURE 5-2
Income Statement

Other Marketing Expenses

Besides managing the advertising program and your sales force, your firm will incur several other types of expenses associated with the marketing function.

General Selling Expenses (GSE)

The general selling expenses entry on your firm's Income Statement includes a fixed, a semi-fixed and a variable component. The fixed portion of $150,000 per quarter represents marketing administration and overhead costs. The semi-fixed portion consists of $4,000 per quarter over and above salary and commission to support each active salesperson. The variable portion consists of 20 cents per unit in administrative costs for each unit of product sold. Thus

GSE = $150,000 + $4,000 x (salespeople) + $0.20 x (units sold)

The more units that are sold, the lower is the general selling expense per unit because the fixed and semi-fixed costs are spread over more and more units.

Transportation Expense

Products shipped for sale within the same area where they were produced cost 10 cents per unit. Shipments <u>to</u> Area 4 or <u>from</u> a plant in Area 4 cost 40 cents per unit. Units shipped to Areas 1, 2 or 3 from a plant in another of the three areas cost 70 cents per unit.

Your firm has established the following transportation policy to control shipping costs. If your firm builds and oper- ates a plant in a non-home area, orders within the area will be filled prior to shipping units outside the area. If additional inventory is available, orders will be filled in the other non- home areas. Any remaining inventory will be used to meet demand in the home area if the home area plant cannot satisfy its de- mand. Shipments from the home area plant will be made to other areas to satisfy any remaining unfilled orders if inventory is available. The net effect of the transportation policy is to give you the lowest total transportation bill commensurate with the location of your production facilities and the geographical source of orders.

Other Selling Expenses

Most of the other selling expenses involve training new salespeople or transferring old ones. As stated above, it costs

$5,000 per quarter to train a new salesperson. This sum includes the salary paid to the salesperson during the training period. Transferred salespeople receive a $5,000 moving allowance charged to other selling expense.

Inventory Storage Expense

Each production plant (home and nonhome area) has internal warehouse space to store 300,000 units of finished product. Thus your firm begins Year 3 with storage space for 300,000 units in your home-area plant. If additional plants are built, they also will include storage for 300,000 units. It costs 10 cents per unit to store unsold inventory in your plant(s) for a quarter. If your inventory exceeds the available storage space in a plant, your firm will rent space in a public warehouse in the area to store the additional units of product. Units will not be shipped to other areas for storage. Public warehouse storage costs amount to 30 cents per unit of product. Units in storage in the public warehouse will be sold prior to units stored in your plant. All storage costs for a quarter are paid at the beginning of the next quarter.

Implicit Cost of Stockouts

If your firm has sufficient inventory on hand to meet consumer demand, its sales will be limited by demand. On the other hand, if consumer demand exceeds your firm's production for the quarter plus beginning inventory, its sales will be limited by the volume of goods available for sale. Some of your customers who want to buy more units of your product than you can supply will become dissatisfied and are likely to take their business elsewhere. The demand for your product will tend to be reduced somewhat in the future over what it would have been if the stockout had not occurred. A stockout results not only in a loss of present sales, it generally results in the loss of a certain amount of future sales. Thus when developing an inventory plan, your firm needs to weigh the costs of storing inventory vs. the costs of a stockout.

Maintaining a low inventory level reduces both the cost of funds required to finance the inventory and the storage costs incurred. However, low inventory levels increase the likelihood of stockouts which inflict an implicit cost that can be measured only in terms of lost sales and profits in the current quarter and lower levels of demand in subsequent quarters. Firms normally develop an inventory plan which includes some level of safety stock, a buffer to meet unexpected variations in demand. The level of safety stock selected is arrived at by balancing the cost of carrying the extra inventory with the cost of stocking out in the quarter.

Summary of Relationships

1. An increase in <u>advertising expenditures</u> usually will result
in increased sales. Such expenditures are subject to the law of
diminishing returns, and sharp fluctuations in expenditures are
likely to harm your company's image.

2. <u>Sales salaries</u> and <u>commissions</u> provide incentive for your
salespeople. Usually increases in compensation will result in
increased sales, subject to the law of diminishing returns.
Higher-paying opportunities at competing firms may cause dissatisfaction on the part of your sales force and increase turnover among salespeople.

3. <u>General selling expense</u> (GSE) includes both a fixed and a
variable component. The total may be calculated as

$$GSE = \$150,000 + \$4,000 \times (salespeople) + \$0.20 \times (units\ sold)$$

4. <u>Transportation expenses</u> vary according to the originating
point and destination. For goods shipped:

> within the area = 10 cents per unit
> to or from Area 4 = 40 cents per unit
> to all other areas = 70 cents per unit

5. <u>Other selling expenses</u> consist primarily of training costs--
$5,000 per new salesperson for 2 quarters--and moving allowances
of $5,000 per salesperson transferred.

6. <u>New model introduction</u> is likely to increase your sales, with
an 80 percent chance of an increase, perhaps by as much as 20
percent. This implies a 20 percent chance that sales may actually decline as a result of introducing a new model. A decline is
unlikely to exceed 5 percent of current sales.

7. <u>Production of a new model</u> must be started one full quarter
prior to selling the model. During the start-up quarter, sales
of the old model will continue until the inventory of the old
model is exhausted. If additional units are required to satisfy
demand, units of the new model produced during the quarter will
be sold for the same price as the old model. All units of the
old model remaining at the end of the start-up quarter will be
sold on the first day of the next quarter to a liquidator at 50
percent of cost, for shipment overseas.

8. <u>Inventory storage costs</u> amount to 10 cents per unit for the
first 300,000 units. Beyond that, public warehouse space in the
area is used at a cost of 30 cents per unit to store all inventory exceeding the 300,000 limit. Quarterly storage costs are
paid at the beginning of the following quarter.

CHAPTER 6

MARKETING: SALES FORECASTING

Forecasting Sales

The volume of new orders placed with your firm will depend
upon a number of factors. Among the more important are: the
trend of economic activity, the season of the year, the wholesale
price charged by your firm and by competitors, the level and mix
of marketing expenditures made by your firm and by competitors,
the product introduction decisions made by your firm and by
competitors, and the marketability of the new models. In short,
the number of new orders that will be generated for your firm's
product in a quarter will be a result of the total effect of the
economic environment, your marketing activities, and the marketing activities of your competitors.

<u>Sales Levels and Gross National Product</u>

Econometric studies have shown a significant correlation
between the level of demand for consumer durable goods and the
level of economic activity as represented by real gross national
product (real GNP). Nominal GNP (stated in current dollars,
unadjusted for price level changes) and the Consumer Price Index
(CPI) are reported in the Quarterly Industry Report, together
with other economic indicators. Past levels of nominal GNP and
CPI are shown in Appendix A.

			---Credit Rating---		
GNP Index (Current $)	110.55	Interest Rates:	No. 1	No. 2	No. 3
Consumer Price Index	108.41				
Stock Market Index	109.12	Long-Term	7.60	8.80	9.80
Stock Market Earnings Yield	6.09	Short-Term	6.00	6.40	7.80
3-Month Time CD Rate	4.50				

87

An index of real GNP, adjusted for the impact of inflation, can be calculated by dividing the nominal GNP by the CPI, as follows:

$$\text{Real GNP Index} = \frac{\text{GNP}}{\text{CPI}} \times 100$$

In order to forecast demand effectively, your firm should become familiar with the historical GNP and CPI data for the simulation, as well as the available real GNP forecasts.

Your firm subscribes to ACCUDAT, a statistical service which provides forecasts of real GNP each quarter for the following four quarters. The ACCUDAT forecast is found at the end of your company report.

REAL GROSS NATIONAL PRODUCT FORECAST							
Actual Values for Last 4 Quarters				Forecast Values, Next 4 Quarters			
Qtr 5	Qtr 6	Qtr 7	Qtr 8	Qtr 9	Qtr 10	Qtr 11	Qtr 12
HIGH				105.03	107.94	110.74	113.73
MEAN 98.51	101.02	101.44	101.98	103.99	106.52	108.93	111.50
LOW				102.95	105.10	107.12	109.27

This forecast may be used, reliably, for near-term economic forecasts. However, you are cautioned that while the historical data are accurate, the forecasted values are estimates obtained by pooling the results of a survey of leading economists. The forecast tends to be more accurate for the first quarter immediately ahead, with the accuracy decreasing with each subsequent quarter. The reported values include the mean of the survey as well as the high and low forecasts provided by the group of economists.

Projecting the Trend of Growth

Changes in the overall level of economic activity from quarter to quarter may be separated for analytical purposes into three distinct types of effects: the overall trend, the cyclical effect, and the seasonal effect. In preparing a forecast, we suggest that you separate the problem of forecasting economic growth from the problem of forecasting cyclical and seasonal fluctuations. A good first step is to project the average rate of growth in real GNP which has occurred in your industry world over the past eight quarters. The values that are shown below provide an example.

Quarter	GNP Index	CPI Index	Real GNP
1	100.0	100.0	100.0
2	100.7	101.4	99.3
3	102.0	102.4	99.6
4	103.4	104.1	99.3
5	103.9	105.5	98.5
6	107.2	106.1	101.0
7	109.2	107.6	101.4
8	110.6	108.4	102.0

Quarter	Forecast Real GNP
9	104.0
10	106.5
11	108.9
12	111.5

As you can see, the economy has been emerging from a recession during the last three quarters, and is expected to grow rapidly during the next year. Even though the eight quarters of historical data, together with a four-quarter forecast, provide a relatively small base upon which to make a statistical projection, it still may be done. You probably will wish, however, to revise such a projection as additional data become available during the course of the simulation. Two relatively easy types of projections will be suggested although you may wish to use other methods.

The first and simplest method, though not necessarily the most accurate, is to plot the observed data on a chart and connect the points of observed data. Then "eye-ball" the resulting chart and use a ruler to extend the general trend of the plotted line across the rest of the chart. A more sophisticated and, we might say, more statistically reliable method of projecting a trend is to compute a least-squares trend line based upon the observed historical values of GNP. This may easily be done using a spreadsheet package such as Lotus 1-2-3 or Quattro. The simple plot described above also may be done quickly with a spreadsheet's graphing feature.

Projecting Economic Fluctuations

After computing the overall trend of the GNP, the next step is to estimate how the GNP will fluctuate over the course of the business cycle. During periods of economic upturn, the GNP is very likely to grow at a rate faster than the overall trend, and during periods of economic recession, it is very likely to grow at a slower rate or even decline.

Durable goods have more pronounced cycles with greater fluctuations than the GNP. They also tend to have somewhat longer downswings and shorter upswings. Your biggest problem, as with forecasting in the business world, will probably be correctly identifying in advance the turning point in the business cycle. This involves prior identification of the exact quarter in which the GNP will change direction and move from a period of recession to one of economic upturn or vice versa. Your knowledge of the characteristics of economic fluctuations should help in estimating the likely length of any particular business cycle in your simulated world.

Leading Indicators

Forecasting accuracy may be improved by using economic time series data which forecasting experts consider to be "leading indicators." A leading indicator is a data series that has historically tended to change direction earlier than the change in the general level of economic activity. However, even though certain series tend to lead changes in the GNP most of the time, they do not always do so. Sometimes they change direction when the GNP does not follow suit. Thus, it is possible for leading indicators to signal "false starts." Other times they have been known to change direction after the GNP changes.

Data on several economic indicators are provided to you in the Business Policy Game. Appendix A includes historical information about the level of stock market prices and the behavior of interest rates. Current data will be reported each quarter throughout the course of the simulation.

If interest rates and the stock market index both turn downward, the possibility of an early downturn in the level of GNP should be considered. Such a signal by leading indicators, however, should not be considered in isolation. It will provide a clue, along with other data, about the possible future behavior of economic fluctuations in your simulated world. You probably will want to update your GNP forecast as additional information becomes available during the course of playing the simulation.

Using the Sales Forecast Work Sheets

One sales forecasting approach is to view sales in a future quarter as being equal to last quarter's sales plus an incremental change due to changes in the factors that influence the level of sales. In mathematical terms this relationship might be expressed as follows:

Future sales = Previous sales + Incremental sales

where incremental sales are determined by changes in real GNP, seasonal factors, price, advertising expenditures, sales force activity, new model introduction, and competitors' activities. Incremental sales may be either positive or negative. Mathematically,

$$\text{Incremental sales} = f(GNP, S, M1, M2, \dots, Mn)$$

where GNP stands for real gross national product, S represents seasonal factors, and M1, M2, ..., Mn represent the various marketing factors that affect the sales of a firm and its competitors.

Sales Forecast work sheets have been developed to assist you in forecasting your firm's future sales (see Figure 6-1). The Sales Forecast work sheets utilize this incremental model. You may use one work sheet to forecast total company sales, by quarters, for a full year or you may use separate work sheets to forecast sales for each of your four market areas. Copies of the work sheet are provided in Appendix C. A spreadsheet template of the Sales Forecast work sheet also is available on disk. We suggest that you follow the procedure indicated on the work sheet to develop your sales forecast.

The real GNP forecast serves as the basis for the first entry on the Sales Forecast work sheet. Enter your forecasted change in GNP for the quarter (+2% in our example, taken from the Accudat forecast shown above).

The next step is to enter the actual sales (in thousands of units) from the previous quarter on the "Sales, previous quarter" line of the work sheet. For your first forecast this will be the sales figure for Year 2, Quarter 4 from the historical data in Appendix B or from a computer printout provided by your administrator for that quarter. If you plan to forecast total sales for your firm, enter the number of units your firm sold last quarter. If you plan to forecast sales by market area, enter the number of units sold in a market area last quarter. For our example shown in Figure 6-1, we will assume that sales in the previous quarter were 345,000 units.

Sales of your simulated consumer durable product tend to be affected by changes in the level of economic activity in your simulated world. In an upturn, sales rise somewhat faster than the GNP, and in a downturn they fall somewhat faster. You need to estimate the affect which changes in the level of economic activity have upon your company's sales. Regression analysis of historical relationships between GNP and sales may give you some clues as to the amount of change to expect in your sales with a given change in GNP. If you undertake statistical analysis, remember that your price changes and other marketing activities, as well as the marketing activities of your competitors will affect the level of sales. Allowance must be made for these factors in addition to the effect of changes in GNP.

THE BUSINESS POLICY GAME
SALES FORECAST WORK SHEET[a,b,c]

Company ____	Year ____			
	Qtr 1	Qtr 2	Qtr 3	Qtr 4
Forecasted GNP change	+2 %	%	%	%
Sales, previous quarter	345			
Estimated sales increments:				
From GNP change	+7			
Seasonal factors	−69			
Price change	+14			
Advertising change	+10			
Sales salary change	0			
Sales commission change	0			
# of salespersons change	+15			
New model introduction	0			
Competitors' actions	−5			
Total incremental change	−28			
Total sales forecast	317			
Expected average price	$ 9.80	$.	$.	$.
Expected sales revenue	$3,107	$	$	$

[a] Unless otherwise indicated, make estimates in thousands of units.
[b] For expected average price, use dollars.
[c] For expected sales revenue, use thousands of dollars.

Figure 6-1
Illustration of the Sales Forecasting Work Sheet

Alternatively, you may decide to make only rough estimates of the effect of GNP changes on the level of sales. All estimates should be refined as more data become available during the course of the simulation.

The ACCUDAT forecast of real GNP for Year 3, Quarter 1 indicates an increase in the index from 101.90 to a mean value of 103.99 (up about two percent), with a range from 105.03 (up about three percent) to 102.95 (up about one percent). Suppose that you wish to be conservative, and accept the low value of about one percent increase as your forecast. And suppose that you estimate that the sales of your durable good product will increase by, perhaps, as much as twice the percentage increase in real GNP. Your unit sales increase, then, would be last quarter's sales times two percent, or

$$345,000 \times 0.02 = 6,900$$

This is rounded to 7,000 for our example, and entered in the Sales Forecast work sheet (Figure 6-1).

Seasonal Factors

Next, an estimate should be made of the likely change in sales caused by seasonal factors. In the Business Policy Game, sales are highest during the second and fourth quarters of each year. During the first and third quarters, they are somewhat lower. ACCUDAT has developed a seasonal index for your world based upon an economic analysis of historical data. The index, which comes with the data package containing the GNP forecast cited above, shows the following seasonal variation:

Quarter	Index
1	.92
2	1.01
3	.91
4	1.16

These index values would indicate that with no change in any other factor affecting sales, first-quarter sales would be about 92 percent of the quarterly average, second-quarter sales about 101 percent, and so forth.

Enter the expected incremental change due to seasonal factors on the next line of the work sheet. The decline from the fourth quarter (116 percent of average) to the first quarter of the next year (92 percent of average) might be expected to be quite large--about 20 percent. If you estimate that seasonal factors would cause sales to decline by 20 percent during the first quarter, other things being equal, enter -69 (69,000

93

units), or a decline of 20 percent times the previous quarter's level of 345,000 units.

Changes in the level of GNP and the seasonal factors that affect your sales level are beyond the control of your company's management. However, the following factors that affect your sales can readily be influenced by your own decisions.

Marketing Activities

Changes in the price of your product, advertising expenditures, sales salaries, commissions, number of salespeople, and the introduction of new models all will influence your levels of sales. The likely effect of your decisions in regard to each of these factors should be estimated and entered on the appropriate line of the sales forecast work sheet.

1. Price Changes. Other things being equal, a decrease in a company's wholesale price will result in generation of sufficient additional sales to increase total sales revenue. Conversely, an increase in the price of the product will cause a large enough reduction in the level of demand that total sales revenues will drop. It can be said, therefore, that the price elasticity of demand for your simulated consumer durable good is positive or elastic. Product quality levels affect the degree of price elasticity. Higher quality products tend to be less sensitive to price changes than lower quality products. Deluxe quality (level number 1) is less price elastic than standard quality (level number 2), and economy quality (level number 3) is more price elastic than standard quality.

The level of demand for a company's product also will be affected by price changes of competitors. For example, if all companies in the industry were to reduce their prices from $10 per unit to $9.50 per unit, total industry sales would rise. The volume of sales for Company 1 would increase, but not by as great a factor as if Company 1 had been the only one to decrease its price. In other words, the average price charged by the firms in the industry will have an effect upon the level of demand for all firms in the industry, in addition to the effect of a price change by an individual company.

Enter the expected change in sales due to price changes on the work sheet. Suppose that you intend to decrease your unit price by 2 percent. After analyzing the historical relationship between sales and price changes, you might believe that a 2 percent price cut would produce a sales increase of 4 percent. Continuing our example, with the previous quarter's sales at 345,000 units, you would estimate an increase of about 14,000 units in the coming quarter and enter +14 on the work sheet.

2. Advertising. Increases in the level of advertising expenditures will tend to increase the level of demand for your company's product, and decreases generally will tend to reduce the level of demand. We suggest that you avoid sharp fluctuations in advertising expenditures. Stick to a well-planned strategy of resource allocations.

If you expect to increase advertising expenditures by 5 percent next quarter, you might anticipate a sales increase of 3 percent, or about 10,000 units in our illustration. This amount has been entered on the work sheet in Figure 6-1.

3. Sales Force and Sales Compensation. In addition to advertising, a company's promotion effort includes the activities of its sales force. The impact of this effort on sales is determined both by the number of active salespeople in the field and by the enthusiasm and perseverance of these salespeople. Again, other things being equal, an increase in your sales effort will tend to increase your volume of sales.

We suggest that you estimate the incremental changes in sales likely to result from changes in sales commission and from changes in the number of active salespeople. In our illustration, we assume no change in compensation levels for the coming quarter, but the expected effect of four new salespeople must be considered. They are not likely to be fully up to speed during their first quarter on the job, but they could be responsible for another 15,000 sales. If you believe this to be true you should enter +15 under "# of salespersons change," as we have done in Figure 6-1.

4. New Model Introduction. Enter the incremental change expected to result from the introduction of a new model. This estimate should include the effect of the quality level of the model. Remember that the new model will go on sale in the quarter following its initial production. Our illustration assumes no new models because no new model is available yet.

Competitors' Actions

The last item listed in the incremental change section of the work sheet is "Competitors' actions," another factor beyond your control. In many instances you will have no way of anticipating what the activities of your competitors will be. You may have reason to believe, though, that your competitors will match a cut in price that you may have made in a previous quarter. If so, you know that such an action will partially negate the increased sales that you otherwise could expect from your own price cut. Any incremental effect that you can foresee as a result of competitors' activities should be entered on the work sheet.

In our illustration, we assume that our intelligence reports indicate that competitors are likely to cut prices, too, partially negating the effects of our price cut. If we assume that their action would reduce our sales by 5,000 units below what they would otherwise be, -5 should be entered on the work sheet.

Completing the Forecast

Completing the remainder of the Sales Forecast work sheet is a matter of simple arithmetic. The sales from the previous quarter plus the estimated total incremental change equals the forecasted total sales for the quarter. Total sales are multiplied by the average price that you expect to charge. The result is your estimate of expected sales revenue for the quarter.

Don't be surprised if your actual sales during the first quarter of Year 3 deviate somewhat from your forecast. And remember that the values estimated for the example are not really inside information regarding the relationships between product demand and the various marketing factors. You may find that the actual relationships are somewhat different, and you are encouraged to make your own estimates. As you gain additional experience in forecasting, your estimates are likely to improve considerably. You will learn more about your industry, your competitors, and the impact and results of the decisions that you make. However, your forecasts will never be totally accurate; thus, your management should allow for a margin of safety to protect against errors in your forecasts. You should establish specific policies regarding the minimum level of inventory to maintain, over and above forecasted demand, as a safety stock. Also, a policy is needed to set the minimum amount of cash that you feel will enable you to meet financial obligations, should sales revenue fall below the amount that has been forecasted.

Look Ahead, Now

Now, don't stop with a sales forecast for Year 3, Quarter 1. In our example it was shown that sales can be expected to grow rapidly in Quarter 2 because of the seasonal factor and the projected increase in real GNP. That is going to happen even if you don't plan an aggressive marketing program. Work out the numbers for the rest of the year so that your production department can plan to have enough production capacity on line to meet your needs. If an expansion in capacity will be required, the plans must be made right away because it takes time to expand (See Chapter 8).

Your company's production could be expanded quickly by about 20 percent if all production workers work overtime (See Chapter 7). Beyond that, even adding second-shift production requires a full quarter of production-worker training before anything can be produced. And investing in more capacity may take from two to five quarters of construction, depending on which investment alternative is chosen.

So plan ahead--now! Start by completing your sales forecast for the rest of Year 3. Then make estimates of capacity requirements for the following year so that your production department can get started.

Summary of Relationships

1. Gross National Product in the Business Policy Game is patterned after an index of economic growth in your country. Interest rates and the stock market index usually are considered to be leading indicators related to GNP.

2. Future sales may be forecast by use of a model that is illustrated with the sales forecast work sheets found in Appendix C.

Future sales = Previous sales + Incremental sales

Incremental sales in this model can be described as a function of real gross national product (GNP), seasonal factors (S), and various marketing factors that have been described (M1, M2, ... Mn). These factors include price changes, advertising, sales salaries and commissions, number of salespeople and new model introductions of a firm and its competitors. Thus,

Incremental sales = f(GNP, S, M1, M2, ...Mn)

CHAPTER 7

PRODUCTION: PLANNING, SCHEDULING, AND COSTS

Your firm's production department should begin the simulation by setting functional-level production goals and objectives and developing production strategy to accomplish these goals. Production goals should support the overall goals developed at the business level, and should focus upon what production can contribute to achieving the business-level goals. The following business-level goal was used as an example in Chapter 4:

Maintain a cumulative rate of return on stockholders' initial investment (goal) of at least 20 (hurdle) percent (index) through year seven (time).

Production goals and objectives that support this business-level goal might be:

Goal: Limit inventory storage costs (goal) to one (hurdle) percent (index) of sales (time implicit).

Objective: Maintain an inventory level (goal) at the end of each quarter (time) equal to four weeks (hurdle) of sales (index)

Goal: Maintain sufficient production capacity (goal) to meet the growth (hurdle) in customer demand (index) during management's tenure (time).

Objective: Increase production capacity (goal) by 30 (hurdle) percent (index) during year four (time).

Other goals and objectives may focus upon production costs and capacity utilization.

Production strategy should be designed to enable your production department to attain its goals and objectives. The strategy should plan for the allocation of production resources to gain maximum efficiency while meeting market demand. The strategy for the inventory goal would focus upon production scheduling. The strategy for matching capacity with demand would involve all options for expansion and contraction of capacity. An effective production strategy should include all of the production variables which require resources.

The quarter to quarter tactical decisions which your production management must make are described below. These decisions should be considered in the light of your firm's sales forecast and guided by your production strategy and overall company policy. This chapter will provide suggestions for planning current and future production needs, discuss the scheduling of production for the current quarter, and outline the costs associated with various production alternatives.

Production Planning and Scheduling

Existing Capacity

Your firm has six production lines available for use as you assume management responsibilities at the beginning of Year 3. Each of the lines is capable of producing 4,000 units during a forty-hour week. Thus, normal production per line is 52,000 units during a thirteen-week quarter. With six lines operating at normal capacity, your plant will produce about 312,000 units during each quarter.

Actual production, however, may vary from this amount by up to 5 percent because of factors beyond your control. For example, if production machine down-time is greater than normal, your plant might produce as few as 296,000 units. Conversely, efficiency of your production workers could turn out to be very high in another quarter, and the six lines might produce as many as 327,000 units.

While your current production capacity is somewhat fixed, you have a number of alternatives for adjusting capacity. A temporary reduction in the production schedule may be arranged if you wish to shut down one or more lines for the entire quarter. During a shutdown period, workers are temporarily furloughed and may be recalled on short notice. For a shutdown period lasting more than 13 weeks, it sometimes is more cost effective to deactivate a line completely. Workers are discharged when a line is deactivated and some of the machinery is secured so that reactivation will require one quarter's advance notice to train new workers and prepare the machinery for active use. The costs associated with shutdown and deactivation procedures are outlined below.

Production may be expanded by scheduling overtime work, by adding a second shift in your home area plant, by adding additional lines in an existing plant, by construction of additions to a plant, or by construction of new plants in other marketing areas. Overtime costs are described below, and the necessary procedures and cash outlays required for other forms of expansion of production facilities are described in Chapter 8.

With these various production alternatives in mind, and considering the costs associated with each alternative, the next step is to determine the strategy that your firm will use to produce sufficient units to meet your sales demand. Suggestions were made in Chapter 4 for completing a sales forecast. This forecast should serve as the basis for the production plans that you will make.

Level Versus Seasonal Production

There are two basic approaches to production planning for a product that has sharp seasonal fluctuations in its sales. One strategy is to plan production during each period of operations that will be approximately equal to the expected sales during that period. Because of higher seasonal demand in the second and fourth quarters, your firm could undertake heavy production schedules during those quarters each year, while shutting down some lines or otherwise reducing the amount of production during the first and third quarters.

This type of plan has the obvious advantage of enabling your firm to operate with a minimum investment in inventory. Storage costs could be held at relatively low levels, and the cost of funds necessary to finance inventory accumulations would be minimal. The disadvantage to such a plan is that production costs are likely to be considerably higher. Sharp seasonal fluctuations in production will require adding large numbers of workers to your labor force during the second and fourth quarters of each year and operating your production facilities at or above normal capacity during those quarters. Conversely, during the first and third quarters many of the workers would be temporarily laid off and a significant portion of your production facilities would be standing idle.

In developing your firm's policies regarding production, you will wish to compare the costs and relative flexibility of seasonal production with a strategy that sometimes is called a level-production plan. A simplified version of the level-production plan would require you to estimate the total volume of expected sales during the coming year and divide that amount by four. Production during each quarter of simulated operation then should be equal to approximately one-fourth of expected annual sales. During the first and third quarters, your firm would produce more goods than are necessary to meet expected sales, and inventories would accumulate to meet the larger demands of the second and fourth quarters.

Obviously, inventory storage costs will be higher than with seasonal production, and more cash will be necessary to finance the inventory buildup. On the other hand, level production will enable you to maintain a stable work force and to better utilize your production capacity. A projection of production costs, inventory storage requirements, and the cost and availability of funds to finance those inventories will assist you in deciding which type of production plan will best meet the needs of your firm.

Inventory Storage Costs

Each production plant (home and non-home area) has room to store 300,000 units of finished product. Thus your firm begins Year 3 with storage space for 300,000 units in your home-area plant. If additional plants are built, they also will include storage for 300,000 units. It costs 10 cents per unit to store unsold inventory in your plant(s) for a quarter. If your inventory exceeds the available storage space in a plant, your firm will rent space in a public warehouse in the area to store the additional units of product. Units will <u>not</u> be shipped to other areas for storage. Public warehouse storage costs amount to 30 cents per unit of product. Units in storage in the public warehouse will be sold prior to units stored in your plant. All storage costs for a quarter are paid at the beginning of the next quarter.

Production Plan Work Sheets

Work sheets are provided in Appendix C for developing a production plan and estimating production costs. A spreadsheet template of the Production Plan work sheet also is available on disk. These work sheets will assist your firm in planning your production requirements, scheduling the necessary production, and estimating costs. If your sales forecasts indicate a need for expanding your production facilities, you also will find these work sheets extremely useful in planning the rate at which you should expand and the type of expansion that you should undertake. Investment alternatives for expansion of your plant are detailed in Chapter 8, along with the costs that are associated with each alternative.

Each work sheet has space for one year, or four quarters, of operations. Thus, you may want to use a series of work sheets to forecast production requirements over several years. As the competition progresses, the accuracy of your production forecast can be assessed, and forecasts of future production requirements can be revised.

An example of a Production Plan work sheet is shown in Figure 7-1. The top section of the work sheet will assist you in determining the amount of production that must be scheduled for each quarter of operation. Suppose that you have forecast sales in the first quarter of Year 3 to be about 317,000 units, as in the illustration of Figure 6-1. Your sales estimate should be entered (in thousands of units) on the first line of the Production Plan work sheet, as shown in Figure 7-1.

If your management has adopted a seasonal production strategy, you may wish to maintain a relatively small safety stock on hand, say 125,000 units. Add this to your sales forecast to show the total number of units needed for the quarter. The minimum number of units needed to meet your expected sales and still maintain your safety stock will be

$$317,000 + 125,000 = 442,000 \text{ units.}$$

If your firm had 134,000 units of inventory on hand at the end of Year 2, Quarter 4, enter this amount for Beginning Inventory. Then subtract your beginning inventory to show the minimum number of units needed to produce during the quarter.

$$442,000 - 134,000 = 308,000$$

As production is scheduled in lumps of 52,000 units per line for a normal 40 hour week, you may decide to schedule all six lines, producing 52,000 each, to total 312,000 units.

$$6 \times 52,000 = 312,000$$

This would leave the total number of units available for sale as the sum of the beginning inventory plus production scheduled for the quarter.

$$134,000 + 312,000 = 446,000$$

This is slightly higher than the amount required to match the sales forecast plus minimum safety stock, but only slightly. Don't stop with your production plan for Year 3, Quarter 1. Sales may be expected to grow rapidly in Year 3, Quarter 2 because of the seasonal factor and expected increase in real GNP (see Chapter 6), so don't let yourself be caught short. Production may be increased quickly by about 20 percent if all production workers work overtime. Beyond that, you must plan ahead (see Chapter 8). Even second-shift production requires a full quarter to train production workers before anything can be produced. New production lines or added plant capacity take even longer.

Plan your production requirements now for the rest of Year 3 and Year 4 so that you will have time to plan for expansion of your productive capacity if you need to.

THE BUSINESS POLICY GAME
PRODUCTION PLAN WORK SHEET

Co. _1_ World _1_ Yr _3_	Quarter 1	Quarter 2	Quarter 3	Quarter 4
Sales forecast (000s)	317			
Safety stock	125			
Total units needed	442			
Beginning inventory	134			
Minimum production	308			
Production scheduled	312			
Total prod. & inv.	446			

	Quarter 1		Quarter 2		Quarter 3		Quarter 4	
	Unit Cost	Total Cost	Unit Cost	Total Cost	Unit Cost	Total Cost	Unit Cost	Total Cost
Labor Cost								
Materials Cost								
Maintenance Cost								
Shutdown Cost								
Training Cost								
Total Cash Expenditure								
Equipment Depreciation								
Plant Depreciation								
Total Production Cost								

FIGURE 7-1
Illustration of the Production Plan Work Sheet

Scheduling

On each quarterly decision form, <u>all available production lines in each plant and for each shift must either be scheduled for production, shut down or deactivated</u>. If a line is available for production but is not scheduled to produce, it must be shut down or deactivated. Unless all available lines are accounted for on the decision form, the computer program will reject your decision set with an error message requiring you to account for all available lines.

    1. <u>Schedule lines</u>. Production lines to be scheduled for first-shift operation should be entered on the decision form on the row for the marketing area in which they are located. Enter the number of production lines that are to be producing (not more than the maximum available) and the number of hours that are to be scheduled per week (from 40 to 48). Make sure your entry is for a marketing area (or areas) in which you have a plant. If your entry is in the wrong area, the decision values will be rejected by the decision-entry program.

Limits: Lines -- 0 to maximum number of lines available
           Hours -- 0, 40 to 48 (per week)

Production Scheduling	Production Lines Hours
Area 1	#____ #____
Area 2	#____ #____
Area 3	#____ #____
Area 4	#____ #____
2d Shft	#____ #____

    2. <u>Second shift</u>. Production on a second-shift operation is possible only in a firm's home-area plant. Enter the number of second-shift lines that are to be producing (up to the maximum number of lines available) and the number of hours that are to be scheduled each week (from 40 to 48). As with the first shift, all available second-shift lines must either be scheduled for production, shut down, or deactivated.

104

NOTE: Second-shift lines are not available and may not
be scheduled until production workers have been trained
to operate the lines.   The training process is described in Chapter 8.   Training of new second-shift
workers requires one quarter before production may
begin.   Advance planning is required, at least one
quarter before you intend to begin production.   Thus,
if you wish to begin production on one or more second-
shift lines in Year 3, Quarter 2, you must make an
entry under "New Lines" for Year 3, Quarter 1.

Limits: Lines -- 0 to maximum number of lines available
          Hours -- 0, 40 to 48 (per week)

    3.   Shut down lines.   Production lines that are available
but not scheduled for production and have not been deactivated
should be shut down.   Enter the number of lines which you plan to
shut down on the decision form under "Production Scheduling--
Shutdown."   Make sure that all first-shift lines are accounted
for and all second-shift lines are accounted for.   If you shut
down a first-shift line, a corresponding second-shift line must
be shut down or deactivated unless there remain at least as many
first-shift lines as second-shift lines.   A second-shift line may
not continue operating unless there is a corresponding line on
the first shift.   Check to make sure your entry is for the area
in which you want to shut down lines.

Limits: 0 to number of lines available

Production Scheduling			
	Shut-down	Deac-tivate	Reac-tivate
Area 1	#____	#____	#____
Area 2	#____	#____	#____
Area 3	#____	#____	#____
Area 4	#____	#____	#____
2d Shft	#____	#____	

NOTE: If your firm decides to operate its plant at
less than normal capacity, lines that are not used must
be shut down or deactivated.   Lines that have been shut
down are immediately available for production in the
following quarter or they may be shut down again at

that time if you need to maintain reduced production levels.

4. <u>Deactivate lines</u>. Any line that is available for production may be deactivated and removed from production until such time as you choose to reactivate the line. Enter the number of lines that you desire to deactivate in the appropriate area on the decision form under "Production Scheduling--Deactivate." Deactivated lines may not be scheduled again for production until they have been reactivated (see paragraph 6 below).

Deactivated lines provide less flexibility because they may not be used for production again until they have been reactivated, which takes a full quarter of preparation. Deactivated lines incur a one-time cost of $100,000 (applies to second-shift as well as first-shift lines and is charged under "Other Expenses" on the Income Statement) when they are taken out of production. Reactivation requires an expenditure of $50,000 for training of workers during the quarter of preparation before the line is available again for production. (This charge is reported under Training Costs in the Production Cost Analysis section of the Operating Information Report.) Remember, all costs are subject to increases due to inflation.

The only restriction on your ability to shut down or deactivate production lines is that the number of second-shift lines may not exceed the number of producing lines on the regular shift. In other words, if first-shift lines are shut down, any second-shift line utilizing the same equipment must be shut down at the same time. If first-shift lines are deactivated, corresponding second-shift lines must be terminated.

Limits: 0 to the number of lines available for production

5. <u>Terminate second shift</u>. Production lines available for second-shift production may be terminated, or "deactivated" by entering the number of lines you wish to terminate under the "Production Scheduling--Deactivate" column for the "2nd Shft" row on the decision form. Second-shift lines must be terminated if the corresponding lines on the first shift are deactivated. Terminated second-shift lines are not carried as "previously deactivated" in the same manner as first-shift lines (see below), so they may not be "reactivated." In order to again schedule a second shift on a line after the line has been terminated, you must start from scratch. Follow the same procedure as described in Chapter 8 for original preparation of lines for second-shift operation. If you wish to continue to have a second-shift line available for production next quarter, even though not producing this quarter, shut it down as in paragraph 3, above.

Limits: 0 to number of second-shift lines available

6. <u>Reactivate lines</u>. First-shift production lines that have been previously deactivated (but not second-shift lines that have been terminated) may be reactivated and made available for production. Such lines, if any, are reported in the Operating Information Report.

	Area 1	Area 2	Area 3	Area 4
Lines Previously Deactivated	0	2	0	0

Reactivation requires one quarter of preparation before a line may be scheduled for production. Enter the number of lines to be reactivated under the appropriate area on the decision form. Lines may not actually be scheduled for production until the following quarter.

Limits: 0 to number of lines previously deactivated

Research and Development

At the close of Year 2, each firm in your world was spending approximately $140,000 per quarter on research and development. A little more than half of this money was going to product development with the remaining funds allocated to process development. Money spent on <u>product development</u> funds a research team which is developing advanced designs of your current product. From time to time, this effort will yield a new model of your firm's product which may be introduced into the marketplace when your management team believes the time is right. While there may not be a linear relationship between the amount of funds spent on product development and the time it takes to develop a new model of the firm's product, the more money spent, the quicker a new model is likely to be developed. Of course, after a certain point additional funds will not lead to any appreciable decrease in the time it takes to develop a product. The law of diminishing returns has not been repealed.

Funds allocated to <u>process development</u> support a research team working on manufacturing methods in an attempt to develop improved manufacturing processes which will reduce manufacturing costs. From time to time, the team will develop a new process or an improved method of an existing process which will reduce production costs. This cost reduction becomes especially important when new products are developed as new products tend to cost more to produce than do older products. Increases in funding for the process research team will tend to shorten the time it takes to develop improvements in production processes. However, the law of diminishing returns applies here also.

The personnel working in your R & D department are highly skilled professionals. They are difficult to find and thus cannot be easily replaced once they leave the firm. Dramatic swings in the R & D budget from quarter to quarter will likely have a negative impact upon the morale of the department causing some of your best people to leave. If severe budget cuts are experienced, a new model which is close to release or a process improvement which is nearly developed may be scrapped for lack of funds. Later increases in funds may restart the project; however, the time required to complete the project will be much longer than if the project had been carried through to completion originally. The additional time is due to the time required to replace personnel who were previously working on the project, as well as the time required to bring existing personnel who were working on the project back up to speed.

Projects completed by the process team of your R & D department will be reported in the Operating Information Report. The report consists of new basic cost levels per unit for labor and materials, which include the cost savings which may have been realized. When available, these cost savings are applied to any product model your firm decides to produce. The savings will be reflected in future reports of basic labor and material costs for new models the firm may develop. An effective research and development program is an essential element of a firm's success. Without such a program, your firm would have no new products to introduce into the marketplace. Your product offering would become obsolete relative to your competitors. Your production processes would become less efficient relative to your competitors. You would earn the dubious distinction of being the high-cost competitor. Your company would be doomed to failure! We urge you to support a strong, continuous research and development program.

Production Costs

Basic <u>standard unit costs</u> for model number 1 (your current model) at the end of Year 2 are as follows:

Labor	$2.40
Materials	1.20
Maintenance	.25
Total	$3.85

Standard cost levels may be different for each model--usually being higher for a new model than for an existing model. Also, standard costs vary according to quality levels, with labor and materials costs for quality 1 being 10 percent higher than for quality 2, and 10 percent lower for quality 3.

As new model availability is reported in your Operating Information report, the new standard costs will be reported at the same time. In this way, you can plan the availability of funds required to produce the new model if you should put it into production. For example, the availability of model 2 might be reported to you, as follows:

```
Latest Model Developed:  2      Model Produced This Quarter:  1  Quality: 2
Standard Cost per Unit for Next Quarter (includes inflation, cost savings):
     Model  2 Quality 2 Labor Cost:  2.64  Materials Cost:  1.37
     Model  1 Quality 2 Labor Cost:  2.46  Materials Cost:  1.23
```

The costs reported are those for the same quality level that you currently are producing. In the case of model 1, that is quality level 2. If you should choose, for example, to introduce model 2 with a higher quality (level 1) then 10 percent should be added to the reported costs for model 2, quality 2. If you choose quality 3, subtract 10 percent from the reported costs for quality 2.

All production costs are subject to inflation and will escalate at a rate approximately equal to the rate of change in the Consumer Price Index (CPI). Materials costs and labor costs will change each quarter by a percentage equal to the percentage change in the CPI during the previous quarter. The effects of inflation are incorporated in the reported levels of standard costs for all models and these costs are those that will be in effect in the quarter following the report.

<u>Process Research and Development</u> focuses upon finding ways to reduce labor and materials costs through modification of the production process. Once developed, the new processes and their resulting cost savings will be available to reduce basic cost levels <u>for any model</u> below the level that otherwise would occur. For example, suppose that your R & D department has successfully developed a process that would reduce labor costs by 20 cents per unit. The basic standard costs for models number 1 and 2 would be 2.26 and 2.44, respectively, instead of those reported above.

```
Latest Model Developed:  2      Model Produced This Quarter:  1  Quality: 2
Standard Cost per Unit for Next Quarter (includes inflation, cost savings):
     Model  2 Quality 2 Labor Cost:  2.44  Materials Cost:  1.37
     Model  1 Quality 2 Labor Cost:  2.26  Materials Cost:  1.23
```

The costs, of course, will rise in subsequent quarters to reflect the impact of inflation as shown by changes in the Consumer Price Index. Suppose that you continue this quarter producing model 1, even though model 2 is available. If the labor cost savings of 20 cents per unit were to be realized and the

Consumer Price Index were to rise by another 2 percent, the following report would be shown the next quarter in the Operating Information Report.

```
Latest Model Developed:  2      Model Produced This Quarter:  1  Quality: 2
Standard Cost per Unit for Next Quarter (includes inflation, cost savings):
      Model  2 Quality 2 Labor Cost:  2.49  Materials Cost:  1.40
      Model  1 Quality 2 Labor Cost:  2.31  Materials Cost:  1.25
```

To extend the example a little further, suppose that you then begin production of model 2, quality 2. In that quarter your firm develops a new model, model number 3, with labor and materials costs about 10 percent higher than for model number 2, and the Consumer Price Index rises by another 2 percent. The following report would be included in the Operating Information Report for that quarter:

```
Latest Model Developed:  3      Model Produced This Quarter:  2  Quality: 2
Standard Cost per Unit for Next Quarter (includes inflation, cost savings):
      Model  3 Quality 2 Labor Cost:  2.79  Materials Cost:  1.57
      Model  2 Quality 2 Labor Cost:  2.54  Materials Cost:  1.43
```

Note that costs for model 2 are the same as in the previous quarter, except for an inflation adjustment. Model number 3 costs are more than for model number 2, but are lower than they would have been without the development of a cost-saving process. Cost savings apply to all models that may be available, or become available in the future.

If subsequent models (number 4, 5, etc.) are developed without changing the model number being produced, only the costs of the two most recently developed models will be reported. Following development of model number 3 in the previous illustration, suppose that your management chooses not to introduce it but instead maintained full production of model number 2. Then, a few quarters later, your Research and Development Department reports model number 4 available. The following quarter's costs for models number 3 and 4 would be reported, but you would have to estimate the costs for model number 2, which would change proportionately to those of model number 3.

NOTE: Increases in costs for all models will be due to inflation, and decreases would be due to successful process research activities resulting in labor or materials cost savings, or perhaps both.

Standard unit costs are based upon a forty-hour work week with
output levels at normal capacity. Production is at a rate of 100
units per line per hour. Actual costs are calculated as indicated below and will be reported quarterly in the Operating
Information Report. All costs are subject to inflation adjustments. An illustration of production costs is provided in Figure
7-2.

```
+-------------------------------------------------------------+
|               PRODUCTION COST ANALYSIS                      |
|                                                             |
|                    --Actual Cost--      Standard Cost       |
|                   TOTAL   PER UNIT        Per Unit          |
|                   ($000)     $               $              |
|                                                             |
| Labor Cost          749     2.40           2.40             |
| Materials Cost      374     1.20           1.20             |
| Maintenance Cost     77      .25            .25             |
| Shutdown Cost         0      .00                            |
| Training Cost         0      .00                            |
|    Total Cash Expenditures  1200   3.85                     |
| Equipment Depreciation  110   .35                           |
| Plant Depreciation       32   .10                           |
|    Total Production Cost 1342  4.30                         |
+-------------------------------------------------------------+
```

FIGURE 7-2
Reported Costs of Production
Quarterly Operating Information Report

Production Cost Components

Your finance department will need estimates of the amounts
of the various components of production cost in order to estimate
cash flows and provide sufficient cash to cover these costs,
along with other expenditures that will take place during the
upcoming quarter. In addition, these estimates will be used in
preparation of pro forma financial statements for the quarter.
The lower part of the Production Plan work sheet will be useful
in providing these estimates. This part of the Production Plan
is illustrated in Figure 7-3.

1. Total labor costs per hour for straight-time production
amount to 100 times the basic cost level ($240 per hour for model
number 1 at the end of Year 2) for each production line. The
union contract provides for a 10 percent premium for workers on a
second-shift operation, or $264 per hour for model number 1 at
the end of Year 2. Overtime work (more than 40 hours per week)
is paid at one and one-half times the normal rate, or $360 per
hour for model number 1 during Year 2, Quarter 4. Contract
restrictions make impractical any operations at less than forty
hours per week or more than forty-eight hours per week.

	Quarter 1		Quarter 2		Quarter 3		Quarter 4	
	Unit Cost	Total Cost	Unit Cost	Total Cost	Unit Cost	Total Cost	Unit Cost	Total Cost
Labor Cost	2.42	755						
Materials Cost	1.21	378						
Maintenance Cost	.26	81						
Shutdown Cost	0	0						
Training Cost	0	0						
Total Cash Expenditure	3.89	1,214						
Equipment Depreciation	.36	111						
Plant Depreciation	.10	32						
Total Production Cost	4.35	1,357						

FIGURE 7-3
Illustration of the Production Plan Work Sheet

An easy way to estimate labor costs is to multiply the cost per unit by the number of units to be produced during the quarter. For straight-time production, this involves using the reported standard labor costs. The cost of units to be produced on overtime or with second-shift operations needs further adjustment to provide for the premium pay on those shifts. Continuing our example, and using the reported costs from Appendix B, if your company is to schedule 6 lines of production at 40 hours per week (about 312,000 units), using the reported labor costs of $2.42 per unit for model 1, total labor costs for the coming quarter would be estimated as:

$$\$2.42 \times 312,000 = \$755,040$$

This value should be rounded to $755,000 and entered under Labor Cost in the work sheet, in thousands of dollars.

If overtime or second-shift production were to be undertaken, make the appropriate additions to this amount. Units produced on overtime would have labor costs 50 percent higher, or $3.63 per unit. Second-shift labor costs are 10 percent higher than for first-shift--$2.66 per unit for straight time and $3.99 per unit for overtime.

2. <u>Materials costs</u> for raw materials used in the manufacturing process are equal to the basic cost level ($1.20 for model number 1 at the end of Year 2) for each unit of production. New models generally have higher materials costs.

If materials costs for model 1 are reported to be $1.21 per unit for next quarter, the cost to produce 312,000 units would be $377,520.

$$\$1.21 \times 312,000 = \$377,520$$

Rounded to thousands of dollars, enter 378 for Materials Cost on the work sheet.

3. <u>Maintenance costs</u> average $25 per hour at the end of Year 2 for each production line that is operating, or $0.25 per unit.

If next period's maintenance costs are expected to increase to $0.26 per unit because of inflation, to produce 312,000 units would require

$$\$0.26 \times 312,000 = \$81,120$$

Round this to thousands of dollars, and enter 81 on the work sheet for Maintenance Cost.

4. <u>Shutdown costs</u> are standby costs for lines that have been shut down. At the end of Year 2, standby costs for shutdown lines amount to $4,000 per line per week. If one line is shut down for thirteen weeks, standby costs total $52,000 and output is reduced by about 52,000 units.

Continuing our example, all six available lines are scheduled for production, so there will be no shutdown costs.

5. <u>Training costs</u> for new production workers are incurred when a new line is constructed, a second-shift line is added, or a previously-deactivated line is reactivated. When a new line is activated (see Chapter 8), the training costs for workers amount to $100,000 per line at prices in effect at the end of Year 2. These costs are spread over two quarters at $50,000 per line per quarter. Training costs associated with new lines added to the second shift are paid in the quarter immediately preceding activation at a rate of $100,000 (Year 2 prices) per line. Reactivation training costs are also paid in the quarter immediately preceding activation at a rate of $50,000 (Year 2 prices) per line.

As there currently are no deactivated lines, and in our example no new lines are scheduled to be prepared for production, enter 0 on the work sheet under Training Cost.

6. <u>Total Cash Expenditure</u> is merely the sum of items 1 to 5 above. For our example, add the values and enter the total:

$$755 + 378 + 81 + 0 + 0 = 1,214$$

Dividing $1,214,000 by the 312,000 units to be produced gives a unit cost for cash expenditure of $3.89, somewhat higher than the $3.85 reported for Year 2, Quarter 4 and $1,214,000 is higher than the $1,200,000 total cash expenditure because of inflation. The value for total cash expenditure should be reported to the finance department for inclusion in the cash flow budget for the coming quarter (see Chapter 10).

7. <u>Equipment Depreciation</u>. Equipment is depreciated on a straight-line basis over 7 years. That is, current-quarter depreciation charges are calculated as 1/28th (3.5714 percent) of the original book value of all equipment in place during the quarter. It should be noted that this is not the same as taking 1/28th of the value of net equipment on the balance sheet. Net equipment is the <u>depreciated</u> value of equipment in place rather than the original book value.

Without a complete list of equipment purchases and write-offs for past years it will be difficult for you to estimate this value exactly. It can be estimated very closely, however, by adjusting last period's depreciation charges, shown in the Production Cost Analysis section of the Operating Information Report. To those charges, add 1/28th (3.5714 percent) of the cost of equipment purchases during the quarter (both new equipment and replacement equipment), and subtract 1/28th of the cost of equipment replacement write-offs. The purchase of replacement equipment would cost the same as the retired equipment, except for the effect of higher prices on the new equipment. Higher prices of new equipment result from inflation, and price levels will continue to rise in proportion to the change in the Consumer Price Index.

For our example, equipment depreciation charges for Year 2, Quarter 4 were $110,000. If no new equipment is to be purchased during the quarter, the only equipment purchases will be for replacement. Because the replacement equipment will cost a little more than the original equipment that is being replaced, the equipment depreciation charges will be slightly higher next quarter than then were this quarter. An estimate of $111,000 will be pretty close, accounting for the inflation factor on depreciation for the replaced equipment. Enter 111 on the work sheet for Equipment Depreciation.

114

If, in addition to purchasing replacement equipment, construction were to start on one new line, increase the previously-estimated equipment depreciation charges by 1/28th of the first quarter's payment for construction on that line. The full amount of the payment will be capitalized in the coming quarter and, therefore, must also be depreciated. If the inflation factor is a one percent increase from Year 2, Quarter 4, the additional amount for equipment depreciation for each new line would be about $9,000.

$$.035714 \times \$250,000 \times 1.01 = \$9,018$$

Thus, for one new line, adding about $9,000 to the earlier estimate of $111,000 would cause us to enter 120 here on the work sheet. In addition, should a new line be under construction, there would be $50,000 in training costs to be entered above.

8. <u>Plant Depreciation charges</u> are computed and added to the cost of production. Buildings are depreciated on a straight-line basis over a period of 31.5 years in the simulated world, or at a rate of 0.7937 percent of their original book value for each quarter. The existing plant was valued originally at $4 million and is being depreciated at a rate of $32,000 per quarter.

If a <u>new plant</u> is constructed in another marketing area (see Chapter 8), the depreciation charges are handled in the following manner: At the end of each quarter of construction, payments made to the contractor are capitalized and depreciation charges are increased by 0.7937 percent of the amount of the payments made. If a ten-line plant is under construction, for example, quarterly payments of $800,000 (plus inflation) will be capitalized at the end of the quarter and depreciation charges will be increased by about $6,000 per quarter.

$$0.007937 \times \$800,000 = \$6,349$$

After five quarters of construction, when the plant is available for use, the total depreciation charges would consist of about $64,000 per quarter--$32,000 on the preexisting plant and about $32,000 (plus inflation) on the new plant. Once the plant has been completed, depreciation charges do not change with inflation because they are based on original cost.

The same procedure is followed for computing depreciation charges on <u>additions</u> to existing plants. Quarterly payments of $300,000 are capitalized and depreciation charges are increased by about $2,000.

$$0.007937 \times \$300,000 = \$2,381$$

The only difference is that construction of new additions is completed in three quarters of simulated operations while new plant facilities require five quarters of construction before completion.

9. <u>Total Production Cost</u> is the sum of Total Cash Expenditure plus Equipment and Plant Depreciation. For our example,

$$1,214 + 111 + 32 = 1,357 \text{ (or \$4.35 per unit)}$$

This amount should be reported to the finance department for inclusion in the pro forma income statement (See Chapter 10). It will form the basis for the estimate of cost of goods sold for next quarter.

Cost Variance

Actual costs may vary somewhat from those shown above. While production normally is at a rate of 100 units per hour per line, or 4,000 units per week, this rate may not be realized. A seemingly random variation of as much as <u>5 percent</u> in either direction may occur because of efficiencies or inefficiencies experienced in actual operation. Absenteeism may be higher than normal, down-time of machinery more than expected, and raw material deliveries delayed. All of these factors would cause production levels to be somewhat lower than anticipated. Actual expenditures, therefore, would be slightly lower than those scheduled. Unit costs (total production costs divided by the number of units produced) would be somewhat higher because total labor and maintenance costs will remain at the same level while the number of units produced has declined. These variations are beyond the control of your management.

Operations of new plants in other areas will be subject to the same cost functions as those of the existing plant in the home area. A second shift is not possible outside of the home area, however, because of a shortage of supervisory personnel.

Illustration of Overtime Costs

Figure 7-4 illustrates the current quarterly costs of first-shift production at straight time and at various amounts of overtime. The costs are for one line operating for one quarter and are based on the standard unit costs for model number 1 at the end of Year 2. Plant depreciation costs are based upon use of six operating lines, with the amount shown being one-sixth of $32,000.

| | Hours Scheduled | | | | |
	40	42	44	46	48
Labor	$124,800	$134,160	$143,520	$152,880	$162,240
Materials	62,400	65,520	68,640	71,760	74,880
Maintenance	13,000	13,650	14,300	14,950	15,600
Equip't depreciation	18,166	18,166	18,166	18,166	18,166
Plant depreciation	5,333	5,333	5,333	5,333	5,333
Total cost	$223,699	$236,829	$249,959	$263,089	$276,219
Output (in units)	52,000	54,600	57,200	59,800	62,400
Unit cost	$4.30	$4.34	$4.37	$4.40	$4.43

FIGURE 7-4
First-Shift Production Cost Per Line

It should be noted that total unit production costs increase rapidly as the amount of overtime increases. Labor costs for all additional units produced after 40 hours per week are higher due to the overtime premium. The higher unit labor costs more than offset the fact that the fixed depreciation charges are averaged over the larger number of units produced. If labor costs were proportionately higher than depreciation charges, as they may be for some models, the unit cost differential between straight time and overtime would be even greater.

Summary of Relationships

1. <u>Basic unit costs</u>: reported standard costs which include inflation-related cost increases as well as process savings that may have been realized

2. <u>Labor costs, regular shift</u>, per hour:
   straight-time rate = 100 times basic labor cost
   overtime rate = 150 times basic unit labor cost

3. <u>Labor costs, second shift</u>, per hour:
   same as straight-time rate + 10 percent premium

4. <u>Materials costs per unit</u>: basic unit material cost

5. <u>Maintenance costs</u>, per line:
   $25 per hour, or $0.25 per unit (subject to inflation)

6. <u>Standby costs for shutdown line</u>:
   $4,000 per line per week, or $52,000 per quarter, subject to inflation (output reduced by about 4,000 units per week, or 52,000 units per quarter)

117

7. Training costs, per line (subject to inflation):
        for newly constructed lines = $100,000 (paid at $50,000
            per quarter)
        for new second-shift lines = $100,000 (paid in one
            quarter)
        for reactivated 1st-shift lines = $50,000 (paid in one
            quarter), 2nd-shift must be rebuilt to reactivate

8. Equipment depreciation charges:
        calculated on a straight-line basis over 7 years, or
        3.5714 percent of original book value each quarter

9. Plant depreciation charges:
        calculated on a straight-line basis over 31.5 years
        for existing plant = $32,000 per quarter
        for new plant or addition = 0.7937 percent per quarter
            of cost of construction in place

10. Deactivation costs: one-time charge of $100,000 per line,
        applies both to first-shift lines and second-shift
        lines separately (second shift lines cannot be
        reactivated)

11. Inventory storage costs amount to 10 cents per unit for the
        first 300,000 units, the maximum storage capacity of a
        plant. Beyond that, public warehouse space is used to
        store all inventory exceeding the 300,000 limit, at a
        cost of 30 cents per unit. Quarterly storage costs are
        paid on the number of units in beginning inventory.

CHAPTER 8

PRODUCTION: CAPACITY CHANGES

Your management team will need to make an early decision
regarding expansion of production capacity. All of the plants in
your industry world have been operating fairly close to capacity.
Sales in the industry have been increasing at a rate that soon
will require additional facilities if the demand for your product
is to be met.   Questions that need to be answered before making
an investment decision include: 1. "How much additional productive capacity will be required?" and 2. "Which, if any, of the
expansion options should our firm undertake?"

Your estimate of production requirements (see Chapter 7)
should assist you in answering the first question. The answer
should be to expand capacity enough to meet expected sales demand
as long as the expansion contributes toward meeting the goals of
your firm and contributes to its profitability. An answer to the
second question requires an evaluation of the expansion options
listed in this chapter, a comparison of their costs, and the time
required to implement them.   In addition, there must be sufficient cash available to finance the investments that you decide
to undertake. Various investment options are described below in
the order of the time required for their implementation.

In an inflationary economy, one expects prices generally to
follow the level of price changes in the economy. All construction, hiring, and training costs outlined in this chapter are
those in effect at the end of Year 2, as you assume management of
the company. The costs in effect in a specific quarter will be
adjusted for changes in the Consumer Price Index through the
preceding quarter. All construction contracts include a provision for cost increases due to inflation.

Investment Options

Overtime

Working your production crews overtime is the fastest way to expand production. Furthermore, it is the only way in which production can be expanded without a delay of at least one quarter. By scheduling overtime, it is possible to increase output by about 20 percent over the normal forty-hour week production level. Restrictions in the union contract make it impossible to schedule production for less than <u>forty hours</u> or for more than <u>forty-eight</u> hours per week.

Units produced while crews are working overtime are somewhat more expensive than those manufactured during the normal work-week. Production employees are paid time-and-a-half for overtime work. Unit labor costs are thus 50 percent more for goods produced when production lines are running overtime. These extra labor costs are partially offset by depreciation charges being spread over a larger number of units of production. Overtime costs are detailed in Chapter 7.

Second Shift

A second shift of workers may be scheduled for production lines in your <u>home area plant</u>. This will enable you to double production without any additional investment in plant facilities or equipment. Second-shift workers, however, receive a 10 percent premium for working nights.

It costs $100,000 (end of Year 2 prices) and requires one quarter to hire and train workers to operate a second shift on a production line. If you wish to schedule production for a second shift on one or more of your existing production lines in Quarter 2 of Year 3, you must, in Quarter 1, enter the number of lines desired in the "2d Shft" row under New Lines in the Construction section of the decision form. During the first quarter of Year 3, workers will be hired and trained with the costs appearing as Training Cost in your firm's Operating Information report. The second shift will be available to begin production on the line(s) during the second quarter of Year 3. A second shift may be added to all producing lines in the home-area plant. There is no provision in the model for second-shift operations in other plants.

Once workers have been hired and trained and a second-shift line is available for production, the second-shift either must be scheduled for production, shut down or terminated. Scheduling rules and shutdown costs are the same as for single-shift operations, except that a second-shift line may not be operated while the corresponding first-shift line is shut down or deactivated (see Chapter 7).

To add second-shift lines, enter the number of lines on the decision form under "New Lines, 2d Shft." The line(s) will be available for production during the <u>following</u> quarter.

Limits: 0 to number of 1st shift lines operating in home area

	Construction		
	New Lines	New Add	New Plant
Area 1	#___	#___	#____
Area 2	#___	#___	#____
Area 3	#___	#___	#____
Area 4	#___	#___	#____.
2d Shft	#___		

Additional Production Lines

The existing plant in your home area was built to house eight production lines. To date, only six lines have been built. Thus, there is space for two additional lines as indicated in the Operating Information Report.

	Area 1	Area 2	Area 3	Area 4
Space Available for New Lines	2	0	0	0

New production lines have the same operating characteristics, costs and output capabilities as existing lines. <u>Two quarters</u> are required to install the necessary equipment and to hire and train workers for new production lines. In order to have additional lines available for production during the third quarter of Year 3, it would be necessary to begin construction of these lines in Quarter 1.

A capital expenditure of $500,000 (end of Year 2 prices) is required to purchase new equipment for each line that is added. In addition, it costs $100,000 (end of Year 2 prices) to hire and train new employees to work on each new production line. One-half of the capital expenditures and one-half of the hiring and training costs are incurred during each of the two quarters of construction. For each quarter of construction, your Cash Flow Statement will show an expenditure for equipment of $250,000 per line and the Operating Information report will show a production cost increase of $50,000 per line to cover hiring and training costs. These costs are subject to inflation.

Equipment is depreciated on a straight-line basis over seven years, with no salvage value. Quarterly depreciation charges equal 1/28th (3.5714 percent) of the original cost. New equipment expenditures are capitalized at the end of each quarter of construction and depreciation charges increased immediately. Thus, an expenditure of $250,000 would increase equipment depreciation charges for the quarter by about $9,000.

$$0.035714 \times \$250,000 = \$8,928$$

In addition, because the total value of equipment in place would have increased by about $250,000, replacement equipment expenditures would rise, too. Your company's equipment replacement policy requires quarterly replacement of 1/28th (3.5714 percent) of all equipment in place. Therefore, equipment replacement costs would rise by about $9,000, too.

$$0.035714 \times 250,000 = \$8,928$$

The only limitation on the number of lines which can be under construction at one time is the availability of space in the plant. Your firm could increase its production capacity by one-third as early as the third quarter of Year 3 by adding lines 7 and 8 to your existing plant. While operating costs of new lines are the same as for existing lines, unit production costs will be somewhat lower because plant depreciation charges will be spread over the larger number of units produced in the plant during the quarter.

To begin construction, enter the number of new lines to be added on the decision form. The entry should be made in the marketing area where a plant with additional space is located. After the construction has begun, no further entry is necessary until the lines are ready and available for production. Entries in subsequent quarters will result in starting additional new lines at that time (if space is available, otherwise the entries will be rejected by the decision-entry program). When ready for production, and not before, new lines must be scheduled for production, shut down, or deactivated.

Limits: 0 to space available

Addition to Existing Plant

When the plant in your home area was built, sufficient land was reserved to permit the building of an addition on each of two sides of the plant. Each addition will provide space for two production lines and represents an increase of 25 percent of the presently available space for production capacity. Three quarters are required to complete construction of a new addition.

The installation of production lines in the addition may be started during the second quarter of addition construction so that the lines will be available for production as soon as the plant addition is completed. Construction may begin on only one two-line addition in any plant during any quarter. If desired, however, construction may be started on another addition while the first is still under construction, provided that such construction will not cause the maximum plant capacity of twelve lines to be exceeded.

Construction of a new addition requires a capital expenditure of $900,000 (end of Year 2 prices), which must be paid to the contractor in three installments over the construction period. Your Funds Statement will show a capital expenditure of $300,000 or more during each quarter of construction. These amounts will be capitalized and depreciated at the same rate as the existing plant. Depreciation is on a straight-line basis over 31.5 years, with no salvage value. Quarterly depreciation charges amount to 0.7936 percent of the original cost of all construction in place at the end of each quarter. After completion, construction of one new two-line addition will cause depreciation charges to be increased by at least $7,142 per quarter.

To begin construction, enter "2"--the number of lines of capacity--under "New Add" on the decision form in the marketing area in which you wish to construct the new lines. After construction has begun, no further entries are necessary except to begin construction of the production lines so that the lines will be available for production when desired. New-line construction may be started as soon as the second quarter of construction of the new addition, or any time thereafter.

Limits: 0 or 2 lines (to a maximum capacity of 12 lines)

Construction of a New Plant

The final option for expanding production capacity is to locate a new plant in another marketing area. Your company may locate a plant in any area you desire, provided that you do not already have a plant in that area. You may move into a competitor's home area or into Area 4. Plant construction requires five quarters to complete. A plant may be built with a capacity

of either six, eight or ten lines. Additions may be built later
to increase plant size to a maximum capacity of twelve lines.
Construction and added depreciation costs for each plant size are
shown below. Costs are those in effect at the end of Year 2, and
are subject to inflationary changes. Depreciation is on a
straight-line basis over 31.5 years, with no salvage value.
Quarterly depreciation charges are calculated as 0.7936 percent
of the original cost.

Sizes	Construction Cost	Quarterly Depreciation
6 lines	$2,600,000	$20,633
8 lines	3,300,000	26,188
10 lines	4,000,000	31,744

Construction costs must be paid to the contractor in five
installments during the construction period. If a ten-line plant
is being built, your Cash Flow Statement will show a capital
expenditure of at least $800,000 during each quarter of construc-
tion, with the total expenditure amounting to $4,000,000 or more.
Construction payments are capitalized and subject to depreciation
in the quarter in which they are paid. The quarterly depreciation charges shown above represent the total additional depreciation incurred once the new plant has been completed, assuming
end-of-Year-2 costs.

Building a plant shell, by itself, will not permit you to
produce any goods. In order for production to begin, production
lines must be installed at a cost of at least $600,000 each
(including hiring and training costs for new workers). If you
plan to schedule production as soon as the plant is finished, you
must begin installation of production lines during the fourth
quarter of plant construction. The plant and new lines will be
completed during the fifth quarter of plant construction. Any
number of lines up to the full capacity of the plant may be
installed. Space availability for new lines will be reported in
the Operating Information Report as soon as construction may
begin.

Operating costs and production capabilities for a new plant
will be the same as those for the existing plant in your home
area. Second-shift operations, however, are not feasible in non-
home areas because of a shortage of supervisory personnel.

Your firm will realize transportation cost savings after
completing a new plant. Shipments from a new plant to a destination within the same marketing area cost 10 cents per unit. If
the new plant is located in Areas 1, 2, or 3, the savings for
shipments within the same area will be 60 cents per unit.
Shipments to other areas, except to Area 4, will continue to cost

seventy cents per unit. If the plant is located in Area 4, the savings for shipments within Area 4 will be 30 cents per unit. Shipping from a plant in Area 4 to any other area costs 40 cents per unit.

To begin construction of a new plant, enter the number of lines of capacity that are desired (6, 8, or 10) in the marketing area in which the new plant is to be located. It takes five quarters to complete the construction of a new plant. After construction has begun, no further entry is required except to begin construction of new lines prior to the start of production. New production lines may be started as soon as the fourth quarter of plant construction.

Limits: 0 in home area; 0, 6, 8, 10 lines in other areas

Summary

Investment Options

1. <u>Overtime work</u> may increase production by about 20 percent. Labor costs for working more than 40 hours per week are 50 percent higher than normal. Fixed costs are spread over more units. There is no delay in implementation.

2. A <u>second shift</u> may be added to lines in your home plant. Labor costs are 10 percent higher. There is a one-quarter delay while workers are hired and trained at a cost of $100,000. Second-shift production lines may be terminated at any time without delay or restriction at a cost of $100,000 per line.

3. <u>Additional production</u> lines may be added, space permitting, at a cost of $500,000 each. Hiring and training of new workers costs $100,000 per line. Construction requires two quarters. One-half of construction, hiring, and training costs ($300,000) are charged during each quarter of construction.

4. <u>Additions to existing plants</u> may be made so long as the maximum plant size of twelve lines capacity is not exceeded. Each addition has capacity for two production lines and costs $900,000. Construction requires three quarters, and costs are charged at the rate of $300,000 per quarter.

5. A <u>new plant</u> may be constructed in any marketing area where your company does not already have a plant. Construction requires five quarters to complete and one-fifth of the total cost must be paid during each quarter of construction. Costs of a six-line plant total $2,600,000 ($520,000 per quarter); an eight-line plant costs $3,300,000 ($660,000 per quarter); and a ten-line plant costs $4 million ($800,00 per quarter).

All costs shown are those in effect at the end of Year 2, and are subject to inflationary increases in proportion to changes in the Consumer Price Index.

CHAPTER 9

FINANCE: STRATEGY AND INVESTMENT ANALYSIS

The management of your firm's financial affairs provides a major challenge for your team. You must coordinate the financial requirements of marketing, production and expansion decisions. You must provide the cash to pay for company operations, to cover production expansion costs, to make interest payments on borrowed funds, to repay financial obligations promptly, to pay taxes when due, and to make dividend payments to stockholders. In addition, your management should provide a sound capital structure, give assurance to creditors that your obligations will be met promptly, plan for and help to provide a reasonable level of profitability, and assure a reasonable return to your stockholders. Measures of the success of your financial management include your stock price, your return on investment and your credit rating.

Prior to making specific financial decisions, your firm's financial managers should set financial (functional level) goals and objectives and develop financial strategy to accomplish these goals (see Chapter 5 for a discussion of goal and objective setting and strategy development). Financial goals should support the overall goals developed at the business level. The financial goals should focus upon what finance can contribute to achieving the business-level goals. The following business-level goal was used as an example in Chapter 5:

Maintain a cumulative rate of return on stockholders' initial investment (goal) of at least 20 (hurdle) percent (index) through year seven (time).

Supporting finance goals and objectives might be:

Goal: Develop a financial structure with a debt-to-equity ratio (goal) of 35 (hurdle) percent (index) by the end of year seven (time).

127

Objective: Increase the debt-to-equity ratio (goal) by 5
                  (hurdle) percent (index) during year three (time).

Goal: Upgrade the firm's credit rating (goal) to number
                  (index) one (hurdle) by the beginning of the fifth
                  year (time).

Objective: Maintain a $500,000 (hurdle & index) cash balance
                  (goal) during each quarter of year three(time).

Other goals and objectives may focus upon other financial ratios
and your firm's financial structure.

     Financial strategy should be designed to enable your finance
department to attain its goals and objectives. The strategy
should plan for the allocation of financial resources to gain
maximum efficiency while meeting market demand. The strategy for
the debt-to-equity goal would focus upon the sources used for
external funding. The strategy for upgrading the credit rating
would involve maintaining sufficient cash reserves, a strong
earnings growth and regular dividend payments. An effective
finance strategy should include all of the finance variables used
in managing resources.

     The quarter-to-quarter tactical decisions which your finance
managers must make are described below. These decisions should
be based upon your firm's sales forecast and production plan and
the resulting need for resources. Decision-making should be
guided by your financial strategy and company policy (See Chapter
5 for a discussion of strategy and policy).

     A considerable amount of planning is required prior to
making financial decisions, as the impact of many financial
decisions will extend over a considerable period of time. Tools
which we encourage you to use in financial planning include the
capital budget, cash budget, pro forma income statement, and pro
forma balance sheet. These tools will be described below along
with a description of the items that will be reported in your
financial statements. But first we will begin with a discussion
of the financial decisions your firm will be making.

Finance Decisions

Bank Loan

     Your firm has established a $2.5 million line of credit with
your friendly local banker. You may draw against this line of
credit by floating a short-term bank loan to be repaid at the
beginning of the following quarter. Interest is charged at the
short-term rate that is available during that quarter to a

company with your credit standing. Interest, amounting to one-fourth of the annual rate (because the loan is for 3 months) is paid during the quarter that the loan is outstanding.

To execute a loan, enter the amount desired (in thousands of dollars) under "Bank Loan" on the decision form. Because short-term loans are made for a period of only three months, your banker has agreed to automatically deduct the repayment amount from your bank account during the following quarter.

Bank loans are secured by inventory and receivables, and may not exceed 50 percent of the value of receivables plus inventory at the end of last quarter. Your line of credit requires an annual cleanup, so a loan request will be denied if your firm has had a loan outstanding during each of the past three consecutive quarters.

If sufficient funds are not provided to meet all obligations, an emergency bank loan will be provided at five percentage points above the normal interest rate. In addition, your banker and the bond credit analysts will review your credit standing. Emergency borrowing automatically will result in a reduction of your company's credit rating. If required, an emergency loan will be granted automatically without making an entry on the decision form. As with standard bank loans, emergency loans are automatically repaid from your bank account on the first day of the following quarter. Interest is charged, at the premium rate, during the quarter when the loan is outstanding.

Maximum loan: 50 percent of receivables plus inventory up to $2.5 million

Maximum loan: 0 if a loan was outstanding in each of the previous three quarters

Limits: 0 to 2500 (in thousands of dollars)

```
+--------------------------------+
|            (000s)              |
|   Bank Loan    $_____      |
|                                |
|   Bond Issue   $_____      |
|                                |
|   Stock Issue#_____        |
|                                |
|   Dividends    $_____      |
|                                |
|   Time CDs     $_____      |
+--------------------------------+
```

Sale or Redemption of Bonds

1. **Bond Issue**. Your firm's long-term debt may be increased by issuing bonds in multiples of $1,000,000. New issues are callable ten-year secured bonds carrying the current long-term rate of interest that is available to a company with your credit rating. Bonds must be <u>secured by plant and equipment</u> and the <u>value of existing bonds plus new bonds to be issued may not exceed 75 percent of net fixed assets</u>. Furthermore, your investment banker will consider an issue too risky to underwrite if the existing bonds, plus new bonds to be issued, exceed 50 percent of total equity (consisting of the previous quarter's total equity plus the proceeds of new shares to be sold simultaneously with the bonds). Enter the amount of new bonds to be sold (<u>in thousands of dollars</u>) on the decision form under "Bond Issue." If you decide to issue $4,000,000 worth of bonds, for example, enter 4000 on the decision form. Do <u>not</u> include commas in your entry.

Maximum issue: 50 percent of equity or 75 percent of net fixed assets, whichever is less

Limits: 0 to 9000 (in thousands of dollars), in million dollar lots

2. **Bond redemption**. Bonds that are outstanding may be called and redeemed in amounts that are multiples of $100,000 except that there is a restriction in the bond indenture that prohibits the redemption of more than $500,000 of the face amount of bonds in any one quarter. You will be required to pay a five percent call premium on all bonds that are called. If your firm has more than one bond issue outstanding, the bonds carrying the highest interest rate will be redeemed first. If bonds are to be redeemed, enter the face amount of the bonds for which redemption is desired (in thousands of dollars), <u>preceded by a minus sign</u> under "Bond Issue" on the decision form. If you decide to redeem $500,000 worth of bonds, enter -500 on the decision form. The five percent call premium will be charged automatically.

Maximum redemption: Total amount of bonds outstanding (if less than $500,000)

Limits: -500 to 0 (in thousands of dollars) in hundred thousand dollar lots

Sale of Common Stock

1. **Stock Issue**. New shares of common stock may be issued through an investment banker in multiples of 100,000 shares, provided the new issue will be large enough to raise at least <u>$1</u>

million. The investment banker will make a firm offer at any time of a price that will be determined by the following formula:

$$\text{Issue price} = \frac{(\text{shares outstanding}) \times (\text{latest market price})}{(\text{shares outstanding}) + (\text{shares to be issued})}$$

If your firm's credit rating is 2, this is the issue price. If your firm's credit rating is 3, subtract 10 percent of the formula value from the issue price. If your credit rating is 1, add 10 percent.

Enter the number of new shares to be issued (in thousands of shares) on the decision form under "Stock Issue." If your firm decides to issue 4,000,000 shares of stock, enter 4000 on the decision form. Do not include commas in your entry.

Minimum issue: Enough shares to raise $1 million
Limits: 0 to 9000 (in thousands of shares) in 100,000 share
    blocks

   2.   Stock Repurchase. Shares of your firm's common stock may be repurchased by placing a purchase order with the firm's stock broker. The shares will be purchased at a price that is 10 percent above the market price reported at the end of the previous quarter. Stock is repurchased by entering the number of shares to be repurchased preceded by a minus sign in the "Stock Issue" section of the decision form. Repurchase must be made in multiples of 100,000 shares. If your firm decides to repurchase 500,000 shares of stock during the current quarter, enter -500 on the decision form. Your corporate charter requires that there be at least 3 million shares outstanding so repurchases are limited to an amount that would leave at least 3 million shares after the repurchase. Shares may not be repurchased if there are insufficient retained earnings to fund the repurchase.

Maximum repurchase: number of shares outstanding minus 3 million

Limits: -900 to 0   (in thousands of shares)

Dividends

   Cash dividends may be paid to stockholders; but a restrictive bond covenant provides that the dividends paid in any quarter, taken together with dividends paid in the previous three quarters, may not exceed the total amount of earnings in the previous four quarters of operations. Thus if total earnings in the previous four quarters amounted to $200,000 and dividends already paid in the previous three quarters amounted to $190,000, the maximum dividend that could be paid in the current quarter would amount to $10,000. Enter the amount of cash dividends to be paid (in thousands of dollars) under "Dividends" on the decision form. If your firm decided to declare the permissible amount of $10,000 in dividends in the above example, you would enter 10 on the decision form. Dividends may not be declared if the retained earnings account on the balance sheet has a negative balance.

Maximum: Net income last 4 quarters minus dividends last 3 quarters

Maximum: 0, if retained earnings are negative

Limits: 0 to 9999 (in thousands of dollars)

Certificates of Deposit

Three-month time Certificates of Deposit (CDs) may be purchased in multiples of one hundred thousand dollars. Purchases may be made at the beginning of any quarter. CDs mature at the beginning of the next quarter, three months later. Interest will be earned on deposits at the rate reported in the industry report for 3-month time CDs during the quarter in which they will be invested. Interest will be credited to your account on the last day of the quarter in which the deposit is made, with quarterly interest calculated at one-fourth of the annual rate. Note that while interest is credited on the last day of the quarter that the deposit is made, the funds from the deposit itself are not available until the next day--the first day of the subsequent quarter. Thus if your firm should need emergency cash during the quarter in which the funds are invested in CDs, the funds will not be available to meet the need.

To purchase time CDs, enter the amount of the purchase in thousands of dollars on the decision form under "Time CDs." If your firm decides to purchase $400,000 worth of CDs, enter 400 on the decision form. Do not include commas in your entry. Repayment of the CDs as well as crediting your account with earned interest will be done automatically by the bank.

Limits: 0 to 9900 (in thousands of dollars), in hundred thousand dollar lots

Investment Analysis

One of the most critical strategic decisions your firm must make is how to adjust production capacity to meet the forecasted demand for your product. The expenditures required for expansion of production facilities are very large relative to those required to implement most operating decisions. A decision to build a new plant with six lines of capacity requires a total expenditure of at least $6,200,000 (including construction of production lines and training of new workers). This amount is almost equal to the total equity invested in your firm at the end of Year 2. The commitment is for a long period of time, and the effect of such a decision will continue to influence the profitability of your firm for the rest of the simulation.

There are three dimensions involved in the evaluation of investment options. The evaluation requires (1) an estimate of expected financial returns to the firm, (2) an evaluation of the time sequence of expected receipts and expenditures, and (3) a determination of the appropriate discount rate to apply to those expected returns. The analysis required for the proper consideration of each of these dimensions will be the focus of this section of the chapter.

After you determine the relative value and risk associated with the various investment options under consideration, a decision must be made.

Several methods of evaluation have been suggested by different authors or used by business managers. These methods include pay-back, the average rate of return, the internal rate of return and net present value. We suggest that you review a standard textbook on financial management to help you choose the most appropriate method for your firm. The discussion in this chapter will focus upon the net-present-value approach utilizing the Capital Investment Analysis work sheet. Copies of the work sheet are provided in Appendix C. A spreadsheet template of the Capital Investment Analysis work sheet also is available on disk.

Flexibility and Risk

The net-present-value method requires an estimation of numerical values to determine the likely effect a proposal will have on your firm's profitability. Certain attributes of investment proposals are difficult, sometimes impossible, to quantify. Their impact is often difficult to assess. However, they must be considered in the decision-making process as factors that will affect the success of the investment decision.

For the Business Policy Game, these factors include flexibility and risk. Some of the investment options provide more flexibility than others. The construction of an addition with new lines for your home area plant provides the option of adding a second-shift with relative ease. Should the production capacity of your first-shift operations turn out to be insufficient to meet demand, the capacity of your expansion can be quickly doubled by adding a second shift. Construction of a new plant, on the other hand, will provide only the production capacity of the installed first-shift lines. A second shift is not available outside of your home area. The flexibility of each investment proposal must be weighed against the relative costs and estimated returns from the proposal.

There are risks associated with your sales forecast and the resulting accuracy of your estimated future returns. If your sales forecast turns out to be too high, your estimate of returns from a given investment proposal probably will be too high, also. Profits from the new investments thus will turn out to be less than anticipated. On the other hand, if your estimates are too low, you may not provide sufficient production capacity to meet your actual needs. Your profits will suffer because of lost sales that you might otherwise have made.

Capital Investment Analysis Work Sheet

We have designed the Capital Investment Analysis work sheet to assist you in determining which production expansion project is best for your simulated firm. The capital investments that are available range from adding new production lines in your existing plant to building new plants in your marketing area. The costs associated with each type of project are outlined in Chapter 8. Now it is time to illustrate the analysis of a capital investment project to expand production capacity. The discussion below refers to the evaluation of expenditures for building a six-line plant in Area 4 and installing the equipment necessary to operate all six production lines. The work sheet in Figure 9-1 is used to illustrate the analysis.

We suggest that your firm complete a work sheet for each investment option that your management believes will provide the desired flexibility at an acceptable risk. Your investment horizon should not be limited to the tenure of your firm's present management--that is, the length of the Business Policy Game. An investment decision may continue to affect your firm's profits for many years after your management has moved on to greener pastures. The continued viability of your firm after you depart will enhance the reputation of your management and likely will affect the way in which your team is judged.

Estimation of Incremental Cash Flows

To evaluate investment options, you need to estimate the net incremental cash flows expected from each of the options under consideration. Incremental cash receipts are the additional cash receipts to be received by your firm from implementing an investment option, over and above those which would otherwise be received if you did not expand production capacity. Incremental cash expenditures are the additional cash payments expected to be made by your firm in implementing an investment option, over and above those which would otherwise be paid. Net incremental cash

134

flows equal incremental receipts minus incremental expenditures. Only receipts and expenditures expected to directly result from the investment project being considered should be counted. Net incremental cash flows then should be discounted at an appropriate cost of capital to estimate the net present value of the investment option.

The first step in this evaluation process is to estimate the expected incremental receipts for a specific investment option. We suggest that your estimates cover the entire expected useful life of the investment. You may consider the useful life of a new plant to be twenty-five years, even though it is depreciated for tax purposes over a longer life. The useful life of equipment for new lines is seven years, but company replacement policy will provide the means to keep them active over the entire life of the plant. Therefore, replacement expenditures for the additional equipment to be installed must be considered as part of the analysis. Space has been provided on the work sheet to estimate values separately for each of the next five years. For our illustration, those would be Years 3 through 7 of the simulation. Because of the difficulty of accurately estimating receipts and expenditures beyond that point, we suggest you assume that anticipated revenues and expected costs will continue at about the same rate for each of the subsequent years, up to the end of the project's useful life. For the new plant of the illustration, with an expected useful life of 25 years, that would be Years 8 through 27 of the simulation. Paragraph numbers below refer to line numbers on the work sheet.

1. Estimated demand. Enter the estimated sales demand for your product (in thousands of units) on the first line of the work sheet. This value can be copied from your sales forecast (See Chapter 6). For this illustration, demand is estimated at 1,500,000 units for Year 3, increasing to 2,500,000 in Year 5 and continuing at that level in succeeding years. (These estimates are for illustration only. They are not necessarily related to the actual demand that your firm will experience in the coming years. For your own analysis, you will need to do your own forecasting.)

2. Capacity with expansion. Next enter on line 2 the total production capacity (in thousands of units) that will be available with this investment option. The investment project in our example is the immediate construction of a new six-line plant, with three of the production lines to be completed in time to be available for production in the second quarter of Year 4 and the other three lines to be completed for production by the first quarter of Year 5. Production capacity in Year 3 would be 1,248,000 units (four quarters times your existing capacity of 312,000 units per quarter).

$$4 \times 312,000 = 1,248,000$$

135

FIGURE 9-1
INVESTMENT ANALYSIS WORK SHEET

Company __1__ World __1__	Project: New 6-line plant, Area 4 3 lines for Y4, Q3, 3 lines for Y5, Q1					

Year	3	4	5	6	7	After
RECEIPTS						
1. Estimated demand	1,500	1,800	2,500	2,500	2,500	2,500
2. Capacity with expansion	1,248	1,716	2,496	2,496	2,496	2,496
3. Price with expansion($)	10.00	10.00	10.00	10.00	10.00	10.00
4. Revenues with expansion	12,480	17,160	24,960	24,960	24,960	24,960
5. Capacity w/o expansion	1,248	1,248	1,248	1,248	1,248	1,248
6. Price w/o expansion ($)	10.50	10.50	10.50	10.50	10.50	10.50
7. Revenues w/o expansion	13,104	13,104	13,104	13,104	13,104	13,104
8. Incremental receipts (4 - 7)	(624)	4,056	11,856	11,856	11,856	11,856
INCREMENTAL EXPENDITURES						
9. Investment expenditures	2,980	3,382	432	432	432	432
10. Production costs	0	1,802	4,805	4,805	4,805	4,805
11. Selling costs	0	304	811	811	811	811
12. Tot incremental expenditures	2,980	5,488	6,048	6,048	6,048	6,048
13. Net cash flow b/tax (8 - 12)	(3604)	(1432)	5,808	5,808	5,808	5,808
TAX ADJUSTMENTS						
14. Incremental depreciation	68	380	516	516	516	516
15. Net incremental taxable income (8-10-11-14)	(692)	1,570	5,724	5,724	5,724	5,724
16. Incremental taxes	(269)	612	2,232	2,232	2,232	2,232
17. Net cash flow a/tax (13 - 16)	(3335)	(2044)	3,576	3,576	3,576	3,576
PRESENT VALUE CALCULATIONS						
18. Present value factor	.870	.756	.658	.572	.497	3.111
19. PV of net cash flow (17 x 18)	(2901)	(1545)	2,353	2,045	1,772	11,125
20. NPV of project (sum of values on line 19)						$12,849

It would increase to 1,716,000 units in Year 4 (existing capacity for the full year plus an additional 156,000 units for each of the last three quarters of the year).

$$1,248,000 + (3 \times 156,000) = 1,716,000$$

For Year 5 and each year thereafter your firm would expect to have an annual capacity of 2,496,000 units. Twelve production lines, each with a quarterly capacity of 52,000 units equals a quarterly capacity 624,000 units. Multiplying 624,000 by four yields the annual capacity.

$$4 \text{ quarters} \times 12 \text{ lines} \times 52,000 \text{ units} = 2,496,000 \text{ units}$$

3. <u>Price with expansion</u>. Enter the price you expect to charge for your product on line three. You may decide on a different price if you decide to expand, than if you don't expand capacity. We have entered $10.00 for each cell in line 3, assuming that you plan to continue the existing price of your product. You could enter a different average price for each year in another analysis.

4. <u>Revenues with expansion</u>. Multiply the price on line 3 by the number of units you expect to sell in each year (the smaller of the values on lines 1 and 2), to obtain total expected revenues. If your expected production capacity is less then your sales forecast, you only will be able to sell the amount to be produced. If the forecast is less than expected capacity, you will not be able to sell the entire amount of production. It is important to attempt to balance the amount of production capacity with the forecast of the amount of goods that you expect to be able to sell. Enter the value of expected revenues with the new project (in thousands of dollars) on line four. If you maintain a price of $10.00, total expected revenues, assuming all units produced are sold, would be $12,480,000 in Year 3, $17,160,000 in Year 4, and $24,960,000 in each year thereafter. We simplified this example by assuming constant costs and selling prices. The effects of inflation on costs will likely cause you and your competitors to raise prices over the course of time. Margins get pretty slim when prices and costs converge. While the exercise becomes more difficult, your analysis will be much more accurate if you build inflation into your cost and price estimates.

5. <u>Capacity without expansion</u>. To calculate estimated revenues without expanding production capacity, enter 1,248,000 units per year (in thousands) on line five for all years. This is your current capacity of 312,000 per quarter.

$$4 \times 312,000 = 1,248,000$$

6. <u>Price without expansion</u>. You may decide to increase price somewhat if you decide not to expand, since demand is so

much higher than production capacity. You would expect to sell fewer units, but sales will be limited by production capacity, anyway. Let's assume that your firm expects to sell its total output for $10.50 per unit. Enter this price on line six for all years.

7. Revenues without expansion. Multiply capacity without expansion (line 5) by price without expansion (line 6) to obtain the projected revenues for each year. In our example this amounts to $13,104,000 per year, which is entered (in thousands) on line seven. As with the estimates of revenue with expansion above, building inflation into your costs and prices will increase the accuracy of your estimates.

8. Incremental receipts. To determine expected incremental receipts from the proposed expansion, subtract revenues expected without expansion (line 7) from those expected with the completion of a new six-line plant (line 4). We project a decline of $624,000 in net receipts for Year 3.

$$\$12,480,000 - \$13,104,000 = (\$624,000)$$

For Year 4 the expansion should produce a $4,056,000 gain,

$$\$17,160,000 - \$13,104,000 = \$4,056,000$$

and for each year thereafter the gain may be expected to amount to $11,856,000.

$$\$24,960,000 - \$13,104,000 = \$11,856,000$$

Estimation of Incremental Expenditures

The incremental expenditures of an expansion include only the additional cash outlays associated with building and operating the new facility. Investment expenditures and incremental production and selling costs should be totaled separately and entered on the work sheet on the appropriate line. Don't forget to estimate the impact of inflation on your costs. As noted above, this example assumes constant costs for simplicity.

9. Investment expenditures. The costs of building a new six-line plant are detailed in Chapter 8. An example of the timing of these costs and associated depreciation charges is shown in Figure 9-2. To begin construction in the first quarter of Year 3, your firm must pay the contractor about $520,000, with payments continuing each subsequent quarter for a total of $2,080,000 (at Year 2 prices) during Year 3. A payment of about $520,000 also will be required during the first quarter of Year 4.

In addition, production lines must be installed at a cost of about $500,000 each, plus $100,000 per line for hiring and training workers. Payments for equipment and training will be split evenly between the two quarters of construction. Construction of three new lines should be started during the last quarter of Year 3 so that production can begin in the second quarter of Year 4, as soon as the plant is completed. Thus, quarterly payments of $750,000 for equipment,

$$3 \text{ lines times } \$250,000 = \$750,000$$

plus $150,000 for hiring and training workers,

$$3 \text{ lines times } \$50,000 = \$150,000$$

must be made during the last quarter of Year 3 and during the first quarter of Year 4.

Construction of the remaining three lines should begin during the third quarter of Year 4 so that production can begin in Year 5, when demand is expected to be high enough to sell the additional goods to be produced. Payments of $750,000 for equipment and $150,000 for hiring and training workers are required during the third and fourth quarters of Year 4.

	Year 3				Year 4				Year 5			
	Q1	Q2	Q3	Q4	Q1	Q2	Q3	Q4	Q1	Q2	Q3	Q4
Investment:												
New Plant	520	520	520	520	520	0	0	0	0	0	0	0
Equipment	0	0	0	750	750	0	750	750	0	0	0	0
Training	0	0	0	150	150	0	150	150	0	0	0	0
Replacement	0	0	0	0	0	54	54	54	108	108	108	108
Totals	520	520	520	1,420	1,420	54	954	954	108	108	108	108
Annual totals		2,980				3,382				432		
Depreciation:												
New Plant	4	8	12	17	21	21	21	21	21	21	21	21
Equipment				27	54	54	80	108	108	108	108	108
Totals	4	8	12	44	75	75	101	129	129	129	129	129
Annual Totals		68				380				516		

FIGURE 9-2
Timing of Investment Costs and Depreciation Charges

In addition, equipment replacement costs will rise because of the expansion (see Chapter 10). An amount is required to replace 1/28th (3.5714 percent) of all equipment each quarter at current prices according to company policy. After the first three new lines are available for production in Year 4, Quarter 2 (each line costs about $500,000), quarterly equipment replacement costs will increase by about $54,000.

$$3 \times .035714 \times \$500,000 = \$53,571$$

The other three lines will start producing in Year 5, Quarter 1, adding another $54,000 per quarter for a total of $108,000.

$$\$54,000 + \$54,000 = \$108,000$$

The equipment replacement policy will maintain the new equipment capacity throughout the life of the plant.

Adding the quarterly totals for Year 3 in Figure 9-2 indicates an expected investment cash outlay during that year of $2,980,000.

$$\$520,000 + \$520,000 + \$520,000 + \$1,420,000 = \$2,980,000$$

Investment payments during Year 4 amount to $3,382,000.

$$\$1,420,000 + \$54,000 + \$954,000 + \$954,000 = \$3,382,000$$

For Year 5 and each year thereafter, investment expenditures for this project will be $432,000, consisting only of equipment replacement costs continuing indefinitely.

$$\$108,000 + \$108,000 + \$108,000 + \$108,000 = \$432,000$$

Enter the investment expenditures on line 9 of the work sheet.

10. <u>Production costs</u>. The easiest way to estimate incremental production costs is to estimate the production cost per unit and multiply that value by the number of <u>additional</u> units likely to be produced. Cash outlays for production costs at the end of Year 2 amount to about $3.85 per unit (see Chapter 7). This includes unit labor costs of $2.40, materials costs of $1.20, and maintenance costs of 25 cents at normal production levels. (Depreciation charges do not require a cash outlay.)

If we assume for our example that unit production costs will remain stable, we should multiply $3.85 by the expected output of the new plant in Area 4. Incremental production in Year 4 is expected to be 468,000 units for three lines producing during the last three quarters of that year.

$$3 \text{ lines} \times 52,000 \text{ units} \times 3 \text{ quarters} = 468,000 \text{ units}$$

This will yield the expected incremental production cost of
$1,802,000 for that year.

$$468,000 \text{ units } \times \$3.85 = \$1,801,800$$

The total for Year 5 and each year thereafter is expected to be
$4,805,000, when all six new lines will be producing for the
entire year.

$$6 \text{ lines } \times 52,000 \text{ units } \times 4 \text{ quarters } = 1,248,000 \text{ units}$$

$$1,248,000 \text{ units } \times \$3.85 = \$4,804,800$$

These values are entered on line 10. No additional production
was scheduled for Year 3 because the plant will still be under
construction. Your evaluation will be more accurate if you
include an inflation component as well as increases due to new
model introductions in unit production cost estimates.

11. <u>Selling costs</u>. Your incremental selling and administrative
costs will depend, in part, upon the decisions that your firm
makes. (See Chapter 5 for a detailed explanation regarding calculation of these costs.) For purposes of our example, we will
assume that you will not change your advertising expenditures nor
the number of salespeople employed due to the construction of the
new plant in Area 4. We will also assume that commission rates
will remain at present levels (20 cents per unit). Thus, incremental commissions paid to salespeople will total 20 cents per
unit. The variable component of general selling expenses also is
20 cents per unit.

Transportation costs on units shipped from the new plant in
Area 4 will amount to 10 cents per unit for goods shipped to
points in Area 4, and 40 cents per unit for goods shipped to all
other areas. To estimate transportation costs, we must estimate
the likely geographic distribution of sales for units produced in
the new plant. If we assume that half of the new production will
be sold in Area 4 and the other half in other non-home areas,
transportation costs will average about 25 cents per unit.

Incremental selling costs thus would total about 65 cents
per unit.

$$20¢ \text{ commission } + 20¢ \text{ GSE } + 25¢ \text{ transportation } = 65¢$$

The incremental number of units sold during Year 4 can be
calculated by subtracting the value on line 5 from the value on
line 2, resulting in 468,000 units.

$$1,716,000 - 1,248,000 = 468,000$$

141

Multiplying incremental unit selling costs by incremental sales of 468,000 units in Year 4 yields $304,000 incremental selling costs.

$$\$0.65 \times 468,000 = \$304,200$$

Selling costs for the 1,248,000 additional units in Year 5 and subsequent years will be about $811,000.

$$\$0.65 \times (2,496,000 - 1,248,000) = \$811,200$$

These costs are entered on line 11 (in thousands of dollars). Of course, if you decide to increase advertising expenditures, increase the number of salespeople, or change the commission rates or other expenditures as a result of the expansion, the incremental values should be estimated and entered here.

12. Total incremental expenditures. Total incremental expenditures equal the sum of the investment required for the project (line 9), incremental production costs (line 10), and incremental selling costs (line 11). In our example these will total $2,980,000 in Year 3, $5,407,000 in Year 4, and $5,832,000 in Year 5 and each year thereafter. Enter total incremental costs on line 12 (in thousands).

13. Net incremental cash flow before tax. Calculate net incremental cash flow before tax by subtracting total incremental costs (line 12) from incremental receipts (line 8). In our example, there is a reduction in net cash flow before taxes of $3,604,000 in Year 3, a decline of $1,351,000 in Year 4 and an increase of $6,024,000 in Year 5 and each year thereafter. Enter net incremental cash flow before tax on line 13 (in thousands).

Tax Adjustments

Incremental taxes must be computed so that we may estimate the net cash flow after taxes that is expected to result from expansion. Taxes are levied against net income, which does not include deductions for investment outlays, but does include deductions for depreciation charges. Incremental taxes amount to 39 percent of the difference between incremental receipts and incremental expenditures, after adjustment for investment expenditures and depreciation charges. Note that the investment outlays that were computed on line nine of the work sheet are not deductible expenses for tax purposes. The depreciation charges, which we are about to estimate, are deductible, even though they require no cash outlays. The timing of depreciation charges is estimated in Figure 9-2.

14. Incremental depreciation. Depreciation charges on new plant construction during the simulation are computed each quarter as 0.7936 percent of the value of payments made by the end of the

quarter (see Chapter 7). The cash outlay required for our new six-line plant is $520,000 per quarter for each of five quarters. By rounding to the nearest thousand, depreciation charges will total about $4,000 during the first quarter of Year 3, shown in Figure 9-2.

$$0.007936 \times \$520,000 = \$4,127$$

Depreciation will be about $8,000 in the second quarter,

$$0.007936 \times 2 \times \$520,000 = \$8,253$$

$12,000 in the third quarter,

$$0.007936 \times 3 \times \$520,000 = \$12,380$$

and $17,000 in the fourth quarter,

$$0.007936 \times 4 \times \$520,000 = \$16,507$$

for a total of about $41,000 during the year.

$$\$4,000 + \$8,000 + \$12,000 + \$17,000 \cdot= \$41,000$$

In Year 4 and each year thereafter, incremental plant depreciation charges will be about $21,000 each quarter.

$$0.007936 \times \$2,600,000 = \$20,634$$

This will amount to a total of about $84,000 per year.

To this should be added the incremental equipment depreciation charges, amounting each quarter to 3.5714 percent of the cost of equipment in place. The first new equipment depreciation charges occur in Year 3, Quarter 4, with the beginning of construction of the first new line. Added depreciation charges that quarter amount to 3.5714 percent of the $750,000 equipment expenditures, or about $27,000. These also are shown in Figure 9-2.

$$.035714 \times \$750,000 = 26,786$$

Another $27,000 is added in Year 4, Quarter 1, for a total of $54,000. The $54,000 amount will be the same in Year 4, Quarter 2. Then, in Year 4, Quarter 3 with the beginning of construction of another 3 lines, there will be $2,250,000 of new equipment in place.

$$3 \times \$750,000 = \$2,250,000$$

The depreciation charges on this amount of new equipment will be about $80,000.

$$.035714 \times \$2,250,000 = \$80,356$$

And by Year 4, Quarter 4, the total amount of new equipment in place with all six lines completed, each costing a total of $500,000, will be $3,000,000.

$$6 \times \$500,000 = \$3,000,000$$

Additional equipment depreciation charges thus will total about $108,000 per quarter by then.

$$.035714 \times \$3,000,000 = \$107,142$$

Adding incremental quarterly depreciation charges for both new plant and new equipment, the annual totals are $68,000 for Year 3, $380,000 for Year 4, and $516,000 for Year 5 and each year thereafter. Enter total incremental depreciation charges on line 14 (in thousands of dollars) of the work sheet, as shown in Figure 9-2.

15. <u>Net incremental taxable income</u>. Calculate net incremental taxable income by subtracting production costs (line 10), selling costs (line 11) and incremental depreciation (line 14) from incremental receipts (line 8). Enter the value on line 15 (in thousands). This is the amount that will be used to calculate incremental taxes because of the expansion project. Values have been entered in Figure 9-2. Net incremental taxable revenues, for example, have been calculated for Year 3 as a negative value, because of lower sales revenue resulting from the lower ($10.00) price.

$$(-624) - 0 - 0 - 68 = (-692)$$

For Year 4, the balance becomes positive as revenues rise faster than production and selling costs.

$$4,056 - 1,802 - 304 - 380 = 1,570$$

Amounts for Years 5 and subsequent years are estimated for the work sheet as $5,724,000.

$$11,856 - 4,805 - 811 - 516 = 5,724$$

16. <u>Incremental taxes</u>. Incremental taxes are the additional taxes which you must pay due to the net incremental taxable income that your firm receives from the investment option. If our assumptions hold true, your firm's taxable net income will decline by $692,000 in Year 3, will increase by $1,570,000 in Year 4, and by $5,724,000 in Year 5 and each year thereafter. As

the tax rate is 39 percent of net income in the Business Policy
Game, your firm will realize a tax saving of $269,000 in Year 3,
and owe additional tax payments of $612,000 in Year 4, and
$2,232,000 in Year 5 and the following years, over and above what
would have been paid without considering the expansion project.
Enter incremental taxes on line 16 (in thousands of dollars).
Each value entered on line 16 of the work sheet has been calculated as 39 percent of the value on line 15.

17. Net cash flow after taxes. Your net cash flow after taxes
is estimated by subtracting incremental taxes (line 16) from your
net cash flow before tax (line 13). These amounts are entered on
line 17 of the work sheet (in thousands) and are the values in
which we are most interested. To find the net present value of
these cash flows we need to discount the amounts to the beginning
of Year 3, using an estimate of your firm's cost of capital.

Present Value Calculations

You now need to estimate the cost of capital for your
simulated firm. Use the cost of capital to discount the present
value of expected net cash flows from the investment option. Add
together the discounted cash flows over the life of the project,
to yield the net present value of the proposed investment project. The net present value of a project will enable you to
compare the profitability of that option with others. A positive
net present value indicates a project likely to add value to your
company. A negative net present value indicates a project which
probably will reduce the value. When several mutually exclusive
projects are being considered, the one with the largest positive
net present value should yield the greatest additional value to
your firm, and provide the greatest increment to owners' wealth.

If all of your funds requirements could be met by borrowing,
the cost of capital to your firm would simply be the after-tax
interest cost for the use of the borrowed funds. Interest rates
are deductible for tax purposes, so the after-tax cost of borrowing funds in the Business Policy Game would be equal to 61
percent of the interest rate (100 percent minus the tax rate of
39 percent). If the interest rate for your firm is 12 percent,
the after-tax cost would be 7.32 percent.

.61 x 12 percent = 7.32 percent

This relatively low cost of borrowed funds, however, is not the
appropriate rate to use for your cost of capital under normal
circumstances.

You may want to meet a substantial portion of your funds
requirements through retention of earnings and the sale of common
stock. The cost of obtaining funds from equity sources is a
little more difficult to estimate. There is no specific account-

ing cost assigned to the use of funds provided by stockholders. However, there is an opportunity cost which should be considered. You may view the cost of equity capital as the return that investors would require if they were to purchase your company's stock.

We suggest that you consult a financial management textbook for help in estimating the required rate of return on equity capital. To keep our illustration simple, we will use a rule of thumb adopted by some analysts. Because an investment in a company's stock entails more risk than an investment in the firm's bonds, investors will require a higher rate of return to invest in stock than in bonds. The rule of thumb is that the returns on stock investments must be 4 to 6 percent higher than the interest rate on bond investments in the same company. Therefore, if we assume that the interest rate on your company's newly issued bonds is 12 percent, we would expect stock investors to require a return on their more-risky stock investment between 16 and 18 percent. We will use the mid-point of this range, or 17 percent, for an estimate of your cost of equity capital.

You may combine the cost of debt capital and the cost of equity capital into a <u>weighted-average cost of capital</u> for your analysis. Assume that your management has a policy requiring 20 percent of your capital requirements to be met by borrowing and 80 percent to be met by retention of earnings or the sale of common stock. If your firm must pay 12 percent for borrowed funds (before taxes) and equity investors expect a return of 17 percent, your weighted-average cost of capital will be just over 15 percent. The calculation is shown below:

	Before Tax	After Tax	Weight	Col. 2 X 3
Cost of debt capital	12%	7.32%	.20	1.46%
Cost of equity capital		17.00%	.80	13.60%
Weighted average cost of capital				15.06%

18. <u>Present value factor</u>. In Figure 9-1, line 17 shows a net outflow of $3,335,000 for Year 3, a net outflow of $2,044,000 for Year 4, and a net inflow of $3,576,000 for Year 5 and each year thereafter. Each of these values now must be discounted to their present value at the beginning of Year 3. Present value factors for line 18 may be found in any financial management textbook, or computed as the discounted value of $1 for the time period involved. The appropriate formula to find the present value factor (PVF) of a lump sum is

$$PVF = 1/(1 + r)^n$$

where r is the discount rate and n is the number of periods over which the discounting occurs. The discount rate should be your weighted-average cost of capital, approximately 15 percent. For the first year (Year 3), the present value factor is 0.870.

$$PVF = 1/(1 + .15)^1 = 0.870$$

For the second year, the value is 0.756.

$$PVF = 1/(1 + .15)^2 = 0.756$$

Present value factors for the third, fourth and fifth years of the analysis (Years 5, 6, and 7) are calculated in the same manner, and have been entered on line 18 of the work sheet.

To find the present value of the equal annual cash flows shown beyond Year 7, it is convenient to consider the annual flows as an annuity. The annuity would run for the remaining twenty years of the life of the project. The present value factor for this 20-year annuity, as of the end of Year 7, may be found in a table of annuity present values, or calculated as the sum of the 20 individual present value factors. This factor is 6.259.

But the factor of 6.259 only will discount those cash flows to the end of Year 7. We need to discount them further to the end of Year 3. This may be done by multiplying the present value annuity factor (6.259) by the present value lump sum factor appropriate for lump-sum values to be received in Year 7 (0.497).

$$6.259 \times 0.497 = 3.111$$

Thus, 3.111 is the present value factor that will discount the annual cash flows beyond Year 7 to a present value at the beginning of Year 3. It has been entered in the work sheet's last column on line 18.

19. <u>Present value of net cash flows</u>. The present value of the net cash flows received in each year is obtained by multiplying the value on line 17 by the value entered on line 18 (the present value factor). These present values have been entered in the work sheet on line 19.

20. <u>Net present value of project</u>. The net present value of this project, $12,849,000, is an estimate of the value that this project may add to the value of your company. It is obtained by summing the present value of net cash flows for each year of the analysis, as shown on line 19. The sum is entered on line 20. The net present value is positive and therefore it should be a profitable investment for your firm, even though it results in negative cash flows for the first two years.

147

Reliability of Assumptions

A word of caution is in order at this point. The net present value of the project in our illustration was computed after making a number of important assumptions about the sales forecast, production costs, price to be charged, and expected selling cost. The cost of capital used to discount the estimated net cash flows was based upon assumptions about interest rates and their relationship to required returns on equity capital, as well as an assumption about the relative proportions of debt to equity funds to be used. If the estimates and assumptions that have been made in computing the net present values have been overly conservative, the net present value will be considerably understated. On the other hand, an estimate of expected revenues that is overstated will cause the net present value to be overstated. You may want to conduct a sensitivity analysis on some of the values based upon certain critical assumptions. Use of the spreadsheet template for this work sheet will make the chore easier than filling out numerous work sheets with different sets of assumptions.

Comparison of Options

We recommend that you perform a present value analysis for each investment project that your firm is seriously considering, whether it be new plants, new plant additions, new lines, or installation of a second-shift operation. If desired, an analysis of combinations of projects may also be made. For example, you may wish to build a larger plant in Area 4 than is necessary and then deactivate some of the production lines in your home-area plant after the new plant is completed. This would provide some transportation cost savings by shifting production for the non-home areas from your home-area plant to the Area 4 plant. Do some brainstorming to develop project recommendations that may be feasible. Then test them with an investment analysis similar to the one described above.

The investment option, or combination of options, that has the greatest net present value is the one that likely will add the most value to your company. You should reject any project that shows a negative net present value as it likely will end up reducing the value of your company and the wealth of its stockholders.

When undertaking this type of analysis, you need to remember that substantial changes in your sales forecasts may change the relative ranking of some investment proposals. On the other hand, minor changes in incremental production and selling costs, and in cost-of-capital computations, may not be as likely to change the relative ranking of the investment proposals. This may be true if the same assumptions were used for each proposal, even though the absolute values of the estimated returns may change substantially. Also, it may not be true in particular circumstances. This is the kind of conclusion, though, that is better left to a sensitivity analysis of the particular assumptions that are in question.

Provisions for Adequate Funds

Your expansion plans are not complete until you have completed a capital budget for the required funding! Plans must be made so that sufficient funds will be available to meet your expenditure requirements, if any, for new plant and equipment. There also may be times when you firm wants to undertake a new project, but it may not be able to raise sufficient capital to fund the project. Procedures for raising funds by borrowing and by selling stock were discussed earlier in this chapter, along with penalties that will be incurred if you fail to provide sufficient funds to meet your needs.

Summary

Financial decisions

1. Three-month <u>Certificates of Deposit</u> may be purchased in multiples of $100,000, to a maximum amount of $9,900,000. Interest is earned at the rate reported in the previous quarter's Industry Report. Interest is paid during the quarter in which the investment is made. The principal is not available until the following quarter.

2. Secured <u>bank loans</u> are available under a $2,500,000 line of credit subject to a maximum limit of 50 percent of accounts receivable plus inventories, and to a one-quarter annual cleanup requirement in 4 consecutive quarters. Loans are discounted at the current short-term rate of interest and must be repaid in ninety days. Emergency loans, required because of insufficient cash on hand, are charged a penalty rate of interest (five percent above the current rate) and result in a lower credit rating.

3. Secured <u>bonds</u> with a face value of $2 million are outstanding at the end of Year 2. The bonds mature in ten years, carry a coupon rate of 10 percent and are callable with a five percent call premium. New bonds may be issued with a ten-year maturity at the current long-term rate of interest and are callable with a five percent call premium. Bonds may only be issued if the resulting ratio of bonds to equity will be less

than 50 percent. They will be secured by plant and equipment, and must result in a ratio of bonds to net fixed assets of less than 75 percent. Bonds are sold in multiples of $1 million. Outstanding bonds may be called (repurchased) with payment of the call premium in multiples of $100,000 to a maximum of $500,000 in any quarter.

4. Dividends may be declared in any quarter, subject to the restriction that current dividends plus dividends paid during the previous three quarters should not exceed earnings in the previous four quarters. Dividends may not be paid if the payment would result in a negative balance in the retained earnings account.

5. Common stock may be issued at a price to be determined by a formula shown in the text. At the beginning of the simulation, 6 million shares are outstanding. New issues are sold in multiples of 100,000 shares, with a minimum-sized issue being enough shares to raise at least $1 million. Stock that is outstanding may be repurchased at a price 10 percent above the stock price reported at the end of the previous quarter. Repurchases are in multiples of 100,000 shares, to a maximum of 500,000 shares in any quarter. A repurchase is permitted only if the resulting number of shares outstanding will be at least 3 million with positive retained earnings.

Investment Options (See Chapter 8)

1. Overtime work may increase production by about 20 percent. Labor costs for overtime work are 50 percent higher than for a normal 40-hour week, increasing unit costs. Fixed costs are spread over more units, reducing unit costs. There is no delay in implementation.

2. A second shift may be added to lines in your home plant. Labor costs are 10 percent higher. There is a one-quarter delay while workers are hired and trained at a cost of $100,000.

3. Additional production lines may be added, space permitting, with an equipment cost of $500,000 each. Hiring and training of new workers costs $100,000 per line. Construction requires two quarters. One-half of construction, hiring, and training costs (totaling $300,000) is charged during each quarter of construction.

4. Additions to existing plants may be made so long as the maximum plant size of twelve lines capacity is not exceeded. Each addition has capacity for two production lines and costs $900,000. Construction requires three quarters, and costs are charged at the rate of $300,000 per quarter.

5.   A <u>new plant</u> may be constructed in any marketing area
where your company does not already have a plant. Construction
requires five quarters to complete and one-fifth of the total
cost must be paid during each quarter of construction. Costs of
a six-line plant total $2,600,000 ($520,000 per quarter); an
eight-line plant costs $3,300,000 (660,000 per quarter); and a
ten-line plant costs $4 million ($800,00 per quarter).

All costs shown are those in effect at the end of Year 2,
and are subject to inflationary increases in proportion to
changes in the Consumer Price Index.

Evaluation of Options

1.   Work sheets are provided for the net-present-value
method of evaluation of investment options. This method requires
an estimate of incremental cash receipts resulting from the
project over its life, incremental cash expenditures required
because of the project, and an estimate of the time pattern of
receipts and expenditures. Net cash flows then should be discounted to find the net present value at the firm's cost of
capital.

2.   A comparison should be made of the net present value of
each expansion option that seems feasible in light of the company
goals, attitude towards risk, and estimate of demand. The option
with the greatest net present value most likely will provide the
greatest financial return to your firm and the greatest increase
in wealth to your stockholders.

CHAPTER 10

FINANCING: FINANCIAL PLANNING

Capital Budgeting

The evaluation of capital investment options was discussed
in Chapter 9 to help you plan for the potential large expenditures that your firm may make to expand your production facilities. For expansion to take place, funds must be provided to pay
for the construction of buildings, installation of equipment, and
training of workers. The Capital Budget work sheet shown in
Figure 10-2 has been developed to assist you in planning for
funding of production expansion projects. Copies of this form
are provided in Appendix C and also are available in a spreadsheet template on disk.

Capital Expenditures

Construction of a plant or plant additions which your firm
has decided to fund should be listed in the first section of the
work sheet. Enter the costs that will be incurred to complete
the project in the columns under the quarters in which the
payments become due. In the second section, list the planned
installation of new production lines, by plant and number of
lines. Again, enter the cost for the installations under the
quarters in which payments are due. The sum of each column
represents the total funds required for each quarter.

The work sheet in Figure 10-2 continues the six-line plant
example from the Investment Analysis work sheet in Chapter 9.
Investment expenditures for the new 6-line plant, equipment, and
training would extend over the eight quarters of Years 3 and 4.
The work sheet covers one calendar year so it is necessary to use
two work sheet forms. The amount and timing of funds require-

ments for the project are the same as those that were developed in Chapter 9, and are reproduced in Figure 10-1.

	Year 3				Year 4				Year 5			
	Q1	Q2	Q3	Q4	Q1	Q2	Q3	Q4	Q1	Q2	Q3	Q4
Investment:												
New Plant	520	520	520	520	520	0	0	0	0	0	0	0
Equipment	0	0	0	750	750	0	750	750	0	0	0	0
Training	0	0	0	150	150	0	150	150	0	0	0	0
Replacement	0	0	0	0	0	54	54	54	108	108	108	108
Totals	520	520	520	1,420	1,420	54	954	954	108	108	108	108
Annual totals	2,980				3,382				432			

FIGURE 10-1
Timing of Investment Costs

Total capital expenditures required by the project would be $2,980,000 in Year 3 and $3,382,000 in Year 4. These values are entered, in thousands of dollars, in the top section of the Capital Budget work sheet. The additional equipment replacement expenditures from Year 5 onward probably should be budgeted as part of quarterly operations rather than being funded as part of the capital budget.

Sources of Funds

You may be able to fund part of your expansion project internally, by retention of quarterly earnings. This works only if your operations generate sufficient cash that is not required for other things. Because of its size, however, you probably will have to fund a substantial portion of the capital budget from external sources, by selling bonds and/or common stock. The proportion you obtain from each source is a matter for your management to decide. You need to consider the cost of funds from the various sources and the risks involved in utilizing financial leverage through borrowing.

Bond analysts and your friendly banker will expect you to fund a substantial portion of the project with equity, through retention of earnings or by selling common stock. Your investment bankers have indicated that they only will underwrite a new bond issue if the new issue does not boost your bond to equity ratio above 50 percent. Thus total bonds outstanding (new issue plus existing bonds) must not exceed 50 percent of total equity (existing equity plus any new stock issue). You may want to limit the risks of financial leverage by borrowing a smaller

153

THE BUSINESS POLICY GAME
CAPITAL BUDGET WORK SHEET

Company 1 World 1	Funds Required in Year 3				
CAPITAL EXPENDITURES:	Qtr 1	Qtr 2	Qtr 3	Qtr 4	Total
Plant Construction:					
6-line plant in Area 4	520	520	520	520	2,080
New Additions:					
New Production Lines:					
3 lines for Year 4, Qtr 2				900	900
3 lines for Year 5, Qtr 1					
Total Funds Requirement:	520	520	520	1,420	2,980
SOURCES OF FUNDS:					
Quarterly Earnings	100	100	100	100	400
Sale of Bonds					
Sale of Common Stock				3,000	3,000
Temporary Bank Loan	420	840	1,260		
Less Loan Repayment		-420	-840	-1,260	
Total Sources of Funds	520	520	520	1,840	3,400
Quarterly Surplus (Deficit)	0	0	0	420	420

FIGURE 10-2
Illustration of Capital Budget Work Sheet

THE BUSINESS POLICY GAME
CAPITAL BUDGET WORK SHEET

Company 1 World 1	Funds Required in Year 4				
CAPITAL EXPENDITURES:	Qtr 1	Qtr 2	Qtr 3	Qtr 4	Total
Plant Construction:					
6-line plant in Area 4	520				520
New Additions:					
New Production Lines:					
3 lines for Year 4, Qtr 2	900				900
3 lines for Year 5, Qtr 1			900	900	1,800
Equipment replacement		54	54	54	162
Total Funds Requirement:	1,420	54	954	954	3,382
SOURCES OF FUNDS:					
Quarterly Earnings	100	100	100	100	400
Sale of Bonds	1,000				1,000
Sale of Common Stock				1,600	1,600
Temporary Bank Loan			708		
Less Loan Repayment				-708	
Total Sources of Funds	1,100	100	808	992	3,000
Quarterly Surplus (Deficit)	100	146	0	38	38

FIGURE 10-2 (Continued)
Illustration of Capital Budget Work Sheet

proportion of your funds requirements than the maximum amount that is permitted by your investment bankers.

Estimate the approximate amount of <u>cash</u> that you expect to be available each quarter from internal sources and enter that in the "Quarterly Earnings" section of the work sheet. If cash generated from your operations is required for something else, then it may not be used to fund the capital budget, too. The balance will have to be raised by the sale of stock or bonds, or by temporary borrowing from the bank until longer-term funds can be arranged. Bonds provide attractive financing during periods of relatively low interest rates, and stock is attractive during periods of relatively high market prices. A temporary bank loan may be used as long as the terms of your line of credit are not violated (see Chapter 9).

The Capital Budget work sheet has space for you to specify the mix of funds you plan to use to finance the project. The exact proportions of the mix become less firm as you project further into the future. Some adjustment may be needed after the cash budget is completed each quarter. Suppose that your firm has planned to allocate $100,000 of retained earnings (which will be available in cash) each quarter to partially finance the project, with the balance coming from the sale of bonds and common stock.

The first three quarters of Year 3 require investment expenditures of $520,000 each quarter. Because the additional amounts beyond the $100,000 earnings retention are too small to justify a new issue of bonds or stock, you may decide to use a short-term bank loan for the balance of $420,000 per quarter (providing that you have not already overdrawn your line of credit). For the first quarter, $420,000 has been entered in the work sheet for a bank loan.

Because the bank loan must be repaid each quarter, the following quarter's loan includes enough to repay the amount borrowed during the previous quarter plus the external funds required for the construction during the second quarter. Thus, the total loan requirement for the second quarter is $840,000.

$$\$420,000 + \$420,000 = \$840,000$$

If borrowing is to be continued into the third quarter, a total of $1,260,000 must be provided to repay the second quarter's loan of $840,000 and provide another $420,000 for the capital budget.

$$\$840,000 + \$420,000 = \$1,260,000$$

Then the bank loan must be repaid to comply with the annual cleanup requirement for your line of credit. Bank loans must be considered as providing a bridge until the stock issue of about $3,000,000 in the fourth quarter is used to pay off the $1,260,000 loan, as well as to meet the construction payments of $1,420,000 for that quarter. The surplus of $420,000 will fund part of the requirement for the first quarter of Year 4, and should be placed in certificates of deposit, to earn interest, until it is needed.

To summarize the entire year's financing activity, the $400,000 of earnings retained during the year ($100,000 each quarter) plus $3,000,000 from the sale of common stock will provide sufficient funds for the first year's capital budget requirement of $2,980,000, with a surplus of $420,000 to be carried over to Year 4. A temporary short-term bank loan was used as a bridge loan during the first three quarters of the year and repaid with the proceeds of the stock issue in the fourth quarter.

During the first quarter of Year 4, $1,420,000 is required to fund the plant and equipment investment. $420,000 still is available from the common stock issue in the previous quarter. $100,000 is expected to be available from earnings retention and a $1 million bond issue can be used for the balance, leaving a surplus of $100,000, to be invested in certificates of deposit.

Surplus from previous quarter	$420,000
Earnings retention, Quarter 1	100,000
Sale of bonds	1,000,000
Less funds requirement	(1,420,000)
Surplus at end of quarter	$ 100,000

During the second quarter of the year only $54,000 is required for equipment replacement. $100,000 should be available from earnings retention, in addition to the $100,000 surplus from the previous quarter, so there will be a quarterly surplus for the second quarter of $146,000.

Surplus from previous quarter	$100,000
Earnings retention, Quarter 2	100,000
Less funds requirement	(54,000)
Surplus at end of quarter	$146,000

Then, in the third quarter, a payment of $954,000 is due for equipment installation. $146,000 is available from previous financing and $100,000 should be available from retention of earnings during the quarter. The balance of $708,000 can be met with another bridge loan.

```
Surplus from previous quarter     $173,000
Earnings retention, Quarter 3      100,000
Temporary bank loan                708,000
Less funds requirement            (954,000)
Surplus at end of quarter         $      0
```

Note that the loan is available because no loan was made since Year 3, Quarter 3, and the one-quarter cleanup requirement for your line of credit has been more than satisfied. If, for some reason, your operating situation required a short-term loan during three consecutive quarters prior to the need for a bridge loan, the bank loan would not be available. Funds would have to be raised from another source.

In Year 3, Quarter 4 another $954,000 payment is required, and a $708,000 bank loan must be repaid, so financing must be found for at least $1,662,000. Retention of earnings should provide about $100,000. The balance might be raised by issuing $1,600,000 more of common stock. This would leave a small surplus at the end of the year of about $38,000.

```
Surplus from previous quarter $          0
Earnings retention, Quarter 4      100,000
Sale of common stock             1,600,000
Less repayment of bank loan       (708,000)
Less funds requirement            (954,000)
Surplus at end of quarter         $  38,000
```

Summarizing the proposed financing activity for Year 4, first and second quarter payments were financed by the surplus from Year 3 ($420,000), earnings retention ($100,000 each quarter), and a bond issue in the first quarter ($1,000,000). A bridge loan ($708,000) was used to complete payments for installation of new equipment in Quarter 3. A new issue of common stock (about $1,600,000) completed the financing requirements in the fourth quarter, providing enough to repay the bridge loan and meet the fourth quarter's payments for equipment installation. Total new financing for the year, after repayment of the bridge loan, consisted of $3 million, from the sale of bonds in Quarter 1 and the sale of common stock in Quarter 4.

Note: The number of shares to be issued for each stock flotation and the exact amount to be raised from each issue cannot be determined until the selling price of the stock is known at the end of the quarter prior to the issue (see "Sale of Common Stock" in Chapter 9).

Profit Planning and the Income Statement

The management of each firm is judged, in part, by its profit performance. All of your decisions should be weighed in

terms of their effect on your firm's income. While profit is not
the only, or even necessarily the major, criterion of successful
management, poor profit performance is a sure sign of management
failure.

The preparation of a pro forma income statement is one way
to estimate your profit position in the future. We suggest that
you establish a policy of preparing pro forma income statements
for each of the next four quarters. This will enable you to
estimate the impact which your firm's decision will have on
profits before the decision is implemented. A Pro Forma Income
Statement work sheet (shown in Figure 10-3) has been provided for
this purpose. Extra copies are available in Appendix C and a
spreadsheet template of the work sheet is available on disk.

If the projected income on your pro forma income statement
is less than desired, you may want to alter part of your firm's
planned decision. We suggest that you compare the actual results
of operations with your pro forma statement after each quarter
has been run. An analysis of the differences between actual and
forecasted results will help sharpen your forecasting skills and
will provide a control mechanism for your management team.

Sales and Cost of Goods Sold

Expected Gross Revenue from Sales should be estimated from
your sales forecast. Sales revenues can be estimated in two
ways:

(1) Estimate the number of units you expect to sell in
each marketing area and multiply the estimate by the
unit price to be charged in the respective area.

(2) Estimate your firm's total unit sales for the
quarter and multiply the estimate by the average price
your firm will charge.

In the example from Chapter 6, the second method was used.
With a certain set of assumptions, the total number of sales for
Year 3, Quarter 1 was forecast to be 317,000 units (See Figure 6-
1). With an estimated price of $9.80 per unit, expected sales
revenue was forecast to be $3,107,000.

$$317,000 \text{ x } \$9.80 = \$3,106,600$$

This value has been entered on the first line of the Pro Forma
Income Statement work sheet of Figure 10-3. Rounding all values
to thousands of dollars is suggested.

The next step is to calculate the value of Cost of Goods
Sold in order to estimate the gross profit. First, enter the
value of Beginning Inventory on the work sheet. This is the

FIGURE 10-3
PRO FORMA INCOME STATEMENT

Co. _1_ World _1_ Year _3_	Qtr 1	Qtr 2	Qtr 3	Qtr 4
Gross Revenue from Sales	3,107			
LESS COST OF GOODS SOLD:				
Beginning Inventory	576			
Production Cost	1,361			
Goods Available for Sale	1,937			
Ending Inventory	562			
Cost of Goods Sold	1,375			
Gross Profit	1,732			
SELLING EXPENSE:				
Advertising	181			
Sales Salaries	147			
Sales Commissions	63			
General Selling Expense	409			
Transportation Expense	149			
Other Selling Expense	40			
Total Selling Expense	989			
ADMIN & GENERAL EXPENSE:				
Research and Development	147			
Storage Expense	13			
Executive Compensation	150			
Loan Interest	7			
Bond Interest	50			
Other Expense	0			
Total Admin & General Exp	367			
Total Operating Expense	1,356			
PROFIT SUMMARY:				
Operating Profit (Loss)	376			
Other Income: CD Interest	0			
Net Profit (Loss) Before Tax	376			
Less Income Tax	147			
Net Profit (Loss) After Tax	229			
Less Dividends Paid	180			
Addition to Retained Earnings	49			

ending inventory shown on your previous quarter's balance sheet, or on the work sheet when calculating quarters 2, 3 and 4. From the financial statements in Appendix B, your ending inventory for Year 2, Quarter 4 was $576,000 (consisting of 134,000 units).

Enter your <u>Production Cost</u>, including depreciation charges, on the next line. You may obtain this value from your Production Plan work sheet (See Figure 7-3). The value to use is found on the last line of that work sheet, Total Production Cost.

Continuing the example of Chapters 6 and 7, that value was estimated for Figure 7-3 as $1,357,000 (for 312,000 units). If the new plant construction project (analyzed in Chapter 9) is adopted, the production plan of Figure 7-3 should be modified to reflect the additional $4,000 depreciation charges for the new plant, as shown in Figure 9-2. This would increase total production cost by $4,000 to $1,361,000.

The <u>Goods Available for Sale</u> is calculated by adding beginning inventory and production cost.

$$576,000 + $1,361,000 = $1,937,000$$

Enter this value as Goods Available for Sale.

Inventory Valuation

Inventories are valued on a first-in, first-out (FIFO) basis. You may estimate the value of <u>Ending Inventory</u> as follows:

1. Add the number of units you expect to produce during the coming quarter to the number of units in inventory at the beginning of the quarter to obtain the number of <u>units</u> available for sale. Subtract the number of units you expect to sell during the quarter from the number of units available for sale to determine the number of units in your anticipated ending inventory. Continuing our example, the production cost was based on production of 312,000 units. Beginning inventory was 134,000 units, so the number of units available for sale would be 446,000.

$$312,000 + 134,000 = 446,000$$

Our sales forecast showed expected sales to be 317,000 units, so the number of units expected to be in ending inventory is 129,000.

$$446,000 - 317,000 = 129,000$$

2. Divide the expected cost of production in the coming quarter by the number of units you expect to produce. The result

will be your estimate of unit production costs for the quarter. This value already was calculated, and could have been copied from the Production Plan work sheet (Figure 7-3), except that we just increased the expected production costs by $4,000 to cover depreciation charges for the first quarter's construction of the new plant. Our expected unit production costs must be calculated, instead of copied. They are $4.36--one cent per unit higher than the $4.35 from Figure 7-3.

$$\$1,361,000 / 312,000 = \$4.36$$

3. Multiply the number of units in ending inventory by the unit production cost. If the number of units in inventory at the beginning of the quarter is less than expected sales, the result will be the value of ending inventory.

$$129,000 \times \$4.36 = \$562,440, \text{ or } \$562,000$$

For our example, this is the value to enter for Ending Inventory

4. If the number of units in beginning inventory exceeds expected sales, a different calculation will have to be made. Because all of the units to be sold would have been produced in the previous quarter, some of the units in this quarter's ending inventory will have been produced in the previous quarter and some in the current quarter. The value of the beginning inventory should be divided by the number of units in stock to estimate the unit cost of goods on hand when the quarter started. Then multiply the unit cost of beginning inventory by the number of units you expect to sell to determine the cost of units from beginning inventory which will be sold. Subtract this value from your estimate of the cost of goods available for sale (on the line above) to provide an estimate of the value of your ending inventory.

Cost of Goods Sold is computed by subtracting the value of your ending inventory from the value of goods available for sale. For our example, this is $1,375,000.

$$\$1,937,000 - \$562,000 = \$1,375,000$$

Gross Profit

Your gross profit on sales is calculated by subtracting the cost of goods sold from the value of gross sales.

$$\$3,107,000 - \$1,375,000 = \$1,732,000$$

It is wise to check occasionally for consistency. A comparison of this value with the gross profit reported for Year 2, Quarter 4 shows that it is somewhat lower than last quarter. This is to be expected, because sales are expected to be lower (mostly due to the seasonal effect), and production costs are expected to be slightly higher (because of inflation).

Selling Expense

You may want to refer to Chapter 5 for a detailed discussion of selling expenses and how they are calculated.

a. <u>Advertising</u>. Enter the total amount you plan to spend on advertising in all marketing areas. In developing the sales forecast of Figure 6-1, an expected increase in advertising expenditures of five percent was used. Advertising expense in Year 2, Quarter 4 was $172,000, so an increase of five percent would total $180,600, or rounded to thousands of dollars, $181,000.

$$1.05 \times \$172,000 = \$180,600$$

b. <u>Sales Salaries</u>. Multiply the salary you plan to pay the sales force by the number of salespeople you plan to employ and enter the result. Your company had 45 salespeople in Year 2, Quarter 4, and four are in training to begin selling in Year 3, Quarter 1, for a total of 49. If you expect to keep the same salary level as last quarter ($3,000 for each salesperson), and nobody quits, then total sales salaries will rise to $147,000.

$$49 \times \$3,000 = \$147,000$$

c. <u>Sales Commissions</u>. Multiply the sales commission you plan to pay per unit by the number of units you expect to sell and enter the result. If you keep present commissions at 20 cents per unit, sales of 317,000 units will require about $63,000.

$$317,000 \times \$0.20 = \$63,400$$

d. <u>General Selling Expense</u>. Multiply the number of sales-people you plan to employ by $4,000 (the semi-variable portion of general selling expenses). Multiply 20¢ (the variable portion of general selling expenses) by the number of units you expect to sell. Add the above two products to $150,000 (the fixed portion of general selling expenses) and enter the results. For our example, this will total about $409,000.

$$(49 \times \$4,000) + (\$0.20 \times 317,000) + \$150,000 = \$409,400$$

e.   Transportation Expense. The amount of transportation expense depends upon the location and destination of product shipments. See Chapter 5 for a discussion of these expenses. We suggested earlier that you might estimate demand by market area when compiling your sales forecast. Then you would be able to project transportation expense with greater accuracy. Lacking this information, you may wish to look at last quarter's transportation expense and assume that average transportation expenses will continue. Dividing the Year 2, Quarter 4 expense of $161,000 by the 345,000 units sold (See Appendix B) indicates average transportation expense of 47 cents per unit in that quarter.

$$\$161,000 \ / \ 345,000 = \$0.47$$

With expected total unit sales of 317,000 units, transportation expense may be about $149,000 next quarter.

$$317,000 \ x \ \$0.47 = \$148,990$$

f.   Other Selling Expense. This line is used to record selling expense that is not recorded elsewhere. It includes sales training costs, sales force moving expenses and severance pay. If you continue to keep eight salespeople in training (four that started training last quarter and, perhaps, four more to start this quarter), this can be expected to total about $40,000. Sales training costs amount to about $5,000 per person in training.

$$8 \ x \ \$5,000 = \$40,000$$

g.   Total Selling Expense is the sum of advertising, sales salaries, sales commissions, general selling expense, transportation expense, and other selling expense. For our example, it totals $989,000.

$$\$181 + \$147 + \$63 + \$409 + \$149 + \$40 = \$989$$

Advertising expenditures, sales salaries, and commission rates are subject to your management's direct control and may be changed during any quarter. General selling expense, transportation expense, and other selling expense are only indirectly under your control. A successful marketing plan that results in increased sales, for example, will also increase general selling expense and transportation expense. Training new members of the sales force will increase other selling expense.

Administration and General Expense

a. <u>Research and Development</u>. Enter the total amount you plan to spend for process and product R & D on the Research and Development line. If last period's expenditures of $140,000 are to be increased by five percent, for example, enter $147,000.

$$1.05 \times \$140,000 = \$147,000$$

b. <u>Storage Expense</u>. Storage Expenses are computed for inventories on hand at the end of the previous quarter. It costs 10 cents per unit for the first 300,000 units stored in any marketing area that contains a production plant. Units in excess of 300,000 must be stored in a public warehouse at a cost of 30 cents per unit. Last period's ending inventory of 134,000 units thus would require storage expense of about $13,000 this period.

$$\$0.10 \times 134,000 = \$13,400$$

c. <u>Executive Compensation</u> amounted to $148,000 last quarter, and can be expected to increase at about the same rate as the Consumer Price Index. This expense item is not under your direct control. With an increase of about one percent in the Consumer Price Index, executive compensation can be expected to rise to about $150,000.

d. <u>Loan Interest</u> is the interest to be paid on any short-term bank loans. Bank loans normally are charged the short-term interest rate available to a company with your credit rating. You can estimate it as one-fourth of the annual interest rate multiplied by the size of any bank loan that you plan to take out during the coming quarter. In the capital budget example of Figure 10-2, it was estimated that you would need a bridge loan of $420,000 to finance the first stage of construction of a new plant. If you decide to go ahead with this project, interest charges should be estimated.

Short-term interest rates in Year 2, Quarter 4 were 6.40 percent, and rates have been rising. It might be reasonable to estimate that rates would continue to rise to, say, seven percent by next quarter. If they do, quarterly interest expense for that loan would be about $7,000.

$$(\$420,000 \times 0.07) / 4 = \$7,350$$

Inasmuch as you have not yet completed your cash budget, the amount of any bank loan that would be required to meet operating expense is not yet known. If you decide to take out a larger bank loan, return to the pro forma income statement and add the additional interest expense here.

e. Estimate <u>Bond Interest</u> expense by calculating the interest payment for one quarter on new bonds sold during the current quarter and add the result to the quarterly interest payment for bonds outstanding at the end of the previous quarter. Bond interest payments are based upon interest rates at the time the bonds are issued. Interest payments on new bonds may be computed at a quarterly rate equal to one-fourth of the annual interest rate in effect at the time of issue. Interest payments on the bonds that were outstanding at the end of Year 2 are computed at the rate of 2.5 percent of the face value each quarter (10 percent per year).

$$\$2,000,000 \times 0.025 = \$50,000$$

If bonds are repurchased, subtract the amount of interest that would have been paid on those bonds. When bonds are repurchased, those with the highest interest rate will be repurchased first.

For our example, no bond sale or repurchase is contemplated, so bond interest would continue at the rate of $50,000 per quarter.

f. <u>Other Expense</u>. This category covers expenses that are not included elsewhere. The entry represents the total of these expenses. Examples of items that may be included as other expense are:

(1) A <u>deactivation charge</u> of $100,000 per line is assessed if your firm should deactivate any of your production lines (See Chapter 2).

(2) A <u>call premium</u> of five percent is charged on any bonds that may be repurchased (See Chapter 2).

As no other expense is anticipated, a zero has been entered in the work sheet for the example.

g. <u>Total Administration and General Expense</u> is the sum of items a through f. For our example, the total is $367,000.

$$\$147 + \$13 + \$150 + \$7 + \$50 + \$0 = \$367$$

Total Operating Expense

Total Operating Expense is the sum of Total Selling Expense and Total Administration and General Expense. For our example, this is $1,356,000.

$$\$989 + \$367 = \$1,356$$

Profits, Taxes, and Dividends

Operating profit is calculated by subtracting Total Operating Expense from Gross Profit. For our example, the amount is $376,000.

$$\$1,732 - \$1,356 = \$376$$

Other Income consists of interest earned on certificates of deposit. Interest on CD investments is calculated as one-fourth of the annual CD interest rate, reported in the previous quarter's Quarterly Industry Report. The rate reported, shown in Appendix B, is 4.50 percent. If you were, for example, to re-invest the $100,000 that your predecessors invested last quarter you would earn about $1,000, reported as Other Income.

$$(0.045 \times 100,000) / 4 = \$1,125$$

For now, zero is entered here. Until the cash budget is completed, it will not be known if there will be surplus cash to invest. This can be filled in later if you decide to invest surplus cash in certificates of deposit.

Net Profit Before Tax can be estimated by adding other income to operating profit. With no CD investment, enter the same amount as operating profit. For our example, this is $376,000.

Income tax is assessed against net profit at a rate of 39 percent. For the estimates in our example, income tax will be about $147,000.

$$\$376,000 \times 0.39 = 146,640$$

No taxes are assessed on an operating loss. The tax laws in the simulation do not permit a tax-loss carry-back, even for previous quarters in the current calendar year. The entire loss is carried forward to be applied against future profits prior to tax assessment. The loss carryover does not appear on the balance sheet.

Total the tax liabilities and subtract this amount from Net Profit Before Tax to calculate <u>Net Profit After Tax</u>. For our example, Net Profit After Tax is $229,000.

$$\$376,000 - \$147,000 = \$229,000$$

Next, enter the amount of <u>Dividends</u> that you expect to pay during the quarter. Your stockholders expect regular dividend payments, even though none have been paid during the last two years. You need to establish a dividend policy as part of your finance strategy. You may, for example, decide to pay out 50 percent of net profits to stockholders. If this is your policy, you may wish to pay dividends of about $180,000, or about 50 percent of Year 2, Quarter 4 profits.

$$\$362,000 \times 0.50 = \$181,000$$

$180,000 has been entered in the work sheet of Figure 10-3. The payment amounts to three cents per share on the 6 million shares outstanding.

From Net Profit After Tax subtract the amount of Dividends that you expect to pay during the quarter. The resulting <u>Addition to Retained Earnings</u> will be added to the retained earnings shown on the previous quarter's balance sheet to determine the value of total equity on your pro forma balance sheet (see below). For our example, the amount of Addition to Retained Earnings is $50,000.

$$\$229 - \$180 = \$49$$

Cash Budgeting and the Cash Flow Statement

Your management team should keep enough cash on hand to meet all of your financial obligations promptly. We suggest that you plan to maintain a cash balance large enough to meet unexpected cash requirements and to provide a buffer in case your revenues are lower than anticipated. If your firm does not have enough cash to meet your obligations during a quarter, you must take out an <u>emergency bank loan</u>. Your friendly banker has agreed to provide an automatic loan to meet such short-term crises by supplying funds at an interest rate that is <u>5 percentage points higher</u> than the short-term interest rate currently available to your firm. (After all, we can't let your firm go bankrupt.) If your firm's short-term rate is 10 percent, for example, the rate for an emergency bank loan will be 15 percent.

Running out of cash puts you technically in default of your financial obligations. Creditors will lose confidence in your firm and your credit rating will be lowered. The lower credit rating will increase the cost of future borrowing and will reduce the proceeds from the sale of common stock.

To reduce the risk of running out of cash and incurring an emergency loan, we suggest that you prepare a cash budget prior to finalizing the decision for each quarter. A work sheet is provided for this purpose (illustrated in Figure 10-5, with extra copies provided in Appendix C). A spreadsheet template of the Cash Budget work sheet also is available on disk.

The categories on the work sheet match those in the Cash Flow Statement that is reported each quarter as part of your Financial Statements (see Figure 10-4 for an example).

CASH FLOW STATEMENT	$000s
Operating Receipts:	
Accounts Collected	2975
Operating Expenditures:	
Production Cost	1200
Operating Expense	1329
Taxes Paid	0
Net Operating Cash Flow:	446
Investment Receipts:	
CD Interest	1
CDs Matured	0
Investment Expenditures:	
CDs Purchased	100
New Equipment	0
Equipment Replacement	106
Plant Investment	0
Net Investment Cash Flow:	-205
Financing Receipts:	
Loans Received	0
Bond Sale	0
Stock Sale	0
Financing Expenditures:	
Dividends Paid	0
Loans Repaid	0
Bonds Repurchased	0
Stock Repurchased	0
Net Financing Cash Flow:	0
Beginning Cash Balance	934
Net Cash Flow for Quarter	241
Cash Available End of Quarter	1175
Required Loan (incl. interest)	0

FIGURE 10-4
Cash Flow Statement, Year 2, Quarter 4

169

Operating Cash Flow consists of cash receipts and payments directly associated with the operations of your company. Investment cash flows consist of cash receipts from investments and cash payments for new investments. Financing cash flow includes cash receipts and payments directly related to financing activities. These categories enable you to pinpoint problem areas more easily. The values shown in the work sheet of Figure 10-5 continue the example shown above from the Income Statement work sheet of Figure 10-3.

The cash budget should be used both as a planning tool and as a control device. The budget will help you plan your cash requirements so that you may borrow funds or sell stock when necessary. After the quarter is completed, you should analyze the differences between estimated and actual receipts and expenditures in order to perfect your forecasting techniques. In addition, the analysis will help you spot areas in which expenditures should be adjusted.

Cash Budget Work Sheet

Operating Receipts

Accounts collected. Sales in the Business Policy Game are made on credit with the collection period averaging forty-five days. Accounts receivable carried over from the previous quarter will be collected during the current quarter. One-half (45 days) of the current quarter's sales revenue will be collected by the end of the quarter. The other half will be shown on the books as accounts receivable and carried over to the next quarter. All customers in the Business Policy Game are honorable and solvent and thus no provision for bad debts is required.

Enter the accounts receivable value from the previous quarter's balance sheet (or one-half of the projected sales revenue if you are budgeting for more than one quarter) on the Accounts from last quarter line. For our example, this value is $1,725,000, taken from the Year 2, Quarter 4 Balance Sheet (see Appendix B).

Enter one-half of the expected sales revenue for the current quarter on the Accounts from this quarter line. From the Pro Forma Income Statement of Figure 10-3, this value is about $1,554,000.

$$\$3,107,000 \times 0.5 = \$1,553,500$$

Operating Expenditures

1. Production Cost. See Chapter 7 for information on computing production costs. Total production costs entered on

THE BUSINESS POLICY GAME
CASH BUDGET WORK SHEET

Co. __1__ World __1__ Year __3__	Qtr 1	Qtr 2	Qtr 3	Qtr 4
OPERATING RECEIPTS:				
Accounts from last quarter	1,725			
Accounts from this quarter	1,554			
OPERATING EXPENDITURES:				
Production Cost	1,214			
Selling Expense	989			
Admin and General Expense	367			
Taxes Paid (1st qtr only)	464			
Net Operating Cash Flow	245			
INVESTMENT RECEIPTS:				
CD Interest	0			
CDs Matured	100			
INVESTMENT EXPENDITURES:				
CDs Purchased	0			
New Equipment	0			
Equipment Replacement	107			
Plant Investment	520			
Net Investment Cash Flow	(527)			
FINANCING RECEIPTS:				
Loans Received	420			
Bond Sale	0			
Stock Sale	0			
FINANCING EXPENDITURES:				
Dividends Paid	180			
Loans Repaid	0			
Bonds Repurchased	0			
Stock Repurchased	0			
Net Financing Cash Flow	240			
SUMMARY:				
Beginning Cash Balance	1,175			
Net Cash Flow for Quarter	(42)			
Ending Cash Balance	1,133			

FIGURE 10-5
Illustration of Cash Budget Work Sheet

this line of your Cash Budget work sheet should <u>exclude depreciation charges</u> as no cash is required for depreciation. The value for Production Cost appropriate for the Cash Budget work sheet may be copied from the "Total Cash Expenditure" line of your Production Plan work sheet (See Figure 7-3). For our example, the amount is $1,214,000.

2. <u>Selling Expense</u> is the same as described above for the pro forma Income Statement. The value may be copied directly from the Total Selling Expense line of the pro forma Income Statement, as there are no accruals involved. For our example, the amount is $989,000.

3. <u>Administration and General Expense</u> also may be copied from the pro forma Income Statement. For our example, the amount is $367,000.

4. <u>Taxes Paid</u>. The corporate income tax rate is 39 percent of net profits. Taxes are accrued quarterly and <u>paid in full during the first quarter of each year</u>. Be sure to keep sufficient cash on hand during the first quarter of each year to pay the taxes accrued over the previous year. The amount due in the first quarter is the balance of Taxes Payable shown on the fourth quarter's Balance Sheet. This amount was $464,000 at the end of Year 2, and is the value used in our example.

Net Operating Cash Flow

Net Operating Cash Flow is the sum of Operating Receipts minus the sum of Operating Expenditures. The value for our example is $245,000.

($1,725 + $1,554) - ($1,214 + $989 + $367 + $464) = $245

Investment Receipts

1. <u>CD Interest</u>. This value may be copied from the OTHER INCOME: CD Interest line of the pro forma Income Statement. It is the amount that you expect to earn from funds invested in CDs for the current quarter. For our example, because we did not yet estimate surplus cash, the value is zero.

2. <u>CDs Matured</u>. Enter the dollar amount of Time Certificates of Deposit that will mature during the quarter. This is the amount your firm invested in the previous quarter, and may be copied from the last quarter's Balance Sheet. The cash from maturing CDs is available for use during the quarter. The amount for our example is the Time Certificates of Deposit balance from the Year 2, Quarter 4 Balance Sheet, $100,000.

Investment Expenditures

1. <u>CDs Purchased</u>. If you know that you will have surplus cash for the quarter, you may invest surplus funds in time certificates of deposit. Time CDs earn interest at the rate reported in the quarterly industry report. Funds invested in CDs may not be withdrawn during the quarter of the investment to use for other expenditures. <u>Once invested, the funds are tied up until the first day of the following quarter</u>, even though interest is credited to your cash account during the quarter in which the investment is made. For our example, we will enter zero on this line. When the cash budget has been completed, it may be appropriate to come back to make an entry here.

2. <u>New Equipment</u>. Enter the payment required for construction of new lines during the current quarter. This amount may be copied from your Capital Budget work sheet. The amount for our example is $0, taken from the work sheet in Figure 10-2. The first payment for new line construction in our example would occur in the fourth quarter of Year 3.

3. <u>Equipment Replacement</u> costs are controlled by a company policy that requires equipment to be replaced every seven years. Equipment is replaced on a rotating basis so that 1/7th of the equipment is replaced each year or 1/28th is replaced each quarter. Equipment replacement costs are calculated at current (inflation-adjusted) prices, based upon the number of production lines available (both producing and shut down) plus the number of lines deactivated. Because of excellent maintenance policies, equipment used for second-shift operations is not subject to faster replacement. Equipment which is replaced is written off at its depreciated value at time of replacement. The retired equipment has no salvage value.

It should be noted that replacement equipment will cost more than the equipment it is replacing due to inflation. Thus, there is an upward pressure on production costs. By the end of Year 7, all of the equipment (for six production lines) that was on the books at the beginning of Year 1 will have been replaced. When the equipment for new production lines is added during the course of the game, replacement costs will rise according to the number of new lines.

Equipment replacement expenditures amounted to $106,000 in Year 2, Quarter 4. Because of inflation, the amount for Year 3, Quarter 1 is likely to be a little bit higher. For our example, we will estimate $107,000.

4. <u>Plant Investment</u>. Enter the payment required for new plant and new addition construction. The calculation of these amounts is described in Chapter 8. The value may be copied from

your Capital Budget work sheet. For our example the amount is $520,000, taken from Figure 10-2.

Net Investment Cash Flow

Net Investment Cash Flow is the sum of investment receipts minus the sum of investment expenditures. For our example, the work sheet values total -$527,000.

$$(\$0 + \$100) - (\$0 + \$0 + \$107 + \$520) = -\$527$$

Financing Receipts

1. Loans Received. Your banker has extended a $2,500,000, 90-day line of credit to your firm. However, the agreement states that the loan must be secured by accounts receivable and inventory with the loan limited to 50 percent of accounts receivable plus inventory. All loans are discounted at your firm's short-term rate of interest and are automatically paid off in full from your cash account at the bank during the following quarter. There are no compensating balance requirements; but the bank requires an annual "clean-up" with at least one quarter of every four being loan free. Thus if you have borrowed from the bank during the last 3 consecutive quarters, a loan request would be denied during the current quarter. If you fail to meet the cleanup requirements of your credit agreement, you may be forced into taking out an emergency loan.

In estimating operating funds requirements, it is suggested that you leave the loan line blank until you have computed the expected cash available from other sources and compared this amount with your expected cash requirements. The amount of a bank loan, if needed, can then be calculated by subtracting the expected cash requirements, including the desired minimum cash balance, from the amount of cash expected to be available from other sources. If your estimates are reasonably accurate, the result should be the approximate amount of cash that you need to borrow in order to meet your obligations.

For your capital budget requirements, however, the work sheet for the pro forma Income Statement, above, includes interest for a bridge loan of $420,000 to finance the first quarter's payments for construction of a new plant. This amount has been entered as an expected loan. Should operating requirements dictate a different amount, it can be changed later.

2. Bond Sale. During Year 0, your firm issued $2,000,000 in 10 year bonds at an interest rate of 10 percent. Additional bonds, secured by plant and equipment, may be issued with a ten-year maturity date. Your underwriters have agreed to pur-

174

chase your bonds in multiples of $1,000,000 at your firm's current long-term interest rate. The agreement also states that the total bonds outstanding after the sale must not exceed 75 percent of the book value of your firm's net plant and equipment at the end of the previous quarter, and the resulting bonds to equity ratio must not exceed 50 percent. The bonds to equity ratio will be calculated by dividing the sum of the existing bonds plus the new bonds by the sum of the existing equity plus any sale of new stock. Enter the face value of any bonds you plan to sell (in thousands of dollars). For our example, sale of bonds is not contemplated for this quarter, so the value is zero.

3. <u>Stock Sale</u>. Your firm has 6,000,000 shares of no-par-value common stock outstanding at the beginning of Year 3. The stock is traded in the over-the-counter market, and the closing bid price is reported in the industry report at the end of each quarter. The price of new shares you issue is influenced by the closing bid price. The stock underwriters will submit a bid for an entire new issue, with the net proceeds to be paid to your company at once. The underwriters only deal in 100,000 share blocks for new issues and the minimum issue size must raise at least $1 million.

The issue price per share may be estimated by the following formula:

$$\text{Est. issue price} = \frac{(\text{shares outstanding}) \times (\text{latest market price})}{(\text{shares outstanding}) + (\text{shares to be issued})}$$

If you have a Number 2 credit rating, this is the estimated issue price. If your credit rating is Number 3, reduce the issue price by 10 percent. If your rating is Number 1, increase it by 10 percent. Enter the expected proceeds of a stock sale. Proceeds may be estimated by multiplying the issue price by the number of shares you plan to issue. For our example, a sale of stock is not contemplated this quarter, so enter zero.

Financing Expenditures

1. <u>Dividends Paid</u>. Dividends are payable in the quarter in which they are declared. Dividends declared in the current quarter together with the dividends declared during the previous three quarters must not exceed the sum of the net income after taxes earned during the previous four quarters of operation. Dividends may not be declared unless there is a positive balance in the retained earnings account. Enter here the amount of dividends that you plan to pay. Copy the value from the pro forma Income Statement. For our example, the amount is $180,000.

2. Loans Repaid. Enter the amount of any bank loan outstanding at the end of the previous quarter (which must be paid
back in the current quarter). For our example, no bank loan was
outstanding in Year 2, Quarter 4.

3. Bonds Repurchased. Outstanding bonds may be repurchased
with a five percent call premium. If you have floated several
bond issues and decide to call some of the bonds, the bonds
carrying the highest interest rate will be called first. Enter
the principal amount of bonds to be repurchased. The call premium would be entered under Other Expense on the pro forma Income
Statement, and carried in the cash budget as part of Administration and General Expense. For our example, no bond repurchase is
contemplated for Year 3, Quarter 1.

4. Stock Repurchased. Repurchasing stock converts outstanding stock to treasury stock. Your firm's corporate charter
requires the company to maintain a minimum of three million
shares of common stock outstanding. In addition, retained earnings must have a positive balance after the repurchase. Your
investment banker will repurchase the number of shares you specify, consistent with the above requirements, at a price 10% above
the closing price for the last quarter. The 10% premium is
required to obtain the stock in large blocks. Repurchases are in
100,000 share blocks, with a maximum repurchase in any quarter of
500,000 shares. Enter the dollar value of expected stock repurchase (in thousands). Multiply the number of shares to be repurchased by the repurchase price. For our example, no share repurchase is contemplated for Year 3, Quarter 1.

Net Financing Cash Flow

Net Financing Cash Flow is the sum of Financing Receipts
less the sum of Financing Expenditures. For our example, the
amount is $240,000.

$$(\$420 + \$0 + \$0) - (\$180 + \$0 + \$0) = \$240$$

Summary

1. Beginning Cash Balance. Enter the amount of cash on
hand, as shown on the balance sheet from the previous quarter.
For our example, this is $1,175,000. This is a rather large cash
balance and, unfortunately, it earns no interest. Your predeces-
sors might have done well to have put another $1 million in time
CDs in order to earn more interest.

2. Net Cash Flow for Quarter. The estimated net cash flow
for the quarter should be estimated now. It is the sum of Net

Operating Cash Flow plus Net Investment Cash Flow plus Net Financing Cash Flow. For our example, the amount is -$42,000.

$$\$245 - \$527 + 240 = -\$42$$

3.   <u>Ending Cash Balance</u>. The expected ending cash balance is the sum of Beginning Cash Balance plus Net Cash Flow for the Quarter. This calculation will help you decide whether you need additional financing or will have a cash surplus in the coming quarter. If the expected ending cash balance is lower than your minimum cash target, additional funds should be obtained from some source. If the difference shows considerably more cash available than your target, you may want to invest the excess funds in three-month time certificates of deposit, to pay additional dividends or to use some of the cash to increase marketing activities or production capacity.

For our example, the expected ending cash balance is $1,133,000.

$$\$1,175 - \$42 = \$1,133 \cdot$$

At this point you need to consider whether you may wish to revise your financial plans for Year 3, Quarter 1. This is obviously more cash than you will need for the quarter. A starting point would be to go back to your capital budget work sheet and remember that you are starting with a large cash balance. The first quarter's bank loan will not be needed. Perhaps you should consider revising the plan so as not to borrow $420,000. That still would leave a large cash balance. You should consider other aspects of your spending plan, and if such a large cash balance still is likely, invest some of it in time CDs. Be sure not to cut yourself too short, though. Keep a large enough cash buffer to be sure that all contingencies are covered. If you run out of cash, time CDs will not be available and you may be forced to take out an emergency loan.

The Balance Sheet

Your pro forma Balance Sheet can be estimated using values from the balance sheet at the end of the previous quarter, the cash budget, and the pro forma Income Statement. The pro forma Balance Sheet will provide an estimate of the value of each of your balance sheet accounts at the end of the quarter. You may use the pro forma Balance Sheet in lieu of a cash budget, if desired, to determine whether a bank loan will be necessary. To do so, estimate the value of all other balance sheet accounts and "plug" the cash balance to make the balance sheet balance.

This statement also provides a useful vehicle for estimating funds requirements over a longer period of time. We have provided the Pro Forma Balance Sheet work sheet (shown in Figure 10-6) for your use, with extra copies available in Appendix C. A spreadsheet template also is available on disk. The values shown in Figure 10-6 continue our example that was used for the pro forma Income Statement and Cash Budget.

Current Assets

The <u>Cash Balance</u> can be copied directly from the ending cash balance on the last line of the Cash Budget work sheet. For our example, this value is $1,133,000.

Alternatively, if you are using the pro forma Balance Sheet to estimate the funds requirements for future periods, enter the desired minimum cash balance--the amount that you intend to have on hand at the end of the period. Then, when you have finished estimating all of the other accounts, force the balance sheet to balance by using surplus cash to purchase time CDs or borrowing to make up a deficit.

<u>Time Certificates of Deposit</u> also may be·copied directly from the entry in the Cash Budget work sheet. For our example, above, we did not anticipate investing in CDs, but after looking at the large cash balance that seems to be available, you may change your mind about this.

<u>Accounts Receivable</u> at the end of any quarter is equal to one-half of the expected sales for that quarter. In the cash budget work sheet we estimated the half of Year 3, Quarter 1 sales that would be collected to be $1,554,000. The other half, obviously also $1,554,000, would remain on the books as accounts receivable.

<u>Inventory</u> on hand at the end of the period can be copied directly from the <u>pro forma</u> Income Statement, where it was estimated in order to calculate the estimated cost of goods sold. For our example the amount is $562,000, from Figure 10-3.

<u>Total Current Assets</u> is the sum of Cash Balance, Time Certificates of Deposit, Accounts Receivable, and Inventory. For our example, the amount is $3,249,000.

$$1,133 + $0 + $1,554 + $562 = $3,249$$

Fixed Assets

<u>Net Plant</u> is equal to the value of net plant at the end of the previous quarter plus capital investments during the current period minus depreciation charges. The book value of net plant was shown to be $3,044,000 on the balance sheet for Year 2, Quarter 4 (See Appendix B). Payments for new plant investment

THE BUSINESS POLICY GAME
PRO FORMA BALANCE SHEET

Co. __1__ World __1__ Year __3__	Qtr 1	Qtr 2	Qtr 3	Qtr 4
ASSETS:				
Cash Balance	1,133			
Time Certificates of Deposit	0			
Accounts Receivable	1,554			
Inventory	562			
Total Current Assets	3,249			
Net Plant	3,528			
Net Equipment	2,930			
Total Fixed Assets	6,458			
Total Assets	9,707			
LIABILITIES AND EQUITY:				
Taxes Payable	147			
Bank Loan	420			
Total Current Liabilities	567			
Bonds Outstanding	2,000			
Total Liabilities	2,567			
Capital Stock	5,000			
Retained Earnings	2,139			
Total Equity	7,139			
Total Liabilities & Equity	9,706			

FIGURE 10-6
Illustration of the Balance Sheet Work Sheet

for Year 3, Quarter 1 were estimated in our cash budget (Figure 10-5) as $520,000. Plant depreciation charges were estimated in the production plan (Figure 7-3) as $32,000 and an additional $4,000 (From Figure 9-2) was added for the new plant construction project when we calculated the pro forma Income Statement (Figure 10-3. Plant depreciation charges thus were estimated as $36,000.

$$32,000 + \$4,000 = \$36,000$$

The book value of net plant then would be estimated as $3,528,000.

$$3,044,000 + \$520,000 - \$36,000 = \$3,528,000$$

Net Equipment is equal to the value of net equipment at the end of the previous period plus planned capital expenditures for new equipment during the coming period plus equipment replacement expenditures minus equipment depreciation charges.

Equipment is depreciated on a straight-line basis over seven years. That is, current-quarter depreciation charges are calculated as 1/28th of the original book value of all equipment in place during the quarter, including payments made for installation of new equipment.

Thus, the net equipment value is calculated by adding expected expenditures for new equipment during the quarter to the value of the equipment account at the end of the last quarter. Then replacement costs are added and depreciation charges are subtracted to calculate the net equipment value.

The book value of net equipment was $2,934,000 at the end of Year 2, Quarter 4. The cash budget work sheet of Figure 10-5 estimated no new equipment purchases and $107,000 in purchase of replacement equipment. Equipment depreciation charges were estimated for your production plan as $111,000 in Figure 7-3. So for our example, the estimated book value of equipment will be $2,930,000.

$$2,934 + \$107 - \$111 = \$2,930$$

Total Fixed Assets

Total Fixed Assets is the sum of Net Plant plus Net Equipment. For our example, the amount is $6,458,000.

$$3,528 + \$2,930 = \$6,458$$

Total Assets

Total Assets is the sum of Total Current Assets and Total Fixed Assets. For our example, the amount is $9,707.

$$\$3,249 + \$6,458 = \$9,707$$

Current Liabilities

Taxes Payable are calculated for Quarters 2, 3 and 4 by adding 39 percent of the expected net income in the current quarter to the income taxes payable in the previous quarter. During the first quarter of each year, the taxes accrued during the previous year must be paid, so taxes payable at the end of the first quarter would consist only of those accrued during that quarter. The amount of expected income taxes for any quarter may be taken directly from the pro forma Income Statement. For our example, the previous balance of taxes payable, $464,000 from Year 2, Quarter 4, were considered to be paid in Year 3, Quarter 1 (See Figure 10-5). The balance of Taxes Payable for Year 3, Quarter 1, then, would consist of the assessment of $147,000 for the current quarter shown in the pro forma Income Statement (Figure 10-3).

The bank loan is equal to the amount that you plan to borrow during the quarter. In preparing the cash budget work sheet (Figure 10-5), we estimated this amount to be $420,000.

If the pro forma Balance Sheet is being used to estimate funds requirements, we suggest that this category be left blank until the other amounts have been calculated. The bank loan can be utilized as a "plug" figure to make total assets equal total liabilities plus equity. The plug figure will indicate the additional funds that your firm requires during the coming quarter.

Total Current Liabilities

Total Current Liabilities is the sum of Taxes Payable and Bank Loan. For our example, the amount is $567,000.

$$\$147 + \$420 = \$567$$

Long-term Debt

Bonds Outstanding consist of the amount of bonds outstanding at the end of the previous quarter plus or minus any new bonds you plan to issue or redeem in the current quarter. Long-term debt in the Business Policy Game is limited to bonds. As no new issue or repurchase is contemplated in our example, the amount is the same as was reported on the Year 2, Quarter 4 balance sheet, or $2,000,000.

Total Liabilities

Total Liabilities is the sum of Total Current Liabilities plus Bonds Outstanding. For our example, the amount is $2,567,000.

$$\$567 + \$2,000 = \$2,567$$

Equity

Capital Stock is equal to the cumulative value of cash received by your company for the sale of common stock. Your firm's common stock has no par value. Thus, if your firm plans to issue common stock, the expected net proceeds of the issue should be added to the value of capital stock at the end of the previous period. For our example, the value is the same as Year 2, Quarter 4, or $5,000,000.

Retained Earnings are equal to the sum of the retained earnings at the end of the previous quarter plus the net income after taxes earned by your firm in the current quarter minus dividend payments planned for the current quarter. If common stock is to be repurchased, the amount of the repurchase will reduce retained earnings, as sufficient retained earnings to complete the repurchase will first be transferred to the capital stock account. For our example, the value of the Retained Earnings account for Year 2, Quarter 4 was $2,090,000. No common stock repurchase is contemplated in Year 3, Quarter 1. From the pro forma Income Statement (Figure 10-3) the addition to retained earnings was estimated as $49,000. Therefore, the balance of the account will be about $2,139,000.

$$\$2,090 + \$49 = \$2,139$$

Total Equity is the sum of Capital Stock and Retained Earnings, equal to $7,139,000 in our example.

$$\$5,000 + \$2,139 = \$7,139$$

Total Liabilities & Equity

Adding Total Liabilities and Total Equity gives $9,706,000 in our example.

$$\$2,567 + \$7,139 = \$9,706$$

And Total Assets almost equals Total Liabilities and Equity. It should be noted that if you should use different methods of estimation for some of the balance sheet items than for others, as we did, you might not show exact equality for both sides of the balance sheet. Also, because of several different estimation calculations, it is easy for a rounding error to occur. Pro forma statements are not accounting records, keeping track of every penny. They are estimates. If they don't always balance exactly, you will not be in trouble with your CPA. If this imbalance offends your sense of order, you may force a balance by subtracting $1,000 from the expected cash balance. Then total assets will be equal to total liabilities plus equity.

On the other hand, if the difference is large, you probably have made an error, and failed to consider something from one of your estimated statements that was considered on another. Check back over your figures to see what may have been omitted. And always check your pro forma statements against the printed reports that you receive at the end of the quarter. In this way you will find that errors made at the beginning of the quarter will stand out. Your estimating skills can be improved by checking up on their accuracy. But if you are in doubt, be sure to leave a big enough cash balance to take care of funds requirements that you may have overlooked! Don't get caught short on cash and be forced to take out an emergency loan.

If you are using the pro forma Balance Sheet to estimate funds requirements, the difference between total assets and total liabilities plus equity (assuming that you have estimated correctly) would indicate either surplus funds or additional funds requirements. If assets are greater than liabilities plus net worth, then additional funds would be required to finance the assets. If assets are less, then surplus funds would be available, and the difference can be added to the cash account or used to purchase CDs.

We suggest that a pro forma statement be made for the end of each of the next five years. This will enable you to project your long-term funds requirements and permit you to plan for the sale of common stock and bonds as additional funding becomes necessary. Alternatively, more funds may be generated internally than are needed to meet your estimated obligations. In that case, you may want to plan for investment in CDs, for increased dividend payments to stockholders, or to consider other alternative uses for the funds.

Summary

Capital Budget. Work sheets are provided to assist in the preparation of a capital budget. Expansion projects to be undertaken should be listed, funds requirements should be scheduled, and plans should be made for obtaining the required funds.

Pro Forma Income Statement. Work sheets are provided for the preparation of pro forma Income Statements, in which estimates should be made according to generally accepted accounting rules. Calculations of various items are summarized in the text.

1. Sales revenues were estimated from the sales forecast developed in Chapter 6.

2. Goods available for sale were estimated by adding beginning inventory (last period's ending inventory) to total production cost (from the Production Plan work sheet developed in Chapter 7).

3. Inventories are valued on a first-in first-out basis. The value of ending inventory was estimated and subtracted from goods available for sale to estimate the Cost of Goods Sold.

4. Selling Expense includes advertising, sales salaries, commissions, general selling expense, transportation expense, and other selling expense. Calculation of values for these accounts is described in Chapter 5.

5. Research and Development expense is a decision variable, under the control of your management.

6. Storage expense equals 10 cents per unit for the first 300,000 units stored in any plant, and 30 cents per unit for additional units stored in public warehouses. It is computed on the number of units on hand at the beginning of the quarter.

7. Executive compensation is charged quarterly at about $150,000, subject to increase in proportion to changes in the Consumer Price Index.

8. Loan Interest is paid quarterly on any bank loans outstanding at the current short-term rate of interest available to a company with your credit standing. The quarterly rate is one-fourth of the annual rate.

9. Bond Interest is paid quarterly on all outstanding bonds at the long-term rate of interest that was in effect at the time the bonds were issued. The quarterly rate is one-fourth of the annual rate.

10. Other Expense is a category for expenses that are not separately stated, including deactivation charges and call premiums for repurchased bonds.

184

11. Operating Profit is Gross Profit less Total Operating Expense.

12. Other Income consists of interest earned on time certificates of deposit.

13. Income Tax is assessed at a rate of 39 percent of Net Profit.

Cash Budget. A cash budget should be prepared (work sheets are provided) to determine expected receipts and cash outlays for each quarter of operation. This will assist your management in providing sufficient funds to meet its obligations when due.

1. Operating Receipts. Accounts receivable have an average collection period of forty-five days. Receipts in any quarter will equal one-half of sales plus the balance of accounts receivable at the end of the previous quarter.

2. Operating Expenditures consist of Production Cost (taken from the Production Plan work sheet), Selling and Administration Expense (taken from the pro forma Income Statement work sheet) and Taxes Paid (in the first quarter of each year, equal to the Quarter 4 balance of taxes payable). Production costs in this category exclude depreciation charges that do not require a cash outlay.

3. Investment Receipts consist of CD Interest (from the pro forma Income Statement work sheet) and maturing CDs (from the previous period balance sheet).

4. Investment Expenditures consist of CDs purchased (decision variable) and capital expenditures on plant and equipment (taken from the capital budget).

5. Financing Receipts consist of bank loans, bonds sold, and common stock sold.

   Secured bank loans are available under a $2,500,000 line of credit subject to a maximum limit of 50 percent of accounts receivable plus inventories, and to a one-quarter annual cleanup requirement. Loans are discounted at the current short-term rate of interest and must be repaid in ninety days. Emergency loans, required because of insufficient cash on hand, are charged a penalty rate of interest and result in a lower credit rating.

185

Secured <u>bonds</u> with a face value of $2 million are outstanding at the end of Year 2. The bonds mature in ten years, carry a coupon rate of 10 percent and are callable with a five percent call premium. New bonds may be issued with a ten-year maturity at the current long-term rate of interest and are callable with a five percent call premium. Newly-issued bonds are subject to a maximum bonds to equity ratio of 50%. Total bonds outstanding, plus any newly issued, may not exceed 75 percent of net fixed assets at the end of the previous quarter.

<u>Common stock</u> may be issued at a price to be determined by a formula shown in the text. At the beginning of the simulation, 6 million shares are outstanding, with a book value of $5 million. New issues are in multiples of 100,000 shares, subject to a minimum issue of at least $1 million.

6. Financing Expenditures consist of Dividends Paid (taken from the pro forma Income Statement work sheet), Loans Repaid, Bonds Repurchased, and Stock Repurchased.

7. Beginning cash balance equals the previous quarter's ending cash balance.

8. Ending cash balance equals beginning cash balance plus the net cash flow for the quarter.

<u>Pro Forma Balance Sheet</u>. Work sheets are provided for the preparation of a pro forma Balance Sheet. Amounts for this work sheet are estimated using values from the balance sheet at the end of the previous quarter, the cash budget, and the pro forma Income Statement.

1. The Cash Balance is taken from the Cash Budget.

2. Time Certificates of Deposit is taken from the Cash Budget.

3. Accounts Receivable is taken from the Cash Budget, as the value of sales that is not collected by the end of the quarter.

4. Inventory is taken from the pro forma Income Statement.

5. Net Plant is the value of net plant at the end of the previous quarter (previous balance sheet), plus capital investments during the current quarter (Cash Budget), less depreciation charges (Production Plan and pro forma Income Statement).

6. Net Equipment is equal to the value of net equipment at the end of the previous quarter (previous balance sheet), plus planned capital expenditures (Cash Budget), less depreciation charges (Production Plan and pro forma Income Statement).

7. Taxes payable are equal to previous taxes payable (previous balance sheet), plus current tax assessment (pro forma Income Statement), less tax payments (Cash Budget).

8. Bank Loan is taken from the Cash Budget.

9. Bonds Outstanding are equal to previous bonds outstanding (previous balance sheet), plus newly issued bonds (Cash Budget), less bonds repurchased (Cash Budget).

10. Capital Stock is equal to previous capital stock (previous balance sheet), plus newly issued common stock (Cash Budget).

11. Retained Earnings are equal to previous retained earnings (previous balance sheet), plus current additions to retained earnings (pro forma Income Statement), less common stock to be repurchased (Cash Budget).

APPENDIX A

> HISTORICAL DATA FOR YEARS 1 AND 2

TABLE A-1
HISTORICAL DATA FOR YEARS 1 AND 2
THE BUSINESS POLICY GAME

	Year 1				Year 2			
	Qtr 1	Qtr 2	Qtr 3	Qtr 4	Qtr 1	Qtr 2	Qtr 3	Qtr 4
GNP Index (Y1Q1 = 100)	100.0	100.7	102.0	103.4	103.9	107.2	109.2	110.6
CPI Index (Y1Q1 = 100)	100.0	101.4	102.4	104.1	105.5	106.1	107.6	108.4
Loan Interest Rate (%)	8.70	8.70	8.30	8.30	7.70	6.50	5.80	6.40
Bond Interest Rate (%)	8.30	8.80	9.00	9.40	9.40	8.40	8.60	8.80
Stock Market:								
Market Index	100.0	97.2	83.0	90.7	98.8	109.3	109.4	109.1
Mkt Earnings Yield (%)	6.3	6.0	6.7	6.3	5.3	5.4	5.8	6.1
Company Stock Price($)	0.50	0.49	0.43	0.48	1.16	1.31	0.86	1.08
Company EPS ($)	0.017	0.025	0.012	0.032	0.009	0.032	0.021	0.060
Product Prices ($):								
Home Area	10.00	10.10	10.20	10.30	10.40	10.20	10.10	10.00
Nonhome area	10.60	10.60	10.60	10.60	10.60	10.40	10.20	10.00
Nonhome area	10.60	10.60	10.60	10.60	10.60	10.40	10.20	10.00
Area 4	10.30	10.30	10.40	10.50	10.60	10.40	10.20	10.00
Company Salespeople (#):								
Home Area	6	6	6	7	9	10	11	12
Nonhome area	6	6	6	6	7	8	9	10
Nonhome area	6	6	6	6	7	8	9	10
Area 4	7	7	7	8	10	11	12	13
Total	25	25	25	27	33	37	41	45
Company Sales (000s):								
Home Area	50	54	49	62	52	68	67	92
Nonhome area	46	51	47	60	48	60	60	85
Nonhome area	46	51	47	60	48	60	60	85
Area 4	42	46	42	53	43	59	59	83
Total	184	202	185	235	191	247	246	345
Advertising ($000s):								
Home Area	29	`33	37	40	45	45	46	46
Nonhome area	29	32	35	35	36	37	38	40
Nonhome area	29	32	35	35	36	37	38	40
Area 4	29	33	40	42	46	46	46	46
Total	116	130	147	152	163	165	168	172
R & D Expense ($000s):								
Product R & D	50	53	56	59	62	64	68	72
Process R & D	50	52	54	56	58	60	64	68
Total	100	105	110	115	120	124	132	140
Other Items (000s):								
Actual Output	208	208	208	208	260	260	260	312
Ending Inventory	69	75	98	71	140	153	167	134
Total Unit Sales	184	202	185	235	191	247	246	345

TABLE A-2
FINANCIAL DATA FOR YEARS 1 AND 2
THE BUSINESS POLICY GAME

	--------Year 1---------				--------Year 2---------			
	Qtr 1	Qtr 2	Qtr 3	Qtr 4	Qtr 1	Qtr 2	Qtr 3	Qtr 4
Income Statement ($000s)								
Gross Sales	1906	2098	1931	2466	2011	2552	2499	3450
Cost of Goods Sold	845	913	836	1094	863	1083	1098	1530
Gross Profit	1061	1185	1095	1372	1148	1469	1401	1920
Selling Expenses	599	639	671	743	748	824	856	975
Admin and General Exp	292	299	307	315	320	332	342	354
Operating Profit	170	247	117	314	80	313	203	591
Time CD Interest	0	0	0	0	6	0	0	1
Net Profit Before Tax	170	247	117	314	86	313	203	592
Net Profit After Tax	104	151	72	192	53	191	124	362
Cash Flow (CF) Statement ($000s)								
Accounts Collected	1763	2002	2014	2199	2238	2282	2525	2975
Less Production Cost	797	797	798	845	998	999	1049	1200
Less Operating Expense	891	938	978	1058	1068	1156	1198	1329
Net Operating CF	75	267	238	296	-157	127	278	446
Investment Receipts	0	0	0	0	6	400	0	1
Less Investment Expend	99	99	100	101	503	104	105	206
Net Investment CF	-99	-99	-100	-101	-497	296	-105	-205
Financing Receipts	0	0	0	0	0	0	0	0
Less Financing Expend	0	0	0	0	0	0	0	0
Net Financing CF	0	0	0	0	0	0	0	0
Net CF for Quarter	-24	168	138	195	-654	423	173	241
Balance Sheet Items ($000s):								
Cash	491	659	797	992	338	761	934	1175
Time CDs	0	0	0	0	400	0	0	100
Accounts Receivable	953	1049	966	1233	1006	1276	1250	1725
Inventory	311	338	443	336	613	671	764	576
Total Assets	8011	8258	8375	8689	8446	8759	8962	9554
Taxes Payable	66	162	207	329	33	155	234	464
Bank Loans	0	0	0	0	0	0	0	0
Bonds Outstanding	2000	2000	2000	2000	2000	2000	2000	2000
Total Equity	5945	6096	6168	6360	6413	6604	6728	7090
Total Liab and Equity	8011	8258	8375	8689	8446	8759	8962	9554

APPENDIX B

```
+--------------------------------------+
|  REPRODUCTION OF COMPUTER REPORTS    |
|      FOR YEAR 2, QUARTER 4           |
+--------------------------------------+
```

INCOME STATEMENT	$000s	CASH FLOW STATEMENT	$000s
Gross Revenue from Sales	3450	Operating Receipts:	
Less Cost of Goods Sold	1530	Accounts Collected	2975
Gross Profit	1920	Operating Expenditures:	
		Production Cost	1200
Selling Expense:		Operating Expense	1329
Advertising	172	Taxes Paid	0
Sales Salaries	135		
Sales Commissions	69	Net Operating Cash Flow:	446
General Selling Expense	399		
Transportation Expense	161	Investment Receipts:	
Other Selling Expense	39	CD Interest	1
Total Selling Expense	975	CDs Matured	0
		Investment Expenditures:	
Admin and General Expense:		CDs Purchased	100
Research and Development	140	New Equipment	0
Storage Expense	16	Equipment Replacement	106
Executive Compensation	148	Plant Investment	0
Loan Interest	0		
Bond Interest	50	Net Investment Cash Flow:	-205
Other Expense	0		
Total Admin and Gen Exp	354	Financing Receipts:	
		Loans Received	0
Total Operating Expense	1329	Bond Sale	0
Operating Profit (Loss)	591	Stock Sale	0
		Financing Expenditures:	
Other Income:		Dividends Paid	0
CD Interest	1	Loans Repaid	0
		Bonds Repurchased	0
Net Profit (Loss) Before Tax	592	Stock Repurchased	0
Less Income Tax	230		
		Net Financing Cash Flow:	0
Net Profit (Loss) After Tax	362		
		Beginning Cash Balance	934
Less Dividends Paid	0	Net Cash Flow for Quarter	241
		Cash Available End of Quarter	1175
Addition to Retained Earnings	362	Required Loan (incl. interest)	0

BALANCE SHEET

ASSETS	$000s	LIABILITIES	$000s
Cash Balance	1175	Taxes Payable	464
Time Certificates of Deposit	100	Bank Loan	0
Accounts Receivable	1725	Total Current Liabilities	464
Inventory	576	Bonds Outstanding	2000
Total Current Assets	3576	Total Liabilities	2464
Net Plant	3044	Capital Stock	5000
Net Equipment	2934	Retained Earnings	2090
Total Fixed Assets	5978	Total Equity	7090
Total Assets	9554	Total Liabilities & Equity	9554

OPERATING INFORMATION REPORT
BUSINESS POLICY GAME, 3RD EDITION
by Cotter & Fritzsche   Copyright 1991 by Prentice Hall

PRODUCTION COST ANALYSIS

	--Actual Cost-- Total $000s	--Actual Cost-- Per Unit $	Standard Cost Per Unit $
Labor Cost	749	2.40	2.40
Materials Cost	374	1.20	1.20
Maintenance Cost	77	0.25	0.25
Shutdown Cost	0	0.00	
Training Cost	0	0.00	
Total Cash Expenditures	1200	3.85	3.85
Equipment Depreciation	110	0.35	
Plant Depreciation	32	0.10	
Total Production Cost	1342	4.30	

OUTPUT, INVENTORY, AND SALES ANALYSIS
(in thousands of units)

	Total	Area 1	Area 2	Area 3	Area 4
Normal Capacity	312	312	0	0	0
Actual Output	312	312	0	0	0
Ending Inventory	134	134	0	0	0
Total Orders	345	92	85	85	83
Domestic Sales	345	92	85	85	83
Foreign Sales	0				
Industry Sales	2070	524	524	524	498

OTHER OPERATING DATA

Latest Model Developed: 1   Model Produced This Quarter: 1 Quality: 2
Standard Cost per Unit for Next Quarter (includes inflation, cost savings):
    Model 1 Quality 2 Labor Cost: 2.42 Materials Cost: 1.21

	Area 1	Area 2	Area 3	Area 4
Active Salespeople	12	10	10	13
Salespeople in Training, Qtr 1	1	1	1	1
Salespeople in Training, Qtr 2	1	1	1	1
Space Available for New Lines	2	0	0	0

CURRENT PERIOD DECISIONS
BUSINESS POLICY GAME, 3RD EDITION
by Cotter & Fritzsche   Copyright 1991 by Prentice Hall

			Salespeople					
	Price	Adv.	Hire	Trans	Commission	Bank Loan		0
Area 1	10.00	46	1	0	20	Bond Issue		0
Area 2	10.00	40	1	0		Stock Issue		0
Area 3	10.00	40	1	0	Salary	Dividends		0
Area 4	10.00	46	1	0	3000	Time CDs		100

		Production Scheduling					Construction		

Model:			Production		Shut-	Deac-	Reac-	New	New	New
			Lines	Hours	down	tivate	tivate	Lines	Add	Plant
Model 1										
Qual 2		Area 1	6	40	0	0	0	0	0	0
		Area 2	0	0	0	0	0	0	0	0
R & D:		Area 3	0	0	0	0	0	0	0	0
		Area 4	0	0	0	0	0	0	0	0
Prod 72										
Proc 68		2d Shft	0	0	0	0		0		

REAL GROSS NATIONAL PRODUCT FORECAST

	Actual Values for Last 4 Quarters				Forecast Values, Next 4 Quarters			
	Qtr 5	Qtr 6	Qtr 7	Qtr 8	Qtr 9	Qtr 10	Qtr 11	Qtr 12
HIGH					105.03	107.94	110.74	113.73
MEAN	98.51	101.02	101.44	101.98	103.99	106.52	108.93	111.50
LOW					102.95	105.10	107.12	109.27

GNP Index (Current $)	110.55		---Credit Rating---		
				No. 1	No. 2	No. 3
Consumer Price Index	108.41	Interest Rates:	No. 1	No. 2	No. 3
Stock Market Index	109.12	Long-Term	7.60	8.80	9.80
Stock Market Earnings Yield	6.09	Short-Term	6.00	6.40	7.80
3-Month Time CD Rate	4.50				

CO.	STOCK PRICE	EARN- INGS	DIVI- DENDS	INVES- TOR ROI	SHARES ISSUED	BONDS	BANK LOANS	CASH	TIME CDs	CREDIT RATING
1	1.08	0.060	0.000	0.00	6000	2000	0	1175	100	2
2	1.08	0.060	0.000	0.00	6000	2000	0	1175	100	2
3	1.08	0.060	0.000	0.00	6000	2000	0	1175	100	2
4	1.08	0.060	0.000	0.00	6000	2000	0	1175	100	2
5	1.08	0.060	0.000	0.00	6000	2000	0	1175	100	2
6	1.08	0.060	0.000	0.00	6000	2000	0	1175	100	2

CO.	NET INCOME	TOTAL ASSETS	TOTAL EQUITY	INCOME TO EQUITY	INCOME TO SALES	CURR- ENT RATIO	BONDS TO EQUITY	NEW CONSTRUCTION 1	2	3	4	NEW LINES
1	362	9554	7090	5.1	10.5	7.71	28.21	0	0	0	0	0
2	362	9554	7090	5.1	10.5	7.71	28.21	0	0	0	0	0
3	362	9554	7090	5.1	10.5	7.71	28.21	0	0	0	0	0
4	362	9554	7090	5.1	10.5	7.71	28.21	0	0	0	0	0
5	362	9554	7090	5.1	10.5	7.71	28.21	0	0	0	0	0
6	362	9554	7090	5.1	10.5	7.71	28.21	0	0	0	0	0

CO.	SALES $000S	SHARE OF MARKET	DOMES- TIC SALES	FOR- EIGN SALES	MODEL PROD	QUAL ITY	MODEL AVAIL	PRO- DUC- TION	INVEN- TORY	UNIT PROD COST	UNIT SELL EXP
1	3450	16.67	345	0	1	2	1	312	134	4.30	2.83
2	3450	16.67	345	0	1	2	1	312	134	4.30	2.83
3	3450	16.67	345	0	1	2	1	312	134	4.30	2.83
4	3450	16.67	345	0	1	2	1	312	134	4.30	2.83
5	3450	16.67	345	0	1	2	1	312	134	4.30	2.83
6	3450	16.67	345	0	1	2	1	312	134	4.30	2.83

CO.	PRODUCT PRICE 1	2	3	4	NO. OF SALESPEOPLE 1	2	3	4	EST. ADVERTISING 1	2	3	4	R&D
1	10.00	10.00	10.00	10.00	12	10	10	13	40	40	40	40	140
2	10.00	10.00	10.00	10.00	10	12	10	13	40	40	40	40	140
3	10.00	10.00	10.00	10.00	10	10	12	13	40	40	50	50	140
4	10.00	10.00	10.00	10.00	12	10	10	13	40	40	40	40	140
5	10.00	10.00	10.00	10.00	10	12	10	13	40	50	40	40	140
6	10.00	10.00	10.00	10.00	10	10	12	13	40	40	50	50	140

Key: Company 1   ABC Corporation
        Company 2   DEF Corporation
        Company 3   GHI Corporation
        Company 4   JKL Corporation
        Company 5   MNO Corporation
        Company 6   PQR Corporation

Year 2   Quarter 4
06-09-1990
22:07:39

ANNUAL INDUSTRY REPORT
BUSINESS POLICY GAME, 3RD EDITION
by Cotter & Fritzsche   Copyright 1991 by Prentice Hall

Year	1	2
CASH($000s)		
Company 1	992	1175
Company 2	992	1175
Company 3	992	1175
Company 4	992	1175
Company 5	992	1175
Company 6	992	1175
CERTIFICATES OF DEPOSIT($000s)		
Company 1	0	100
Company 2	0	100
Company 3	0	100
Company 4	0	100
Company 5	0	100
Company 6	0	100
ACCOUNTS RECEIVABLE($000s)		
Company 1	1233	1725
Company 2	1233	1725
Company 3	1233	1725
Company 4	1233	1725
Company 5	1233	1725
Company 6	1233	1725
INVENTORY($000s)		
Company 1	336	576
Company 2	336	576
Company 3	336	576
Company 4	336	576
Company 5	336	576
Company 6	336	576
PLANT AND EQUIPMENT($000s)		
Company 1	6128	5978
Company 2	6128	5978
Company 3	6128	5978
Company 4	6128	5978
Company 5	6128	5978
Company 6	6128	5978
TOTAL ASSETS($000s)		
Company 1	8689	9554
Company 2	8689	9554
Company 3	8689	9554
Company 4	8689	9554
Company 5	8689	9554
Company 6	8689	9554

        Year   1   2

TAXES PAYABLE($000s)
    Company 1   329   464
    Company 2   329   464
    Company 3   329   464
    Company 4   329   464
    Company 5   329   464
    Company 6   329   464

BANK LOANS($000s)
    Company 1   0   0
    Company 2   0   0
    Company 3   0   0
    Company 4   0   0
    Company 5   0   0
    Company 6   0   0

BONDS OUTSTANDING($000s)
    Company 1   2000   2000
    Company 2   2000   2000
    Company 3   2000   2000
    Company 4   2000   2000
    Company 5   2000   2000
    Company 6   2000   2000

TOTAL EQUITY($000s)
    Company 1   6360   7090
    Company 2   6360   7090
    Company 3   6360   7090
    Company 4   6360   7090
    Company 5   6360   7090
    Company 6   6360   7090

GROSS SALES($000s)
    Company 1   8401   10512
    Company 2   8401   10512
    Company 3   8401   10512
    Company 4   8401   10512
    Company 5   8401   10512
    Company 6   8401   10512

ADVERTISING EXPENSE($000s)
    Company 1   545   668
    Company 2   545   668
    Company 3   545   668
    Company 4   545   668
    Company 5   545   668
    Company 6   545   668

Year	1	2
RESEARCH AND DEVELOPMENT EXPENSE($000s)		
Company 1	430	516
Company 2	430	516
Company 3	430	516
Company 4	430	516
Company 5	430	516
Company 6	430	516
NET INCOME($000s)		
Company 1	519	730
Company 2	519	730
Company 3	519	730
Company 4	519	730
Company 5	519	730
Company 6	519	730
SHARES OF STOCK OUTSTANDING(000s)		
Company 1	6000	6000
Company 2	6000	6000
Company 3	6000	6000
Company 4	6000	6000
Company 5	6000	6000
Company 6	6000	6000
UNIT PRODUCTION COST($)		
Company 1	4.58	4.41
Company 2	4.58	4.41
Company 3	4.58	4.41
Company 4	4.58	4.41
Company 5	4.58	4.41
Company 6	4.58	4.41
UNIT SELLING EXPENSE($)		
Company 1	3.29	3.31
Company 2	3.29	3.31
Company 3	3.29	3.31
Company 4	3.29	3.31
Company 5	3.29	3.31
Company 6	3.29	3.31
INCOME/EQUITY(PERCENT)		
Company 1	8.16	10.30
Company 2	8.16	10.30
Company 3	8.16	10.30
Company 4	8.16	10.30
Company 5	8.16	10.30
Company 6	8.16	10.30

ANNUAL INDUSTRY REPORT
BUSINESS POLICY GAME, 3RD EDITION
by Cotter & Fritzsche   Copyright 1991 by Prentice Hall

Year	1	2
INCOME/SALES (PERCENT)		
Company 1	6.18	6.94
Company 2	6.18	6.94
Company 3	6.18	6.94
Company 4	6.18	6.94
Company 5	6.18	6.94
Company 6	6.18	6.94
STOCK PRICE($)		
Company 1	0.48	1.08
Company 2	0.48	1.08
Company 3	0.48	1.08
Company 4	0.48	1.08
Company 5	0.48	1.08
Company 6	0.48	1.08
EARNINGS PER SHARE($)		
Company 1	0.087	0.122
Company 2	0.087	0.122
Company 3	0.087	0.122
Company 4	0.087	0.122
Company 5	0.087	0.122
Company 6	0.087	0.122
DIVIDENDS PER SHARE($)		
Company 1	0.000	0.000
Company 2	0.000	0.000
Company 3	0.000	0.000
Company 4	0.000	0.000
Company 5	0.000	0.000
Company 6	0.000	0.000
CURRENT RATIO (TIMES)		
Company 1	7.78	7.71
Company 2	7.78	7.71
Company 3	7.78	7.71
Company 4	7.78	7.71
Company 5	7.78	7.71
Company 6	7.78	7.71
BONDS/EQUITY (PERCENT)		
Company 1	31.45	28.21
Company 2	31.45	28.21
Company 3	31.45	28.21
Company 4	31.45	28.21
Company 5	31.45	28.21
Company 6	31.45	28.21

ANNUAL INDUSTRY REPORT
BUSINESS POLICY GAME, 3RD EDITION
by Cotter & Fritzsche   Copyright 1991 by Prentice Hall

Year	1	2
INTEREST COVERAGE (TIMES)		
Company 1	5.24	6.97
Company 2	5.24	6.97
Company 3	5.24	6.97
Company 4	5.24	6.97
Company 5	5.24	6.97
Company 6	5.24	6.97
SHARE OF MARKET (PERCENT)		
Company 1	16.67	16.67
Company 2	16.67	16.67
Company 3	16.67	16.67
Company 4	16.67	16.67
Company 5	16.67	16.67
Company 6	16.67	16.67

Key: Company 1 ABC Corporation
      Company 2 DEF Corporation
      Company 3 GHI Corporation
      Company 4 JKL Corporation
      Company 5 MNO Corporation
      Company 6 PQR Corporation

APPENDIX C

```
+--------------------------------------+
| BLANK FORMS AND WORK SHEETS          |
+--------------------------------------+
```

CORPORATE CHARTER (1)
DECISION FORMS (10)
PEER EVALUATION FORM (1)
SALES FORECAST WORK SHEET (6)
PRODUCTION PLAN WORK SHEET (6)
INVESTMENT ANALYSIS WORK SHEET (6)
CAPITAL BUDGET WORK SHEET (6)
CASH BUDGET WORK SHEET (6)
PRO FORMA INCOME STATEMENT (6)
PRO FORMA BALANCE SHEET (6)

Business Policy Game
CORPORATE CHARTER

You are authorized to operate the company known as

_____

in the State of Perpetual Knowledge for the duration of the
competition. During that time, you will be expected to operate
your company in keeping with good business practices. You also
are expected to abide by the highest ethical standards. Failure
to do so may result in the revocation of this charter.

Corporate Officers:

Name   Position

_____   _____

_____   _____

_____   _____

_____   _____

_____   _____

_____   _____

Signed this day _____

_____
Simulation Administrator

The BUSINESS POLICY GAME Decision Form

Company _____ World _____ Year _____ Quarter _____

	Price	Adv. (000s)	Salespeople Hire	Trans	Commission	(000s)	
Area 1	$ __ . __	$ __	# __	# __	_____ ¢	Bank Loan	$ __
Area 2	$ __ . __	$ __	# __	# __	Salary	Bond Issue	$ __
Area 3	$ __ . __	$ __	# __	# __	$ __	Stock Issue	# __
Area 4	$ __ . __	$ __	# __	# __		Dividends	$ __
						Time CDs	$ __

Production Scheduling

Model		Production Lines	Hours	Shut-down	Deac-tivate	Reac-tivate
Model# __	Area 1	# __	# __	# __	# __	# __
Qual # __	Area 2	# __	# __	# __	# __	# __
R & D (000s)	Area 3	# __	# __	# __	# __	# __
Prod $ __	Area 4	# __	# __	# __	# __	# __
Proc $ __	2d Shft	# __	# __	# __	# __	# __

Construction

New Lines	New Add	New Plant
# __	# __	# __
# __	# __	# __
# __	# __	# __
# __	# __	# __
# __		

The BUSINESS POLICY GAME Decision Form

Company _____ World _____ Year _____ Quarter _____

	Price	Adv. (000s)	Salespeople Hire	Trans	Commission	(000s)
Area 1	$ __.__	$ _____	# _____	# _____	_____ ¢	Bank Loan $ _____
Area 2	$ __.__	$ _____	# _____	# _____	Salary	Bond Issue $ _____
Area 3	$ __.__	$ _____	# _____	# _____	$ _____	Stock Issue # _____
Area 4	$ __.__	$ _____	# _____	# _____		Dividends $ _____
						Time CDs $ _____

Model

Model # _____

Qual # _____

R & D (000s)

Prod $ _____

Proc $ _____

Production Scheduling

	Production Lines Hours		Shut-down	Deac-tivate	Reac-tivate
Area 1	# _____	# _____	# _____	# _____	# _____
Area 2	# _____	# _____	# _____	# _____	# _____
Area 3	# _____	# _____	# _____	# _____	# _____
Area 4	# _____	# _____	# _____	# _____	# _____
2d Shft	# _____	# _____			

Construction

New Lines	New Add	New Plant
# _____	# _____	# _____
# _____	# _____	# _____
# _____	# _____	# _____
# _____	# _____	# _____
# _____		

The BUSINESS POLICY GAME Decision Form

Company _____ World _____ Year _____ Quarter _____

	Price	Adv. (000s)	Salespeople Hire	Trans	Commission	(000s)
Area 1	$ __ . __	$ ____	# ____	# ____	____ ¢	Bank Loan $ ____
Area 2	$ __ . __	$ ____	# ____	# ____	Salary	Bond Issue $ ____
Area 3	$ __ . __	$ ____	# ____	# ____	$ ____	Stock Issue # ____
Area 4	$ __ . __	$ ____	# ____	# ____		Dividends $ ____
						Time CDs $ ____

Model _____

Production Scheduling

	Production Lines	Hours	Shut-down	Deac-tivate	Reac-tivate
Model # _____					
Qual # _____	# ____	# ____	# ____	# ____	# ____
R & D (000s)	# ____	# ____	# ____	# ____	# ____
Area 3	# ____	# ____	# ____	# ____	# ____
Prod $ _____	# ____	# ____	# ____	# ____	# ____
Proc $ _____	# ____		# ____	# ____	# ____

Area 1, Area 2, Area 3, Area 4, 2d Shft

Construction

	New Lines	New Add	New Plant
	# ____	# ____	# ____
	# ____	# ____	# ____
	# ____	# ____	# ____
	# ____	# ____	# ____
	# ____		

The BUSINESS POLICY GAME Decision Form

Company _____ World _____ Year _____ Quarter _____

	Price	Adv. (000s)	Salespeople Hire	Trans	Commission	(000s)	
Area 1	$ __.__	$ _____	# _____	# _____	_____ ¢	Bank Loan $ _____	
Area 2	$ __.__	$ _____	# _____	# _____	Salary	Bond Issue $ _____	
Area 3	$ __.__	$ _____	# _____	# _____	$ _____	Stock Issue # _____	
Area 4	$ __.__	$ _____	# _____	# _____		Dividends $ _____	
						Time CDs $ _____	

Model

Model	Production Lines	Hours	Production Scheduling Shut-down	Deac-tivate	Reac-tivate	Construction New Lines	New Add	New Plant
Model # _____								
Qual # _____	Area 1	# ___	# ___	# ___	# ___	# ___	# ___	# ___	# ___
	Area 2	# ___	# ___	# ___	# ___	# ___	# ___	# ___	# ___
R & D (000s)	Area 3	# ___	# ___	# ___	# ___	# ___	# ___	# ___	# ___
Prod $ _____	Area 4	# ___	# ___	# ___	# ___	# ___	# ___	# ___	# ___
Proc $ _____	2d Shft	# ___	# ___	# ___	# ___	# ___	# ___		

The BUSINESS POLICY GAME Decision Form

Company _____ World _____ Year _____ Quarter _____

	Price	Adv. (000s)	Salespeople Hire Trans Commission			(000s)
Area 1	$ __.__	$ ____	# ____ # ____ ____¢		Bank Loan	$ ____
Area 2	$ __.__	$ ____	# ____ # ____ Salary		Bond Issue	$ ____
Area 3	$ __.__	$ ____	# ____ # ____ ____		Stock Issue	# ____
Area 4	$ __.__	$ ____	# ____ # ____ $ ____		Dividends	$ ____
					Time CDs	$ ____

Model

Model# ____

Qual # ____

R & D (000s)

Prod $ ____

Proc $ ____

Production Scheduling

	Production Lines Hours	Shut-down	Deac-tivate	Reac-tivate
Area 1	# ____ # ____	# ____	# ____	# ____
Area 2	# ____ # ____	# ____	# ____	# ____
Area 3	# ____ # ____	# ____	# ____	# ____
Area 4	# ____ # ____	# ____	# ____	# ____
2d Shft	# ____ # ____	# ____	# ____	

Construction

New Lines	New Add	New Plant
# ____	# ____	# ____
# ____	# ____	# ____
# ____	# ____	# ____
# ____	# ____	# ____
# ____		

The BUSINESS POLICY GAME Decision Form

Company _____ World _____ Year _____ Quarter _____

Price / Advertising / Salespeople / Finance

	Price	Adv. (000s)	Salespeople Hire	Trans	Commission	Bank Loan (000s) $
Area 1	$ __.__	$ ____	# ____	# ____	____ ¢	Bond Issue $ ____
Area 2	$ __.__	$ ____	# ____	# ____	Salary	Stock Issue # ____
Area 3	$ __.__	$ ____	# ____	# ____	$ ____	Dividends $ ____
Area 4	$ __.__	$ ____	# ____	# ____	____	Time CDs $ ____

Production Scheduling / Construction

Model	Production Lines	Hours	Shut-down	Deac-tivate	Reac-tivate	New Lines	New Add	New Plant
Area 1	# ____	# ____	# ____	# ____	# ____	# ____	# ____	# ____
Area 2	# ____	# ____	# ____	# ____	# ____	# ____	# ____	# ____
Area 3	# ____	# ____	# ____	# ____	# ____	# ____	# ____	# ____
Area 4	# ____	# ____	# ____	# ____	# ____	# ____	# ____	# ____
2d Shft	# ____					# ____		

Model

Model # ____
Qual # ____
R & D (000s)
Prod $ ____
Proc $ ____

The BUSINESS POLICY GAME Decision Form

Company _____   World _____   Year _____   Quarter _____

	Price	Adv. (000s)	Salespeople Hire	Trans	Commission		(000s)	
Area 1	$ __ . __	$ _____	# _____	# _____	_____ ¢	Bank Loan $ _____
Area 2	$ __ . __	$ _____	# _____	# _____	Salary	Bond Issue $ _____
Area 3	$ __ . __	$ _____	# _____	# _____	$ _____	Stock Issue # _____
Area 4	$ __ . __	$ _____	# _____	# _____		Dividends $ _____
						Time CDs $ _____

Production scheduling

Construction

Model		Production Lines	Hours	Shut-down	Deac-tivate	Reac-tivate	New Lines	New Add	New Plant
Model# _____	Area 1	# _____	# _____	# _____	# _____	# _____	# _____	# _____	# _____
Qual # _____	Area 2	# _____	# _____	# _____	# _____	# _____	# _____	# _____	# _____
R & D (000s)	Area 3	# _____	# _____	# _____	# _____	# _____	# _____	# _____	# _____
Prod $ _____	Area 4	# _____	# _____	# _____	# _____	# _____	# _____	# _____	# _____
Proc $ _____	2d Shft	# _____		# _____	# _____	# _____	# _____		

The BUSINESS POLICY GAME Decision Form

Company _____ World _____ Year _____ Quarter _____

	Price	Adv. (000s)	Salespeople Hire	Trans	Commission	(000s):	
Area 1	$ _ . _	$ ___	# ___	# ___	___ ¢	Bank Loan $ ___	
Area 2	$ _ . _	$ ___	# ___	# ___	Salary	Bond Issue $ ___	
Area 3	$ _ . _	$ ___	# ___	# ___		Stock Issue # ___	
Area 4	$ _ . _	$ ___	# ___	# ___	$ ___	Dividends $ ___	
						Time CDs $ ___	

Model

Model# ___
Qual # ___

R & D (000s)
Prod $ ___
Proc $ ___

Production Scheduling / Construction

	Production Lines	Hours	Shut-down	Deac-tivate	Reac-tivate	New Lines	New Add	New Plant
Area 1	# ___	# ___	# ___	# ___	# ___	# ___	# ___	# ___
Area 2	# ___	# ___	# ___	# ___	# ___	# ___	# ___	# ___
Area 3	# ___	# ___	# ___	# ___	# ___	# ___	# ___	# ___
Area 4	# ___	# ___	# ___	# ___	# ___	# ___	# ___	# ___
2d Shft	# ___	# ___	# ___	# ___	# ___	# ___		

The BUSINESS POLICY GAME Decision Form

Company _____   World _____   Year _____   Quarter _____

	Price	Adv. (000s)	Salespeople Hire	Salespeople Trans	Salespeople Commission	(000s)
Area 1	$ __ . __	$ ____	# ____	# ____	____ ¢	Bank Loan $ ____
Area 2	$ __ . __	$ ____	# ____	# ____	Salary	Bond Issue $ ____
Area 3	$ __ . __	$ ____	# ____	# ____	$ ____	Stock Issue # ____
Area 4	$ __ . __	$ ____	# ____	# ____		Dividends $ ____
						Time CDs $ ____

Model

Model# ____
Qual # ____

R & D (000s)

Prod $ ____
Proc $ ____

Production Scheduling

	Production Lines	Hours	Shut-down	Deac-tivate	Reac-tivate
Area 1	# ____	____	# ____	# ____	# ____
Area 2	# ____	____	# ____	# ____	# ____
Area 3	# ____	____	# ____	# ____	# ____
Area 4	# ____	____	# ____	# ____	# ____
2d Shft	# ____	____	# ____	# ____	# ____

Construction

	New Lines	New Add	New Plant
	# ____	# ____	# ____
	# ____	# ____	# ____
	# ____	# ____	# ____
	# ____	# ____	# ____
	# ____		

The BUSINESS POLICY GAME Decision Form

Company _____ World _____ Year _____ Quarter _____

	Price	Adv. (000s)		Salespeople				(000s)
				Hire	Trans	Commission		Bank Loan $ _____
Area 1	$ __.__	$ _____		# _____	# _____	_____ ¢		Bond Issue $ _____
Area 2	$ __.__	$ _____		# _____	# _____	Salary		Stock Issue # _____
Area 3	$ __.__	$ _____		# _____	# _____	$ _____		Dividends $ _____
Area 4	$ __.__	$ _____		# _____	# _____			Time CDs $ _____

Model

Model # _____						
Qual # _____						
R & D (000s)						
Prod $ _____						
Proc $ _____						

Production Scheduling

	Production Lines	Hours	Shut-down	Deac-tivate	Reac-tivate
Area 1	# _____	# _____	# _____	# _____	# _____
Area 2	# _____	# _____	# _____	# _____	# _____
Area 3	# _____	# _____	# _____	# _____	# _____
Area 4	# _____	# _____	# _____	# _____	# _____
2d Shft	# _____	# _____	# _____	# _____	# _____

Construction

	New Lines	New Add	New Plant
	# _____	# _____	# _____
	# _____	# _____	# _____
	# _____	# _____	# _____
	# _____	# _____	# _____
	# _____		

PEER EVALUATION FORM
THE BUSINESS POLICY GAME

TEAM EVALUATION: Please rank the company teams according to the way you judge their overall performance in the <u>Business Policy Game</u> (1=highest, 6=lowest).   A low rank does not necessarily mean poor performance, but rather a lower <u>relative</u> performance than the team with the next highest rank.

<u>Rank</u>	<u>Company number</u>	<u>Rank</u>	<u>Company number</u>
1.	_____	4.	_____
2.	_____	5.	_____
3.	_____	6.	_____

TEAM MEMBER EVALUATION: Please rate the members of your company team according to the way that you judge their contribution to your team's performance.   Rate the following factors:

FACTORS: 1.   Attendance at team meetings
2.   Constructive participation in team meetings
3.   Effort shown outside of team meetings
4.   Ability and willingness to work in a group situation
5.   Overall average

RATINGS: 9-10 = Excellent
7-8 = Good
4-6 = Fair
0-3 = Poor

Name	Attend-ance	Partici-pation	Effort	Contri-bution	Overall Average
Self_____	_____	_____	_____	_____	_____
_____	_____	_____	_____	_____	_____
_____	_____	_____	_____	_____	_____
_____	_____	_____	_____	_____	_____
_____	_____	_____	_____	_____	_____
_____	_____	_____	_____	_____	_____

THE BUSINESS POLICY GAME
SALES FORECAST WORK SHEET[a,b,c]

Company ____	Year ____			
	Qtr 1	Qtr 2	Qtr 3	Qtr 4
Forecasted GNP change	%	%	%	%
Sales, previous quarter				
Estimated sales increments:				
From GNP change				
Seasonal factors				
Price change				
Advertising change				
Sales salary change				
Sales commission change				
# of salespersons change				
New model introduction				
Competitors' actions				
Total incremental change				
Total sales forecast				
Expected average price	$.	$.	$.	$.
Expected sales revenue	$	$	$	$

[a] Unless otherwise indicated, make estimates in thousands of units.
[b] For expected average price, use dollars.
[c] For expected sales revenue, use thousands of dollars.

THE BUSINESS POLICY GAME
SALES FORECAST WORK SHEET[a,b,c]

Company ____	Year ____			
	Qtr 1	Qtr 2	Qtr 3	Qtr 4
Forecasted GNP change	%	%	%	%
Sales, previous quarter				
Estimated sales increments:				
From GNP change				
Seasonal factors				
Price change				
Advertising change				
Sales salary change				
Sales commission change				
# of salespersons change				
New model introduction				
Competitors' actions				
Total incremental change				
Total sales forecast				
Expected average price	$.	$.	$.	$.
Expected sales revenue	$	$	$	$

[a] Unless otherwise indicated, make estimates in thousands of units.
[b] For expected average price, use dollars.
[c] For expected sales revenue, use thousands of dollars.

THE BUSINESS POLICY GAME
SALES FORECAST WORK SHEET[a,b,c]

Company ____	Year ____			
	Qtr 1	Qtr 2	Qtr 3	Qtr 4
Forecasted GNP change	%	%	%	%
Sales, previous quarter				
Estimated sales increments:				
From GNP change				
Seasonal factors				
Price change				
Advertising change				
Sales salary change				
Sales commission change				
# of salespersons change				
New model introduction				
Competitors' actions				
Total incremental change				
Total sales forecast				
Expected average price	$.	$.	$.	$.
Expected sales revenue	$	$	$	$

[a] Unless otherwise indicated, make estimates in thousands of units.
[b] For expected average price, use dollars.
[c] For expected sales revenue, use thousands of dollars.

THE BUSINESS POLICY GAME
SALES FORECAST WORK SHEET[a,b,c]

Company ____	Year _____			
	Qtr 1	Qtr 2	Qtr 3	Qtr 4
Forecasted GNP change	%	%	%	%
Sales, previous quarter				
Estimated sales increments:				
From GNP change				
Seasonal factors				
Price change				
Advertising change				
Sales salary change				
Sales commission change				
# of salespersons change				
New model introduction				
Competitors' actions				
Total incremental change				
Total sales forecast				
Expected average price	$.	$.	$.	$.
Expected sales revenue	$	$	$	$

[a] Unless otherwise indicated, make estimates in thousands of units.
[b] For expected average price, use dollars.
[c] For expected sales revenue, use thousands of dollars.

THE BUSINESS POLICY GAME
SALES FORECAST WORK SHEET[a,b,c]

Company ____	Year ____			
	Qtr 1	Qtr 2	Qtr 3	Qtr 4
Forecasted GNP change	%	%	%	%
Sales, previous quarter				
Estimated sales increments:				
From GNP change				
Seasonal factors				
Price change				
Advertising change				
Sales salary change				
Sales commission change				
# of salespersons change				
New model introduction				
Competitors' actions				
Total incremental change				
Total sales forecast				
Expected average price	$.	$.	$.	$.
Expected sales revenue	$	$	$	$

[a]Unless otherwise indicated, make estimates in thousands of units.

[b]For expected average price, use dollars.

[c]For expected sales revenue, use thousands of dollars.

THE BUSINESS POLICY GAME
SALES FORECAST WORK SHEET[a,b,c]

Company ____	Year ____			
	Qtr 1	Qtr 2	Qtr 3	Qtr 4
Forecasted GNP change	%	%	%	%
Sales, previous quarter				
Estimated sales increments:				
From GNP change				
Seasonal factors				
Price change				
Advertising change				
Sales salary change				
Sales commission change				
# of salespersons change				
New model introduction				
Competitors' actions				
Total incremental change				
Total sales forecast				
Expected average price	$.	$.	$.	$.
Expected sales revenue	$	$	$	$

[a] Unless otherwise indicated, make estimates in thousands of units.
[b] For expected average price, use dollars.
[c] For expected sales revenue, use thousands of dollars.

THE BUSINESS POLICY GAME
PRODUCTION PLAN WORK SHEET

Co. ___ World ___ Yr___	Quarter 1	Quarter 2	Quarter 3	Quarter 4
Sales forecast (000s)				
Safety stock				
Total units needed				
Beginning inventory				
Minimum production				
Production scheduled				
Total prod. & inv.				

	Quarter 1		Quarter 2		Quarter 3		Quarter 4	
	Unit Cost	Total Cost	Unit Cost	Total Cost	Unit Cost	Total Cost	Unit Cost	Total Cost
Labor Cost								
Materials Cost								
Maintenance Cost								
Shutdown Cost								
Training Cost								
Total Cash Expenditure								
Equipment Depreciation								
Plant Depreciation								
Total Production Cost								

THE BUSINESS POLICY GAME
PRODUCTION PLAN WORK SHEET

Co. ___ World ___ Yr___	Quarter 1	Quarter 2	Quarter 3	Quarter 4
Sales forecast (000s)				
Safety stock				
Total units needed				
Beginning inventory				
Minimum production				
Production scheduled				
Total prod. & inv.				

	Quarter 1		Quarter 2		Quarter 3		Quarter 4	
	Unit Cost	Total Cost	Unit Cost	Total Cost	Unit Cost	Total Cost	Unit Cost	Total Cost
Labor Cost								
Materials Cost								
Maintenance Cost								
Shutdown Cost								
Training Cost								
Total Cash Expenditure								
Equipment Depreciation								
Plant Depreciation								
Total Production Cost								

THE BUSINESS POLICY GAME
PRODUCTION PLAN WORK SHEET

Co. ___ World ___ Yr___	Quarter 1	Quarter 2	Quarter 3	Quarter 4
Sales forecast (000s)				
Safety stock				
Total units needed				
Beginning inventory				
Minimum production				
Production scheduled				
Total prod. & inv.				

	Quarter 1		Quarter 2		Quarter 3		Quarter 4	
	Unit Cost	Total Cost	Unit Cost	Total Cost	Unit Cost	Total Cost	Unit Cost	Total Cost
Labor Cost								
Materials Cost								
Maintenance Cost								
Shutdown Cost								
Training Cost								
Total Cash Expenditure								
Equipment Depreciation								
Plant Depreciation								
Total Production Cost								

THE BUSINESS POLICY GAME
PRODUCTION PLAN WORK SHEET

Co. ___ World ___ Yr___	Quarter 1	Quarter 2	Quarter 3	Quarter 4
Sales forecast (000s)				
Safety stock				
Total units needed				
Beginning inventory				
Minimum production				
Production scheduled				
Total prod. & inv.				

	Quarter 1		Quarter 2		Quarter 3		Quarter 4	
	Unit Cost	Total Cost	Unit Cost	Total Cost	Unit Cost	Total Cost	Unit Cost	Total Cost
Labor Cost								
Materials Cost								
Maintenance Cost								
Shutdown Cost								
Training Cost								
Total Cash Expenditure								
Equipment Depreciation								
Plant Depreciation								
Total Production Cost								

THE BUSINESS POLICY GAME
PRODUCTION PLAN WORK SHEET

Co. ___ World ___ Yr___	Quarter 1	Quarter 2	Quarter 3	Quarter 4
Sales forecast (000s)				
Safety stock				
Total units needed				
Beginning inventory				
Minimum production				
Production scheduled				
Total prod. & inv.				

	Quarter 1		Quarter 2		Quarter 3		Quarter 4	
	Unit Cost	Total Cost	Unit Cost	Total Cost	Unit Cost	Total Cost	Unit Cost	Total Cost
Labor Cost								
Materials Cost								
Maintenance Cost								
Shutdown Cost								
Training Cost								
Total Cash Expenditure								
Equipment Depreciation								
Plant Depreciation								
Total Production Cost								

THE BUSINESS POLICY GAME
PRODUCTION PLAN WORK SHEET

Co. ___ World ___ Yr___	Quarter 1	Quarter 2	Quarter 3	Quarter 4
Sales forecast (000s)				
Safety stock				
Total units needed				
Beginning inventory				
Minimum production				
Production scheduled				
Total prod. & inv.				

	Quarter 1		Quarter 2		Quarter 3		Quarter 4	
	Unit Cost	Total Cost	Unit Cost	Total Cost	Unit Cost	Total Cost	Unit Cost	Total Cost
Labor Cost								
Materials Cost								
Maintenance Cost								
Shutdown Cost								
Training Cost								
Total Cash Expenditure								
Equipment Depreciation								
Plant Depreciation								
Total Production Cost								

THE BUSINESS POLICY GAME
INVESTMENT ANALYSIS WORK SHEET

Project: _____

Company _____ World _____

Year						After
═ RECEIPTS ═						
1. Estimated demand						
2. Capacity with expansion						
3. Price with expansion($)						
4. Revenues with expansion						
5. Capacity w/o expansion						
6. Price w/o expansion ($)						
7. Revenues w/o expansion						
8. Incremental receipts (4 - 7)						
═ INCREMENTAL EXPENDITURES═						
9. Investment expenditures						
10. Production costs						
11. Selling costs						
12. Tot incremental expenditures						
13. Net cash flow b/tax (8 - 12)						
═ TAX ADJUSTMENTS ═						
14. Incremental depreciation						
15. Net incremental taxable ═ income (8-10-11-14) ═						
16. Incremental taxes						
17. Net cash flow a/tax (13 - 16)						
═ PRESENT VALUE CALCULATIONS═						
18. Present value factor						
19. PV of net cash flow (17 x 18)						
20. NPV of project (sum of values on line 19)						

THE BUSINESS POLICY GAME
INVESTMENT ANALYSIS WORK SHEET

Project: _____

Company ____ World ____

	Year						After
RECEIPTS							
1. Estimated demand							
2. Capacity with expansion							
3. Price with expansion($)							
4. Revenues with expansion							
5. Capacity w/o expansion							
6. Price w/o expansion ($)							
7. Revenues w/o expansion							
8. Incremental receipts (4 - 7)							
INCREMENTAL EXPENDITURES							
9. Investment expenditures							
10. Production costs							
11. Selling costs							
12. Tot incremental expenditures							
13. Net cash flow b/tax (8 - 12)							
TAX ADJUSTMENTS							
14. Incremental depreciation							
15. Net incremental taxable income (8-10-11-14)							
16. Incremental taxes							
17. Net cash flow a/tax (13 - 16)							
PRESENT VALUE CALCULATIONS							
18. Present value factor							
19. PV of net cash flow (17 x 18)							
20. NPV of project (sum of values on line 19)							

THE BUSINESS POLICY GAME
INVESTMENT ANALYSIS WORK SHEET

Project: _____

Company _____ World _____

Year						After
RECEIPTS						
1. Estimated demand						
2. Capacity with expansion						
3. Price with expansion($)						
4. Revenues with expansion						
5. Capacity w/o expansion						
6. Price w/o expansion ($)						
7. Revenues w/o expansion						
8. Incremental receipts (4 - 7)						
INCREMENTAL EXPENDITURES						
9. Investment expenditures						
10. Production costs						
11. Selling costs						
12. Tot incremental expenditures						
13. Net cash flow b/tax (8 - 12)						
TAX ADJUSTMENTS						
14. Incremental depreciation						
15. Net incremental taxable income (8-10-11-14)						
16. Incremental taxes						
17. Net cash flow a/tax (13 - 16)						
PRESENT VALUE CALCULATIONS						
18. Present value factor						
19. PV of net cash flow (17 x 18)						
20. NPV of project (sum of values on line 19)						

THE BUSINESS POLICY GAME
INVESTMENT ANALYSIS WORK SHEET

Project: _____

Company ____ World ____						

Year						After
= RECEIPTS =						
1. Estimated demand						
2. Capacity with expansion						
3. Price with expansion($)						
4. Revenues with expansion						
5. Capacity w/o expansion						
6. Price w/o expansion ($)						
7. Revenues w/o expansion						
8. Incremental receipts (4 - 7)						
= INCREMENTAL EXPENDITURES=						
9. Investment expenditures						
10. Production costs						
11. Selling costs						
12. Tot incremental expenditures						
13. Net cash flow b/tax (8 - 12)						
= TAX ADJUSTMENTS =						
14. Incremental depreciation						
15. Net incremental taxable income (8-10-11-14) =						
16. Incremental taxes						
17. Net cash flow a/tax (13 - 16)						
= PRESENT VALUE CALCULATIONS=						
18. Present value factor						
19. PV of net cash flow (17 x 18)						
20. NPV of project (sum of values on line 19)						

THE BUSINESS POLICY GAME
INVESTMENT ANALYSIS WORK SHEET

Project: _____

Company ____ World ____

Year						After
RECEIPTS						
1. Estimated demand						
2. Capacity with expansion						
3. Price with expansion($)						
4. Revenues with expansion						
5. Capacity w/o expansion						
6. Price w/o expansion ($)						
7. Revenues w/o expansion						
8. Incremental receipts (4 - 7)						
INCREMENTAL EXPENDITURES						
9. Investment expenditures						
10. Production costs						
11. Selling costs						
12. Tot incremental expenditures						
13. Net cash flow b/tax (8 - 12)						
TAX ADJUSTMENTS						
14. Incremental depreciation						
15. Net incremental taxable income (8-10-11-14)						
16. Incremental taxes						
17. Net cash flow a/tax (13 - 16)						
PRESENT VALUE CALCULATIONS						
18. Present value factor						
19. PV of net cash flow (17 x 18)						
20. NPV of project (sum of values on line 19)						

THE BUSINESS POLICY GAME
INVESTMENT ANALYSIS WORK SHEET

Project: _____

Company _____ World _____

Year						After
RECEIPTS						
1. Estimated demand						
2. Capacity with expansion						
3. Price with expansion($)						
4. Revenues with expansion						
5. Capacity w/o expansion						
6. Price w/o expansion ($)						
7. Revenues w/o expansion						
8. Incremental receipts (4 - 7)						
INCREMENTAL EXPENDITURES						
9. Investment expenditures						
10. Production costs						
11. Selling costs						
12. Tot incremental expenditures						
13. Net cash flow b/tax (8 - 12)						
TAX ADJUSTMENTS						
14. Incremental depreciation						
15. Net incremental taxable income (8-10-11-14)						
16. Incremental taxes						
17. Net cash flow a/tax (13 - 16)						
PRESENT VALUE CALCULATIONS						
18. Present value factor						
19. PV of net cash flow (17 x 18)						
20. NPV of project (sum of values on line 19)						

THE BUSINESS POLICY GAME
CAPITAL BUDGET WORK SHEET

Company ____ World ____	Funds Required in Year ____				
CAPITAL EXPENDITURES:	Qtr 1	Qtr 2	Qtr 3	Qtr 4	Total
Plant Construction:					
New Additions:					
New Production Lines:					
Total Funds Requirement:					
SOURCES OF FUNDS:					
Quarterly Earnings					
Sale of Bonds					
Sale of Common Stock					
Temporary Bank Loan					
Less Loan Repayment					
Total Sources of Funds					
Quarterly Surplus (Deficit)					

FIGURE 8-1
Illustration of Capital Budget Work Sheet

THE BUSINESS POLICY GAME
CAPITAL BUDGET WORK SHEET

Company ___ World ___	Funds Required in Year ___				
CAPITAL EXPENDITURES:	Qtr 1	Qtr 2	Qtr 3	Qtr 4	Total
Plant Construction:					
New Additions:					
New Production Lines:					
Total Funds Requirement:					
SOURCES OF FUNDS:					
Quarterly Earnings					
Sale of Bonds					
Sale of Common Stock					
Temporary Bank Loan					
Less Loan Repayment					
Total Sources of Funds					
Quarterly Surplus (Deficit)					

FIGURE 8-1
Illustration of Capital Budget Work Sheet

THE BUSINESS POLICY GAME
CAPITAL BUDGET WORK SHEET

Company ____ World ____	Funds Required in Year ____				
CAPITAL EXPENDITURES:	Qtr 1	Qtr 2	Qtr 3	Qtr 4	Total
Plant Construction:					
New Additions:					
New Production Lines:					
Total Funds Requirement:					
SOURCES OF FUNDS:					
Quarterly Earnings					
Sale of Bonds					
Sale of Common Stock					
Temporary Bank Loan					
Less Loan Repayment					
Total Sources of Funds					
Quarterly Surplus (Deficit)					

FIGURE 8-1
Illustration of Capital Budget Work Sheet

THE BUSINESS POLICY GAME
CAPITAL BUDGET WORK SHEET

Company ____ World ____	Funds Required in Year ____				
CAPITAL EXPENDITURES:	Qtr 1	Qtr 2	Qtr 3	Qtr 4	Total
Plant Construction:					
New Additions:					
New Production Lines:					
Total Funds Requirement:					
SOURCES OF FUNDS:					
Quarterly Earnings					
Sale of Bonds					
Sale of Common Stock					
Temporary Bank Loan					
Less Loan Repayment					
Total Sources of Funds					
Quarterly Surplus (Deficit)					

FIGURE 8-1
Illustration of Capital Budget Work Sheet

THE BUSINESS POLICY GAME
CAPITAL BUDGET WORK SHEET

Company ___ World ___	Funds Required in Year ___				
CAPITAL EXPENDITURES:	Qtr 1	Qtr 2	Qtr 3	Qtr 4	Total
Plant Construction:					
New Additions:					
New Production Lines:					
Total Funds Requirement:					
SOURCES OF FUNDS:					
Quarterly Earnings					
Sale of Bonds					
Sale of Common Stock					
Temporary Bank Loan					
Less Loan Repayment					
Total Sources of Funds					
Quarterly Surplus (Deficit)					

FIGURE 8-1
Illustration of Capital Budget Work Sheet

THE BUSINESS POLICY GAME
CAPITAL BUDGET WORK SHEET

Company ____ World ____	Funds Required in Year ____				
CAPITAL EXPENDITURES:	Qtr 1	Qtr 2	Qtr 3	Qtr 4	Total
Plant Construction:					
New Additions:					
New Production Lines:					
Total Funds Requirement:					
SOURCES OF FUNDS:					
Quarterly Earnings					
Sale of Bonds					
Sale of Common Stock					
Temporary Bank Loan					
Less Loan Repayment					
Total Sources of Funds					
Quarterly Surplus (Deficit)					

FIGURE 8-1
Illustration of Capital Budget Work Sheet

THE BUSINESS POLICY GAME
CASH BUDGET WORK SHEET

Co. ____ World ____ Year ____	Qtr 1	Qtr 2	Qtr 3	Qtr 4
OPERATING RECEIPTS:				
Accounts from last quarter				
Accounts from this quarter				
OPERATING EXPENDITURES:				
Production Cost				
Selling Expense				
Admin and General Expense				
Taxes Paid (1st qtr only)				
Net Operating Cash Flow				
INVESTMENT RECEIPTS:				
CD Interest				
CDs Matured				
INVESTMENT EXPENDITURES:				
CDs Purchased				
New Equipment				
Equipment Replacement				
Plant Investment				
Net Investment Cash Flow				
FINANCING RECEIPTS:				
Loans Received				
Bond Sale				
Stock Sale				
FINANCING EXPENDITURES:				
Dividends Paid				
Loans Repaid				
Bonds Repurchased				
Stock Repurchased				
Net Financing Cash Flow				
SUMMARY:				
Beginning Cash Balance				
Net Cash Flow for Quarter				
Ending Cash Balance				

THE BUSINESS POLICY GAME
CASH BUDGET WORK SHEET

Co. ____ World ____ Year ____	Qtr 1	Qtr 2	Qtr 3	Qtr 4
OPERATING RECEIPTS:				
Accounts from last quarter				
Accounts from this quarter				
OPERATING EXPENDITURES:				
Production Cost				
Selling Expense				
Admin and General Expense				
Taxes Paid (1st qtr only)				
Net Operating Cash Flow				
INVESTMENT RECEIPTS:				
CD Interest				
CDs Matured				
INVESTMENT EXPENDITURES:				
CDs Purchased				
New Equipment				
Equipment Replacement				
Plant Investment				
Net Investment Cash Flow				
FINANCING RECEIPTS:				
Loans Received				
Bond Sale				
Stock Sale				
FINANCING EXPENDITURES:				
Dividends Paid				
Loans Repaid				
Bonds Repurchased				
Stock Repurchased				
Net Financing Cash Flow				
SUMMARY:				
Beginning Cash Balance				
Net Cash Flow for Quarter				
Ending Cash Balance				

THE BUSINESS POLICY GAME
CASH BUDGET WORK SHEET

Co. ___ World ___ Year ___	Qtr 1	Qtr 2	Qtr 3	Qtr 4
OPERATING RECEIPTS:				
Accounts from last quarter				
Accounts from this quarter				
OPERATING EXPENDITURES:				
Production Cost				
Selling Expense				
Admin and General Expense				
Taxes Paid (1st qtr only)				
Net Operating Cash Flow				
INVESTMENT RECEIPTS:				
CD Interest				
CDs Matured				
INVESTMENT EXPENDITURES:				
CDs Purchased				
New Equipment				
Equipment Replacement				
Plant Investment				
Net Investment Cash Flow				
FINANCING RECEIPTS:				
Loans Received				
Bond Sale				
Stock Sale				
FINANCING EXPENDITURES:				
Dividends Paid				
Loans Repaid				
Bonds Repurchased				
Stock Repurchased				
Net Financing Cash Flow				
SUMMARY: Beginning Cash Balance				
Net Cash Flow for Quarter				
Ending Cash Balance				

THE BUSINESS POLICY GAME
CASH BUDGET WORK SHEET

Co. ____ World ____ Year ____	Qtr 1	Qtr 2	Qtr 3	Qtr 4
OPERATING RECEIPTS:				
Accounts from last quarter				
Accounts from this quarter				
OPERATING EXPENDITURES:				
Production Cost				
Selling Expense				
Admin and General Expense				
Taxes Paid (1st qtr only)				
Net Operating Cash Flow				
INVESTMENT RECEIPTS:				
CD Interest				
CDs Matured				
INVESTMENT EXPENDITURES:				
CDs Purchased				
New Equipment				
Equipment Replacement				
Plant Investment				
Net Investment Cash Flow				
FINANCING RECEIPTS:				
Loans Received				
Bond Sale				
Stock Sale				
FINANCING EXPENDITURES:				
Dividends Paid				
Loans Repaid				
Bonds Repurchased				
Stock Repurchased				
Net Financing Cash Flow				
SUMMARY:				
Beginning Cash Balance				
Net Cash Flow for Quarter				
Ending Cash Balance				

THE BUSINESS POLICY GAME
CASH BUDGET WORK SHEET

Co. ____ World ____ Year ____	Qtr 1	Qtr 2	Qtr 3	Qtr 4
OPERATING RECEIPTS:				
Accounts from last quarter				
Accounts from this quarter				
OPERATING EXPENDITURES:				
Production Cost				
Selling Expense				
Admin and General Expense				
Taxes Paid (1st qtr only)				
Net Operating Cash Flow				
INVESTMENT RECEIPTS:				
CD Interest				
CDs Matured				
INVESTMENT EXPENDITURES:				
CDs Purchased				
New Equipment				
Equipment Replacement				
Plant Investment				
Net Investment Cash Flow				
FINANCING RECEIPTS:				
Loans Received				
Bond Sale				
Stock Sale				
FINANCING EXPENDITURES:				
Dividends Paid				
Loans Repaid				
Bonds Repurchased				
Stock Repurchased				
Net Financing Cash Flow				
SUMMARY:				
Beginning Cash Balance				
Net Cash Flow for Quarter				
Ending Cash Balance				

THE BUSINESS POLICY GAME
CASH BUDGET WORK SHEET

Co. _____ World _____ Year _____	Qtr 1	Qtr 2	Qtr 3	Qtr 4
OPERATING RECEIPTS:				
Accounts from last quarter				
Accounts from this quarter				
OPERATING EXPENDITURES:				
Production Cost				
Selling Expense				
Admin and General Expense				
Taxes Paid (1st qtr only)				
Net Operating Cash Flow				
INVESTMENT RECEIPTS:				
CD Interest				
CDs Matured				
INVESTMENT EXPENDITURES:				
CDs Purchased				
New Equipment				
Equipment Replacement				
Plant Investment				
Net Investment Cash Flow				
FINANCING RECEIPTS:				
Loans Received				
Bond Sale				
Stock Sale				
FINANCING EXPENDITURES:				
Dividends Paid				
Loans Repaid				
Bonds Repurchased				
Stock Repurchased				
Net Financing Cash Flow				
SUMMARY:				
Beginning Cash Balance				
Net Cash Flow for Quarter				
Ending Cash Balance				

THE BUSINESS POLICY GAME
PRO FORMA INCOME STATEMENT

Co. ___ World ___ Year ___	Qtr 1	Qtr 2	Qtr 3	Qtr 4
Gross Revenue from Sales				
LESS COST OF GOODS SOLD:				
Beginning Inventory				
Production Cost				
Goods Available for Sale				
Ending Inventory				
Cost of Goods Sold				
Gross Profit				
SELLING EXPENSE:				
Advertising				
Sales Salaries				
Sales Commissions				
General Selling Expense				
Transportation Expense				
Other Selling Expense				
Total Selling Expense				
ADMIN & GENERAL EXPENSE:				
Research and Development				
Storage Expense				
Executive Compensation				
Loan Interest				
Bond Interest				
Other Expense				
Total Admin & General Exp				
Total Operating Expense				
PROFIT SUMMARY:				
Operating Profit (Loss)				
Other Income: CD Interest				
Net Profit (Loss) Before Tax				
Less Income Tax				
Net Profit (Loss) After Tax				
Less Dividends Paid				
Addition to Retained Earnings				

THE BUSINESS POLICY GAME
PRO FORMA INCOME STATEMENT

Co. ____ World ____ Year ____	Qtr 1	Qtr 2	Qtr 3	Qtr 4
Gross Revenue from Sales				
LESS COST OF GOODS SOLD:				
Beginning Inventory				
Production Cost				
Goods Available for Sale				
Ending Inventory				
Cost of Goods Sold				
Gross Profit				
SELLING EXPENSE:				
Advertising				
Sales Salaries				
Sales Commissions				
General Selling Expense				
Transportation Expense				
Other Selling Expense				
Total Selling Expense				
ADMIN & GENERAL EXPENSE:				
Research and Development				
Storage Expense				
Executive Compensation				
Loan Interest				
Bond Interest				
Other Expense				
Total Admin & General Exp				
Total Operating Expense				
PROFIT SUMMARY:				
Operating Profit (Loss)				
Other Income: CD Interest				
Net Profit (Loss) Before Tax				
Less Income Tax				
Net Profit (Loss) After Tax				
Less Dividends Paid				
Addition to Retained Earnings				

THE BUSINESS POLICY GAME
PRO FORMA INCOME STATEMENT

Co. ____ World ____ Year ____	Qtr 1	Qtr 2	Qtr 3	Qtr 4
Gross Revenue from Sales				
LESS COST OF GOODS SOLD:				
Beginning Inventory				
Production Cost				
Goods Available for Sale				
Ending Inventory				
Cost of Goods Sold				
Gross Profit				
SELLING EXPENSE:				
Advertising				
Sales Salaries				
Sales Commissions				
General Selling Expense				
Transportation Expense				
Other Selling Expense				
Total Selling Expense				
ADMIN & GENERAL EXPENSE:				
Research and Development				
Storage Expense				
Executive Compensation				
Loan Interest				
Bond Interest				
Other Expense				
Total Admin & General Exp				
Total Operating Expense				
PROFIT SUMMARY:				
Operating Profit (Loss)				
Other Income: CD Interest				
Net Profit (Loss) Before Tax				
Less Income Tax				
Net Profit (Loss) After Tax				
Less Dividends Paid				
Addition to Retained Earnings				

THE BUSINESS POLICY GAME
PRO FORMA INCOME STATEMENT

Co. ____ World ____ Year ____	Qtr 1	Qtr 2	Qtr 3	Qtr 4
Gross Revenue from Sales				
LESS COST OF GOODS SOLD:				
Beginning Inventory				
Production Cost				
Goods Available for Sale				
Ending Inventory				
Cost of Goods Sold				
Gross Profit				
SELLING EXPENSE:				
Advertising				
Sales Salaries				
Sales Commissions				
General Selling Expense				
Transportation Expense				
Other Selling Expense				
Total Selling Expense				
ADMIN & GENERAL EXPENSE:				
Research and Development				
Storage Expense				
Executive Compensation				
Loan Interest				
Bond Interest				
Other Expense				
Total Admin & General Exp				
Total Operating Expense				
PROFIT SUMMARY:				
Operating Profit (Loss)				
Other Income: CD Interest				
Net Profit (Loss) Before Tax				
Less Income Tax				
Net Profit (Loss) After Tax				
Less Dividends Paid				
Addition to Retained Earnings				

THE BUSINESS POLICY GAME
PRO FORMA INCOME STATEMENT

Co. ____ World ____ Year ____	Qtr 1	Qtr 2	Qtr 3	Qtr 4
Gross Revenue from Sales				
LESS COST OF GOODS SOLD:				
Beginning Inventory				
Production Cost				
Goods Available for Sale				
Ending Inventory				
Cost of Goods Sold				
Gross Profit				
SELLING EXPENSE:				
Advertising				
Sales Salaries				
Sales Commissions				
General Selling Expense				
Transportation Expense				
Other Selling Expense				
Total Selling Expense				
ADMIN & GENERAL EXPENSE:				
Research and Development				
Storage Expense				
Executive Compensation				
Loan Interest				
Bond Interest				
Other Expense				
Total Admin & General Exp				
Total Operating Expense				
PROFIT SUMMARY:				
Operating Profit (Loss)				
Other Income: CD Interest				
Net Profit (Loss) Before Tax				
Less Income Tax				
Net Profit (Loss) After Tax				
Less Dividends Paid				
Addition to Retained Earnings				

THE BUSINESS POLICY GAME
PRO FORMA INCOME STATEMENT

Co. ____ World ____ Year ____	Qtr 1	Qtr 2	Qtr 3	Qtr 4
Gross Revenue from Sales				
LESS COST OF GOODS SOLD:				
Beginning Inventory				
Production Cost				
Goods Available for Sale				
Ending Inventory				
Cost of Goods Sold				
Gross Profit				
SELLING EXPENSE:				
Advertising				
Sales Salaries				
Sales Commissions				
General Selling Expense				
Transportation Expense				
Other Selling Expense				
Total Selling Expense				
ADMIN & GENERAL EXPENSE:				
Research and Development				
Storage Expense				
Executive Compensation				
Loan Interest				
Bond Interest				
Other Expense				
Total Admin & General Exp				
Total Operating Expense				
PROFIT SUMMARY:				
Operating Profit (Loss)				
Other Income: CD Interest				
Net Profit (Loss) Before Tax				
Less Income Tax				
Net Profit (Loss) After Tax				
Less Dividends Paid				
Addition to Retained Earnings				

THE BUSINESS POLICY GAME
PRO FORMA BALANCE SHEET

Co. ____ World ____ Year ____	Qtr 1	Qtr 2	Qtr 3	Qtr 4
ASSETS:				
Cash Balance				
Time Certificates of Deposit				
Accounts Receivable				
Inventory				
Total Current Assets				
Net Plant				
Net Equipment				
Total Fixed Assets				
Total Assets				
LIABILITIES AND EQUITY:				
Taxes Payable				
Bank Loan				
Total Current Liabilities				
Bonds Outstanding				
Total Liabilities				
Capital Stock				
Retained Earnings				
Total Equity				
Total Liabilities & Equity				

THE BUSINESS POLICY GAME
PRO FORMA BALANCE SHEET

Co. ____ World ____ Year ____	Qtr 1	Qtr 2	Qtr 3	Qtr 4
ASSETS:				
Cash Balance				
Time Certificates of Deposit				
Accounts Receivable				
Inventory				
Total Current Assets				
Net Plant				
Net Equipment				
Total Fixed Assets				
Total Assets				
LIABILITIES AND EQUITY:				
Taxes Payable				
Bank Loan				
Total Current Liabilities				
Bonds Outstanding				
Total Liabilities				
Capital Stock				
Retained Earnings				
Total Equity				
Total Liabilities & Equity				

THE BUSINESS POLICY GAME
PRO FORMA BALANCE SHEET

Co. ___ World ___ Year ___	Qtr 1	Qtr 2	Qtr 3	Qtr 4
ASSETS:				
Cash Balance				
Time Certificates of Deposit				
Accounts Receivable				
Inventory				
Total Current Assets				
Net Plant				
Net Equipment				
Total Fixed Assets				
Total Assets				
LIABILITIES AND EQUITY:				
Taxes Payable				
Bank Loan				
Total Current Liabilities				
Bonds Outstanding				
Total Liabilities				
Capital Stock				
Retained Earnings				
Total Equity				
Total Liabilities & Equity				

THE BUSINESS POLICY GAME
PRO FORMA BALANCE SHEET

Co. _____ World _____ Year _____	Qtr 1	Qtr 2	Qtr 3	Qtr 4
ASSETS:				
Cash Balance				
Time Certificates of Deposit				
Accounts Receivable				
Inventory				
Total Current Assets				
Net Plant				
Net Equipment				
Total Fixed Assets				
Total Assets				
LIABILITIES AND EQUITY:				
Taxes Payable				
Bank Loan				
Total Current Liabilities				
Bonds Outstanding				
Total Liabilities				
Capital Stock				
Retained Earnings				
Total Equity				
Total Liabilities & Equity				

THE BUSINESS POLICY GAME
PRO FORMA BALANCE SHEET

Co. ____ World ____ Year ____	Qtr 1	Qtr 2	Qtr 3	Qtr 4
ASSETS:				
Cash Balance				
Time Certificates of Deposit				
Accounts Receivable				
Inventory				
Total Current Assets				
Net Plant				
Net Equipment				
Total Fixed Assets				
Total Assets				
LIABILITIES AND EQUITY:				
Taxes Payable				
Bank Loan				
Total Current Liabilities				
Bonds Outstanding				
Total Liabilities				
Capital Stock				
Retained Earnings				
Total Equity				
Total Liabilities & Equity				

THE BUSINESS POLICY GAME
PRO FORMA BALANCE SHEET

Co. ____ World ____ Year ____	Qtr 1	Qtr 2	Qtr 3	Qtr 4
ASSETS:				
Cash Balance				
Time Certificates of Deposit				
Accounts Receivable				
Inventory				
Total Current Assets				
Net Plant				
Net Equipment				
Total Fixed Assets				
Total Assets				
LIABILITIES AND EQUITY:				
Taxes Payable				
Bank Loan				
Total Current Liabilities				
Bonds Outstanding				
Total Liabilities				
Capital Stock				
Retained Earnings				
Total Equity				
Total Liabilities & Equity				

INDEX